iOS in the Classroom

 *A Guide for Teaching Students with Visual Impairments*

Larry L. Lewis, Jr.

AFB PRESS

American Foundation for the Blind

Printed in the United States of America

Library of Congress Cataloging-in-Publication Data

Names: Lewis, Larry L. Jr., author.
Title: iOS in the classroom : a guide for teaching students with visual
    impairments / Larry L. Lewis, Jr.
Description: First Edition. | New York : AFB Press, American Foundation for
    the Blind, 2016. | Includes bibliographical references and index.
Identifiers: LCCN 2015050469 (print) | LCCN 2016003331 (ebook) |
    ISBN 9780891287353 (pbk. : alk. paper) | ISBN 9780891287360 (online
    subscription) | ISBN 9780891287377 (epub) | ISBN 9780891287384 (mobi) |
Subjects: LCSH: People with visual disabilities—Education. | iOS (Electronic
    resource) | iPhone (Smartphone) | Computers and people with disabilities.
Classification: LCC HV1626 .L484 2016 (print) | LCC HV1626 (ebook) | DDC
    371.91/145—dc23
LC record available at http://lccn.loc.gov/2015050469

Descriptions provided in this book are based on an iPad running iOS 9. Minor discrepancies may result as updated versions of the operating system are released. Some functionality is only available on third-generation iPad models and later.

The American Foundation for the Blind removes barriers, creates solutions, and expands possibilities so people with vision loss can achieve their full potential.

∞

It is the policy of the American Foundation for the Blind to use in the first printing of its books acid-free paper that meets the ANSI Z39.48 Standard. The infinity symbol that appears above indicates that the paper in this printing meets that standard.

Contents

Introduction

For the past decade, Apple's mobile devices—iPod, iPhone, and iPad products—have led the company to success within the educational, vocational, and home markets. These devices provide versatile opportunities for integrating mobile technologies into the daily activities of users within these environments. Although all of Apple's mobile devices run the same iOS operating system and use touchscreen interfaces, each device offers different functionality.

Apple's pervasive marketing efforts have led school districts across the United States to purchase iPads in bulk, distributing them to students and even integrating them into the classroom curricula. Apple has a longstanding presence within educational computing, a market segment that is quick to explore new methods of acquiring, interacting with, and sharing information. An underlying benefit of Apple's mobile technology is that it includes several accessibility features built directly into the operating system, thereby eliminating the need for installations of third-party software and modifications that other devices require to become accessible to users with visual impairments. The idea of purchasing a single device that might meet the access needs of students with visual impairments, regardless of specific circumstances or level of functional literacy, can be seemingly irresistible to the decision makers who oversee technology purchases for these students.

This book is not designed to tout iOS devices as the last word for students who are blind or visually impaired. As revolutionary as iOS technology has proven to be for people with visual impairments, and as important as it is for your students to be able to flourish using these devices, they are not designed to provide for all of your students' literacy needs. After all, it's not any more reasonable to expect the iPad to serve all your students' needs than it is to expect sighted students to learn to read and write using only an iPad, foregoing the mechanical writing options that have been used over time.

So while iOS devices offer user-friendly out-of-the-box access to its functions, it's important to remember that this technology is constantly evolving and being adapted to meet the needs of students striving to expand their reading and writing skills. The truth is, some of the technology's features work famously while others, such as Siri and high-powered word-processing apps, are still maturing.

For the sake of consistency, this book focuses specifically on the use of the iPad within educational settings. Readers should note that although the book is addressed directly to teachers who will be working with students who are visually impaired, the information is equally useful to parents of those students or even to older students themselves. The iPad was chosen not because it is the most intuitive device for students with visual impairments to use—in fact, the iPad's larger screen, which presents real estate that is unnecessary for tactile navigation, can prove more challenging for orientation for a blind student than the smaller, compact screens offered by iPhones and iPods. However, since most school districts are purchasing iPads in bulk in order to meet as many needs for as many students as possible, you will most likely find yourself in a position to teach your students how to use these devices.

Descriptions provided are based on an iPad running some version of iOS 9. Readers should be aware that Apple frequently updates its operating systems (e.g., versions 9.1, 9.2, and so forth), so that readers may find minor discrepancies in the screens they see on their devices and those described or pictured here. In addition, not all the features discussed appear on earlier iPad models. For the sake of completeness, the book assumes no prior knowledge of other devices running the iOS operating system. An iPad (see Figure 1) is considered a tablet computer, falling somewhere between a smart phone and a laptop computer in terms of power and portability.

FIGURE 1

An iPad Mini on the left next to an iPad on the right.

The screen surface of a standard iPad is nearly the size of a piece of notebook paper, while the iPad Mini has a smaller footprint by a couple of inches for greater portability. Both models provide the same functionality. All iPad models can connect to wireless networks. Some models offer the ability to add cellular data plans primarily for the purpose of sending and receiving data when wireless networks are not present. Within schools, iPads with wireless connectivity only are the norm. iPads typically have a battery life somewhere between 8 and 10 hours of continual use; when left idle for a period of time, iPads will automatically go into a sleep mode in order to prolong battery life.

Adaptive Technology Essentials

This section gives an overview of how information can be accessed and entered on the iPad. There are three ways for students with visual impairments to access information: screen access, speech output, and refreshable braille. There are four ways for students with visual impairments to enter information into an iPad: speech input, braille input, QWERTY keyboard input, and gestures.

Screen Access

Screen Magnification

Built into the iPad is the Zoom screen magnifier, which enables magnification of the entire screen. Couple the iPad's Zoom feature with speech output, as described in later chapters, and one no longer needs to choose between speech and large print. Instead, one can have both. Users can even selectively enable the Zoom feature to "pan," or move through portions of the screen, when using an app. This feature has certainly been a boon for visually impaired users. However, it's also true that the larger the magnification, the smaller the viewing area, which can make panning through complex graphical environments more challenging. Using Zoom is addressed in Chapters 2 and 3.

When a student's visual condition renders screen magnification unhelpful or inefficient, it's time to consider other options for screen access, such as speech output or refreshable braille.

Speech Output

The ability to hear information displayed on a computer screen using adaptive screen-reading software has been around for decades. But a major challenge associated with screen readers is how to organize the information presented within complicated screen layouts. While speech feedback effectively gleans and assimilates information quickly, it does not offer the same access to detail as print does for sighted readers or braille does for blind users. Recognizing this, Apple changed the mobile speech output landscape with its VoiceOver built-in iOS screen reader. This solution logically articulates the given contents on a touch screen and provides alternative methods for interacting with this spoken information. Accessing the iPad with VoiceOver is discussed in Chapters 1 and 2.

Refreshable Braille

Also known as "electronic braille," refreshable braille has been around since the late 1970s. A refreshable braille display (see Figure 2 for an example) is a mechanical line of plastic pins that move up and down to form a line of braille that changes, or refreshes, as it displays what's on the screen. Used in conjunction with speech output, nonvisual learners respond quite favorably to the speed and efficiency of accessing information audibly, while benefiting from the accuracy and learning experience that refreshable braille access offers. Best of all, refreshable braille displays can be wirelessly connected to, and used with, iOS devices, and allow the user to employ intuitive, mnemonic keystroke commands as alternatives to complex touchscreen gestures, as discussed in Chapter 4. (Keystroke commands are specific combinations of keys that, when pressed, provide an alternative method of navigation and input.)

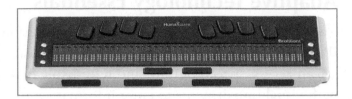

FIGURE 2

Photo of an 8-key, 40-cell refreshable braille display.

Input Methods

Speech Input

iOS devices have two fairly robust built-in dictation features. The first dictation feature, speech input, works directly from the onscreen keyboard when the user is connected to the Internet. Once dictation has been enabled in the Settings menu (see Chapter 7), selecting the microphone key that will then appear to the left of the spacebar on the iOS onscreen keyboard and speaking will enter text in the active field; selecting the microphone key again ends dictation. (Note that dictation is only available on iPad 3 or later.)

The second dictation feature is Siri, a speech-based interface that users can query directly for information or to perform a variety of functions—write an e-mail, send a text, browse the Internet, open an app, and so forth. Once enabled in the Settings menu (see Chapter 3), Siri provides speech feedback and prompts in return. While Siri isn't perfect, its reliability and accuracy improves with every iOS update. (Again, Siri is only available on iPad 3 or later.)

Braille Input

Today's wireless, refreshable braille devices are easily connected to iOS devices, utilizing six- and eight-key braille input keyboards. Students who are comfortable with braille may prefer braille input with these keyboards over other methods. Adaptive technology manufacturers have spent decades developing intuitive keyboard commands, commonly referred to as "chording commands," that enable users to navigate and use various applications efficiently. A chording command is a key combination pressed in conjunction with either the Space, Backspace, or Enter key in order to initiate a given function. For example, pressing the braille keys 1, 2, and 5 (the letter *h*) in conjunction with the Space Bar will move the user to the iOS home screen. Braille input and chording commands are discussed in Chapter 4.

QWERTY Input

iOS devices use onscreen keyboards in the traditional QWERTY layout, which refers to the first six letter keys at the left of the top alphabetic row of the keyboard. While some blind students are proficient at using the onscreen keyboard (as described in Chapter 7), it's not ideal for serious word processing. The good news is, an external, Bluetooth QWERTY keyboard (see Figure 3) can be easily paired with the iPad for writing tasks.

FIGURE **3**

An Apple external Bluetooth QWERTY keyboard with a front view on top and a side view at bottom.

Gestures

Apple has developed and continues to advance a touchscreen, gesture-based access technology that has been readily adapted by multitudes of users who are blind or visually impaired worldwide. A gesture may involve just touching or tapping the screen one or more times with one, two, three, or four fingers, or swiping a certain number of fingers left, right, up, or down. Gestures for visually impaired users, when the assistive technologies discussed in subsequent chapters are enabled, differ from those for fully sighted users. Using gestures, many students who are blind or visually impaired can explore an iPad after only minimal instruction. For adults, this novel way of interacting with a screen may take a bit longer to master. Gestures are discussed in Chapters 1 and 2, and a list of commonly used gestures appears in Sidebar 2.1.

The iOS Revolution

Because Apple incorporates accessibility technology into the actual operating system for its mobile devices, some students with visual impairments can do meaningful work the first day they use an iPad, if provided with the right instruction. All built-in screen magnification and screen-reading access is free to use within Apple's product line, and one does not have to purchase expensive third-party software that historically has cost more than the devices to which they are designed to provide access. All software upgrades for these access components are free; there is no need for costly adaptive technology maintenance or service agreements.

While Apple has done an extraordinary job making the "out-of-the-box experience" inclusive for all, this book addresses extra components that some students will need for staying competitive in the classroom and beyond. Regardless of how any individuals feel about this new technology, the iOS revolution is here in our classrooms and communities, and it must be embraced on behalf of our students.

While those with visual impairments, those who work with people who are visually impaired, and those with visually impaired family and friends will gain something from this publication, this book is addressed to teachers of students with visual impairments. If you are such a teacher, know that this book's purpose is to assist you in introducing and implementing this touchscreen technology in a responsible, caring, and proactive manner.

Getting Started

IN THIS CHAPTER

- Orienting to the iPad without vision
- Acclimating to the various portions of the home screen
- Learning alternative touch gestures
- Connecting the iPad to receive and send data

Most students—with or without visual impairments—possess the sensory skills necessary for navigating a screen by touch, though students with visual impairments may need additional guidance and practice. It is imperative that teachers and service providers who work with students with visual impairments learn how to use touchscreen technology from the perspective of the students they serve.

Studies performed at the University of California[1] show that the human brain typically takes seven days to adapt to new technology, regardless of age. However, students with visual impairments adapting to touchscreen technology may need more time to become familiar with the various components and features of the iPad, along with the gestures required for navigation. Simply put, this technology is completely unlike traditional note-taking solutions. Indeed, there are tasks that visually impaired users can perform more efficiently on an electronic braille notetaker than on an iOS device.

Still, iOS devices possess features and capabilities that blind and visually impaired students need to master to keep pace with their sighted peers. This chapter will provide teachers with the foundation they need to help their students maximize the usefulness of their iOS devices.

---

[1] Small, G. W., Moody, T. D., Siddarth, P., & Bookheimer, S. Y. (2009). Your brain on Google: Patterns of cerebral activation during Internet searching. *American Journal of Geriatric Psychiatry, 17*(2), 116–26. doi: 10.1097/JGP.0b013e3181953a02

Getting Acquainted with the iPad

After removing the iPad from its box, discard the sheet of flexible plastic used to protect the touchscreen. There should be three other components in the box: a USB cable with plugs on both ends, a rectangular power adapter, and a quick-start reference card.

Place the iPad in front of you on a flat surface, oriented vertically, with the home button positioned closest to you. The only physical button on the screen surface, the home button is a small, round button situated within a small indentation in the center of the bottom of the device, below the screen.

Next, along the bottom edge of the iPad in the middle, there is a rectangular slot (larger on iPads 1, 2, and 3 and smaller on the iPad 4 and iPad Air). This slot is called the Dock Connector or Lightning Connector (depending on the model), and it is where the smaller end of the included USB cable is connected. The top left edge of the iPad has a standard audio jack where you can connect a pair of headphones or an external audio speaker. The iPad has an internal speaker, so headphones or an external speaker are not required for use, though some people prefer one or both options. The iPad also has two cameras for taking still images, videos, and videoconferencing via the FaceTime app. The front camera is located at the top of the screen surface, directly in the middle, but does not offer any tactile markings for visually impaired users; however, it is located in the same position at the top of the device as the home button is located at the bottom.

The back-facing camera is located on the back of the device, in the upper left-hand corner, just below the rectangular on/off button. Both the back-facing camera and on/off button provide a visually impaired user with tactile clues. The camera is indented slightly into the device while the on/off button protrudes from the device. The on/off button also functions as the sleep/wake button. Powering the iPad on and off will be discussed later in this chapter.

Along the right edge of the iPad, on the upper right, is the side switch. This tiny switch can be pushed up (away from the user) or down (toward the user), and is used for two purposes: to mute or unmute the device's speaker or lock or unlock screen rotation. Both will be detailed later in this chapter.

Located directly below the side switch is a rocker switch that controls the volume of the iPad. Press the top portion of the rocker switch to turn the volume up; press the bottom portion of the rocker switch to turn the volume down. The next sections will show you how to power up the iPad and start using it.

Powering On and Off

Before powering on, there are a few things worth noting about the on/off button. The button can be used to turn the iPad off completely so that it doesn't use any power at all, which one may wish to do if the iPad will not be in use for a few days. To turn the device off, hold the button down for a few seconds until the onscreen command "slide to power off" appears, indicating the necessary gesture. To perform this gesture, slide one finger near the top of the screen from left to right, keeping the finger on the screen. (If the VoiceOver screen reader is already activated, simply double tap the screen anywhere with one finger, as described later in the chapter. By default, the built-in VoiceOver screen reader is disabled. How to enable it is discussed in subsequent pages, but you may encounter an iPad where it has already been enabled. The double tap is simply two rapid touches with a single finger using the pad of the finger when making contact with the screen. You will follow these same steps using the same procedure to power back up.

These somewhat complicated power on/off sequences are required because these devices are carried around, tossed about, and sometimes handled pretty roughly. Requiring the user to perform a sequence ensures that the iPad isn't inadvertently turned on or off when that is not the user's intention.

Sleep and Wake

The on/off button also can be used to temporarily put the device into a power-saving "sleep" mode by pressing the button quickly. To wake the device, quickly press the button again and perform the slide-to-unlock command with the sliding finger motion along the bottom of the screen. If VoiceOver is active, repeatedly swipe, or "flick" one finger to the right until the word "unlock button" is spoken, then double tap anywhere on the screen with one finger to unlock the screen. These movements are part of the special gestures that are used to navigate the touchscreen with VoiceOver, introduced in the next section; the "flick" gesture is described in more detail in the section on Navigating the Home Screen, where the gesture is called into play.

Touchscreen Gestures

Apple iOS devices are accessible right out of the box, which means students with visual impairments are able to use the touchscreen technology without having to spend time taking a course. However, there is a learning curve, especially when it comes to gestures. Learning a few rudimentary finger gestures that take the place of a mouse or keyboard is essential. A gesture is performed when the pads of the user's fingertips are used to interact with the touchscreen. It's important to utilize the actual *pads* of the fingertips—not the fingertips or fingernails. Aggressively tapping the screen with force accomplishes little or nothing at all. In fact, a user can touch the screen quite gently and it will respond immediately.

Gestures used by sighted users to issue commands to the iPad are quite different from those employed by users who are blind or visually impaired when VoiceOver is activated. For example, a sighted user taps an option on the screen once to select or launch an operation, whereas a blind or visually impaired user follows two steps: a single touch to hear the prompt and then a double tap to activate it. Zoom users employ a few unique gestures, but for the most part use the same gestures as sighted users. Of course, visually impaired students who prefer to use both Zoom and VoiceOver must learn gestures for both. Most students pick up these gestures very quickly. A few gestures are described in this chapter, since they are necessary to getting started with VoiceOver and getting oriented to the iPad. The rest will be discussed in Chapter 2, and Sidebar 2.1 provides a summary list of gestures with descriptions.

Setting Up the iPad for the First Time

School systems using iPads typically have their information technology departments take care of setting up the device. If that pertains to you and your iPad, you can move on to the next section, Activating VoiceOver. If for some reason you need to set up the device for the first time, the following instructions should prove helpful. The staff at any Apple store also can provide assistance.

Steps for Set Up

1. **Power on.** Assuming your iPad has some charge, press and hold down the on/off button for a few seconds. An Apple icon should appear while the unit powers on (this takes a minute or two). (If the iPad is not charged, plug the USB power cord into the slot at the bottom of the device and the other end into a power outlet to charge it.) Unless VoiceOver is activated, you will not hear an auditory cue to indicate that the iPad is powered up; it only speaks when VoiceOver is enabled.

2. **Slide right.** When the iPad is powered up for the first time, a gray screen will appear with the word "iPad" in the middle and an arrow pointing to the right. Using the pad of your index finger—not the tip or fingernail—touch down on the arrow and slide your finger across to the right.

3. **Choose a language.** Next, a screen with foreign words floating in the background and a box near the bottom center of the screen with the word "English" (the default setting) will appear. Once again, using the pad of your index finger, gently tap the word "English" (or tap the arrow for more language choices).

4. **Pick the country of origin.** The default is the United States; tap it (or scroll to your location if you are elsewhere).

5. **Turn on Location Services.** Turning this feature on allows the iPad to pinpoint the device's position on a map or indicate where the user is in relation to another location. Enable Location Services to take full advantage of the many services rendered by GPS-related and social networking apps (discussed in later chapters).

6. **Select a Wi-Fi network.** Locate the default network for your school or home and tap to select it. If it is a secure network, it will ask for the network password.

7. **Choose Set Up.** Once the iPad is activated, you may choose to either use it as a new iPad or restore it from an old iPad configuration. Choose Set Up as New iPad.

8. **Create an Apple ID.** This will be the primary user's e-mail and password for iTunes and the App Store. If you are the primary user and already have an Apple ID, sign in with it now. If not, tap Create a New Apple ID and choose your Apple ID (preferred e-mail) and password. This step may be skipped during set up, but you will not be able to acquire content from the App Store and iTunes without an Apple ID and password. (See Chapter 5 for detailed instructions on how to set up an Apple account.)

9. **Complete or skip e-mail option.** The choice is yours.

10. **Protect against loss or theft.** Find My iPad is a useful feature that allows the user to choose a sound for the iPad to make if it has been misplaced, or to locate the device on a map if it has been stolen. The service also allows for the remote erasing of all data on a stolen iPad. The iPad can only be located if both Location Services and Find My iPad are enabled. (Note: to locate a lost iPad, either use the Find My iPad app on a different iOS device or visit www.icloud.com and select the Find My iPad button.)

11. **Select Dictation.** When asked by the iPad, select the Dictation utility if you would like to hear the letters typed read aloud when the onscreen keyboard is in use. (This feature is available in iPad3 and up.)

12. **Lock it.** You have the option to create a 4-digit passcode that must be entered every time the iPad is powered on or unlocked, thereby protecting the iPad from unwanted users. This 4-digit code should be easy to remember, yet tricky enough to prevent potential thieves from unlocking the device. This step may be bypassed, though it is recommended that you select your passcode and confirm the selection.

By default, if this passcode is entered incorrectly six times in a row, the iPad displays the message: "iPad is disabled." If this happens, connect the device to a computer with the iTunes application and restore the iPad. This re-enables the iPad. Your iTunes Account should be directly tethered to the same Apple ID and password as your iPad. If you've previously synced the iPad with this computer, settings and data will not be affected, but if you have not, you'll need to sync the data via iCloud once the iPad has been re-enabled. (Using iCloud is discussed in Chapter 5.) The iPad also has an optional setting that will erase all data if the passcode is entered incorrectly 10 successive times. This option is turned off by default, but can be changed in the General section of the Settings screen. Caution must be exercised if this option is enabled. Re-enabling the iPad using iTunes will also replace any data lost by entering an incorrect passcode 10 times assuming the iPad has been previously synced with the computer.

13. **Go to the home screen.** When your set up is complete, a "Thank You" screen is displayed, along with a prompt to begin using the iPad. This will take you to the home screen, where you will find all of Apple's preinstalled apps.

Activating VoiceOver

Next you will want to get acquainted with VoiceOver and some of its alternative gestures. Teachers may find that the majority of students who have low vision will prefer to explore for a while without VoiceOver, using Zoom for initial access instead. (Zoom settings are covered in Chapter 3.) Students who are blind, on the other hand, need to learn VoiceOver gestures from the beginning, or at least until they have access to a wireless keyboard or refreshable braille device.

Shortcut for Accessiblity Features

The Accessibility Shortcut, also called "triple click home," is an easy way to turn user-selected iOS accessibility features on or off. It's up to the student and the teacher to decide which functions they want the shortcut to perform. For example, if VoiceOver is selected as the default option, the user may toggle VoiceOver on and off simply by clicking the home button three times in quick succession. This shortcut is particularly useful for teachers who have multiple users of the same iPad, as well as for students who use more than one means of screen access. A visually impaired user can use this option to quickly toggle VoiceOver off before handing it over to a sighted user.

The ability to use Zoom and VoiceOver together was introduced with iOS 6. It's a huge step forward, but it comes with a small price. That is, some gestures change when both options are turned on (see Zoom and VoiceOver Conflicts in Chapter 2). For that reason, this exercise will focus on how to toggle VoiceOver only on and off, but the process would be the same for Zoom or any other feature listed within the Accessibility Shortcut setting.

To what extent VoiceOver is employed depends on the student. Teachers may tailor their approach to meet the individual needs of students with some remaining functional vision. The following steps outline how to set the Accessibility Shortcut to quickly toggle your desired feature on and off. While this feature may be set and adjusted by a visually impaired user with VoiceOver activated, instructions are being provided from the perspective of a fully sighted educator who has yet to activate VoiceOver.

Setting Accessibility Shortcut Options
With VoiceOver disabled, tap the "Settings" icon on the home screen once.

1. When the Settings split screen appears, tap General in the left-hand column once. Find Accessibility in the right-hand column (see Figure 1.1). If your screen does not display this option (which will be the case with certain models of the iPad mini), quickly flick one finger in an upward motion in the right-hand column to scroll and display another list of options, with Accessibility appearing near the bottom. Tap it once, using one finger.

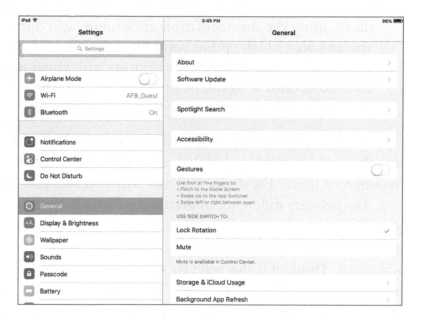

FIGURE **1.1**

The iOS main Settings menu on the left-hand side of the iPad screen and the General menu options on the right. The Accessibility option is the fourth from the top.

2. Now locate the last option on this page, which is the Accessibility Shortcut.

3. Tap Accessibility Shortcut to find this list of options:
   a. VoiceOver
   b. Invert Colors

    c. Grayscale

    d. Zoom

    e. Switch Control

    f. AssistiveTouch

4. Tap VoiceOver with one finger and a checkmark will appear to confirm this selection.

5. Now press the home button once to return to the home screen.

6. Press the home button three times to enable VoiceOver. This will cause the iPad to speak, "VoiceOver on."

7. Press the home button three times again to disable VoiceOver, and the iPad will confirm this by speaking, "VoiceOver off." The other Accessibility Shortcut features work similarly. Again, Zoom will be discussed in subsequent chapters.

8. Activate VoiceOver again by triple clicking the home button.

9. It is possible to select more than one option for the Accessibility Shortcut. When you do so, using the shortcut (triple click home) will display a pop-up screen prompting you to select which option you'd like to enable. Selecting multiple accessibility options can present some difficulty for students with visual impairments if VoiceOver is not enabled because it would be problematic for them to identify or select the desired option from the list on screen without audible cues.

The first time VoiceOver is activated on an iOS device, the user receives a warning that the gestures employed by VoiceOver are different than those used by sighted touchscreen users. The device will ask, "Are you sure you wish to continue?"

The primary difference in gestures is that, when enabled, VoiceOver will speak the item directly under your fingertip as you move it around the screen. Once you find the item you wish to activate with your finger, you double tap anywhere on the screen to activate it. Think of it this way: By touching or tapping an item, you are telling the iPad to bring focus to where your finger is on the screen, thus directing the VoiceOver cursor. (*Focus* refers to which item on the screen is selected and ready to be acted on.) VoiceOver speaks the item and visually highlights it on the screen.

To confirm VoiceOver, double tap anywhere on the screen. If "OK" is in focus, double tap it. If "OK" is not in focus, tap it once and then double tap anywhere on the screen to confirm. (Note: If "Cancel" is in focus and you double tap on the screen, VoiceOver will not be enabled.) Keep in mind that the Accessibility Shortcut alleviates the need to double tap on Okay or Cancel once VoiceOver is enabled for the first time.

Navigating the Home Screen

Now that the iPad has been set up and VoiceOver has been activated, the rest of this orientation to the iPad will continue using VoiceOver, from the point of view of a student who is visually impaired. The home screen is what you encounter whenever you turn the iPad on. Use one finger to gently touch any part of the screen, then slide your finger slowly around the screen to hear VoiceOver announce the item beneath your fingertip. This is commonly referred to as "exploring by touch." VoiceOver users can navigate the screen either by touching the screen and sliding around, or by using a flicking gesture. To "flick" either right or left with one finger, place your fingertip anywhere on the screen and quickly swipe it once to the right; you may also swipe to the left. ("Flick" and "swipe" are generally used interchangeably to describe this gesture.) Do so in a short, straight, horizontal line across the screen. Be sure not to drag the finger when swiping, but quickly flick it, and ensure that your other fingers on the flicking hand do not inadvertently touch the screen, which would interfere with the execution of this gesture. The advantage of flicking through the screen is that the student moves through all the items or apps on the screen sequentially, which gives a good sense of everything that's on that particular screen in a logical order. The disadvantage is that the student doesn't get a holistic perspective of the layout of the screen, and it may take quite a while to find the desired app. Most VoiceOver users rely on a combination of flicking and exploring by touch.

To master the flick, practice gently flicking one finger to the right or left to move forward or backward from one item to another on the screen. Remember to lift the finger off the iPad immediately after the flick. Flicking right advances forward through a list of menu options or apps until the bottom of the screen or list is reached. Flicking left navigates backward through a list of items or apps toward the top of the screen. Remember that your finger doesn't have to be touching a particular option for it to be in focus when using the flick gesture.

One issue to be mindful of is that some blind students have a problem flicking directly left or right and tend to flick in a diagonal direction, particularly when holding the iPad in their lap. They may need to practice horizontal movements across the screen. Alternatively, you may start teaching them this gesture on a tabletop.

Sections of the Home Screen

There are three sections to the iPad home screen: the status bar, the apps screen, and the dock. The status bar (see Figure 1.2 for some examples) runs along the very top of the home screen. Gently touch down on the upper left-hand corner of the screen with one finger. If the first app on the home screen is highlighted, direct the finger up at a left angle to bring focus to this status area.

It's a bit tricky to get the hang of this, but once VoiceOver focus is brought to this status area, the user can access important items. Moving across to the right using the flick gesture, you will hear these items spoken. First is the iPad's connectivity status—either a wireless or cellular network. If the iPad has not been connected to a

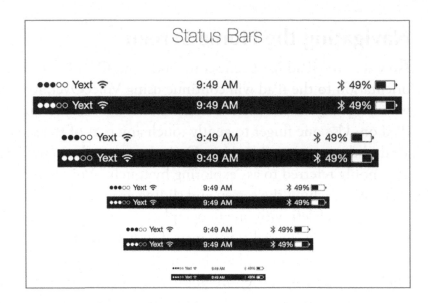

FIGURE 1.2

Photo of five different iOS status bars from large (top) to small (bottom).

wireless network, no network will be displayed. Once a wireless network has been selected, the iPad will connect automatically whenever the iPad is within range of that network. Connectivity is imperative for all iOS devices; it is through a cellular or wireless data connection that apps are installed and updated, e-mails and messages are sent and received, the web is accessed, and information about the device's current location is updated.

Continuing across the status bar, the time is in the middle, and the device's battery status is displayed at the right end of the bar. If you have music or a video playing, this action is presented on the status bar. Note: locked/unlocked orientation, location tracking, and setting up a Bluetooth connection, all of which are announced when activated and displayed on the status bar, will be discussed in later chapters.

There are two important features that a VoiceOver user can access when focus is on any of these status items:

1. **Control Center.** Swiping three fingers up from the middle of the screen activates the Control Center (see Figure 1.3), which provides shortcuts for playing music, sharing files, changing the brightness of the screen, and other options pertinent to the iPad's functionality.

2. **Notification Center.** Swiping three fingers down the screen activates the Notification Center (see Figure 1.4). The Notification Center gives you a snapshot of your

day, displaying any appointments or events scheduled for the day and today's weather. It also lets you know what to look forward to tomorrow.

The second section of the screen—encompassing nearly the entire screen—is where you access the device's apps. When you first begin to use a new iPad, this section will display the pre-installed apps that come with the device, arranged in tidy rows of four across when the iPad is in portrait layout and five across when in landscape layout (see Figure 1.5). The screen can accept up to 20 apps, although the app layout may be conditional upon the model of iPad and iOS version being used. Gently slide your finger pad across each of these to hear their names spoken, or use the flick gesture to sequentially move horizontally across a row. Once the end of a row of apps is reached, VoiceOver automatically moves to the next row on the screen. The flick gesture can be performed anywhere on the screen; the progression will begin wherever VoiceOver is

FIGURE **1.3**

The iOS Control Center at the bottom of the screen.

FIGURE **1.4**

The iOS Notification Center.

focused. (Activation and use of apps is covered in Chapter 5.) Some of the apps may appear on a second page, depending on the layout on your particular model. Following is a list of the pre-installed apps with a summary of what they do:

The iPad home screen in landscape orientation. The Dock is located at the bottom of the screen.

- **Messages.** Send free text messages (using devices running iOS 5 or later).

- **Camera.** Take photographs and videos.

- **Maps.** Search for places and get directions to where you need to go.

- **Clock.** Displays different time zones; allows user to set alarms, timers, and stopwatches.

- **Photo Booth.** Take photos and videos and apply a variety of effects.

- **Calendar.** Look up and schedule appointments.

- **Contacts.** Keep track of contact information in a format similar to an address book.

- **Notes.** Jot notes to yourself.

- **Reminders.** Keep a to-do list.

- **iTunes Store.** Purchase and download audio and video content.

- **News.** Select from a variety of news sources to keep up with the latest breaking news and topics of interest (iOS 9 and above).

- **Videos.** Watch videos that have been downloaded from the iTunes store.

- **App Store.** Purchase and download new apps.

- **Game Center.** Play a variety of games on your device (difficult to use for students with visual impairments).

- **FaceTime.** Make audio or video calls to contacts who also use iOS devices.

- **Settings.** Control all the iPad internal and app settings.

- **Tips.** Find out how to get the most from your iOS device.

- **Find Friends.** See a map of where your friends are in relation to your current location. (Location services for all parties must be enabled for this to be effectively used.)
- **Find iPhone.** Locate your missing iPhone from the iPad when the iPad is tied to an Apple ID and iPhone password.

Finally, along the bottom of the screen resides the Dock (see Figure 1.5), which showcases additional apps. The Dock enables users to have access to the apps located there, regardless of which screen of apps is in focus. As more apps are installed on your iPad, new screens to house these apps are created. The Dock provides a quick and easy way to activate apps in the Dock from any screen on the iPad. The Dock houses four apps to start and can accept up to six; it can be personalized to meet each user's needs. By default the Dock apps are:

- **Safari.** Browse the web.
- **Mail.** Set up multiple e-mail accounts from different providers to send and receive e-mail.
- **Photos.** Store and view photographs.
- **Music.** Download, store, and play music, and listen to Apple Radio.

Locking the Screen Orientation

iOS devices have a unique design feature that automatically shifts the orientation of the screen from portrait to landscape and vice versa every time the device is turned vertically or horizontally. This works fine for visual users who may prefer a taller or wider screen for different tasks, but it can sometimes be maddening for blind or visually impaired users when it automatically rotates with every turn, changing the layout of the screen. VoiceOver announces when the screen orientation changes; for example, when turning the iPad clockwise, VoiceOver says: "Landscape, home button to the left." You will probably want to instruct your students to lock the screen to portrait mode in the beginning. Some students with low vision may eventually prefer to use landscape mode when typing from the onscreen keyboard, viewing video content, or playing games because it provides them with a larger screen area on which to work.

The side switch can be used to either switch between locking and unlocking screen rotation or to switch between muting and unmuting the iPad speaker, but not both. The user gets to decide by making the choice in Settings. Out of the box, this switch is set to toggle between mute and unmute.

For purposes of working with students with visual impairments—since they may prefer additional sound for VoiceOver gestures feedback— go to Settings and designate the side switch button to be used for locking and unlocking screen rotation. Before beginning a few practice exercises to become more comfortable using the iPad, lock the rotation in portrait mode. Remember, if the screen is black (indicating the device is in sleep mode), press the home button or the on/off button quickly, then slide your finger or flick>tap>double tap to unlock the iPad.

FIGURE 1.6

The iOS main Settings menu on the left-hand side of the iPad screen and the General menu options on the right. Text reading "USE SIDE SWITCH TO:" appears at the top of the image above the Lock Rotation and Mute options.

To lock the rotation of the screen with VoiceOver on, follow these steps:

1. Touch Settings on the home screen and then double tap anywhere on the screen.

2. Touch General and double tap.

3. Locate the heading "Use Side Switch To:" (see Figure 1.6), where you'll find two options: Lock Rotation and Mute. Touch and double tap Lock Rotation. Make sure the iPad is positioned in portrait orientation with the home button at the bottom before selecting this option.

4. Now move the side switch (on the upper-right edge of the iPad) down to the locked position. When the screen orientation is locked, the iPad status bar will show a small padlock icon with a circular arrow.

When students with low vision become more familiar with their iOS devices, they may choose to use landscape orientation, especially for reading in Zoom or for typing. In landscape orientation, the onscreen keyboard isn't much smaller than a real keyboard. Students can easily toggle between landscape and portrait screen orientation once the side switch has been properly set.

Waking Up and Staying Up

If the iPad has gone to sleep due to lack of activity, press and release the home button or the power button. With VoiceOver activated, VoiceOver will speak a status item, usually the time. Flick right with one finger until VoiceOver says, "Slide to unlock; slide or double tap." Double tap anywhere on the screen to unlock it. As you get used to performing VoiceOver gestures, you may bring three fingers together and slide them from left to right across the screen in one motion to unlock the iPad as soon as you press the button to wake up the iPad, thus avoiding having to locate the unlock button. You can set your iPad to stay awake for longer intervals in the Settings menu. Here's how to do this using VoiceOver:

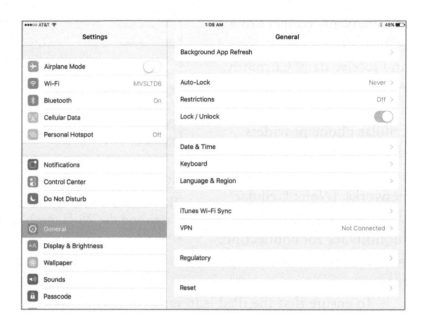

FIGURE 1.7

The iOS main Settings menu on the left-hand side of the iPad screen and the General menu options on the right. Auto-Lock is shown set for Never.

1. Go to Settings on the home screen, then select General.

2. Locate Auto-Lock (see Figure 1.7). Flick right to reach it, and double tap.

3. Flick to select one of these options: 2 minutes, 5 minutes, 10 minutes, 15 minutes, or Never.

4. Make the preferred selection by double tapping on the desired option.

Wi-Fi Connectivity

The last "getting started" topic is Wi-Fi connectivity. There are two types of connectivity for iPads: wireless connectivity (Wi-Fi) and cellular network connectivity. For the educator working with an iPad that has been set up by a school or school district, it's likely that the iPad will only connect to wireless networks.

iPads can be purchased with wireless connectivity or cellular data plans in addition to the wireless option. The cellular data option means that when wireless networks are not present, the iPad can automatically connect to a cellular phone tower to send and receive data. Currently, AT&T, Verizon, T-Mobile, and Sprint are the only U.S. cellular phone providers that allow for iOS device connectivity to their cellular networks. (Note: Cellular data connectivity results in a monthly fee for connecting, sending, and downloading information.)

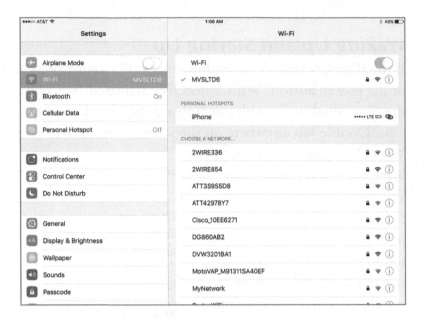

FIGURE 1.8

The iOS main Settings menu on the left-hand side of the iPad screen and the Wi-Fi menu options on the right. Wi-Fi is shown enabled.

To ensure that the iPad is in range of a wireless network, using VoiceOver, follow these steps:

1. Flick to, and double tap Settings from the home screen.

2. Flick and double tap Wi-Fi to enable it (see Figure 1.8)

3. Flick to and double tap the desired network (if the Wi-Fi setting is turned on, the iPad automatically scans for Wi-Fi networks that are within range).

4. Enter the network password (wireless security key), if required, using the QWERTY keyboard that appears on the screen. Because of the complexities of, and strategies for, using the onscreen keyboard when VoiceOver is enabled (discussed in Chapter 2), you may wish to disable VoiceOver by triple clicking the home button before entering the password.

5. Once you've entered the password, tap Join Network to connect.

6. Relaunch VoiceOver by triple clicking the home button again.

Once successful connection to a particular Wi-Fi network takes place, every time the iPad is in range of this network it will automatically connect to it. The status and strength of the connection can be viewed and listened to within the status bar. If later the user wishes for the iPad to "forget" this network, he or she may open Settings and then Wi-Fi by double tapping on both; locate and double tap the More Info button (lowercase *i* in a circle) to the right of the network name; and then locate and double tap the Forget This Network option. Once a network is forgotten, you will need to manually reconnect to it if you want to use it again.

Conclusion

In this chapter, you have had the opportunity to become oriented to the iPad from the perspective of a visually impaired user and to obtain some strategies for orienting such users to the iPad's screen contents. You should now grasp the significance of alternative touch gestures, and have an understanding of how providing a locked screen orientation can provide a springboard for your students to efficiently access information on this device. Now that you are up and running and connected to your preferred wireless network, the next chapter will show you how to become better acquainted with VoiceOver.

CHAPTER 2

Getting Acquainted with VoiceOver and Zoom

IN THIS CHAPTER

- Learning VoiceOver gestures
- Opening, closing, and switching apps
- Making notes, scheduling events, and entering contacts using VoiceOver
- Practicing gestures
- Using Zoom
- Zoom and VoiceOver conflicts

VoiceOver gestures can be more difficult to learn than the standard gestures used by people with functional vision because they are new and different. Using some of the preinstalled apps on the iPad, this chapter will show you how to use VoiceOver gestures to perform a variety of useful tasks. Sidebar 2.1 presents a list of commonly used gestures, their descriptions, and functions that can be used as a reference while reading this book and afterward.

While some preinstalled apps are not frequently used to complete specific educational tasks in the classroom, they can be an effective means for helping teachers and parents of students with visual impairments become more familiar with some of the complexities associated with VoiceOver gestures. Two such apps are the App Store, where users can browse and download applications for use with iOS devices, and the Safari web browser.

Opening, Switching, and Closing Apps

Follow these steps with VoiceOver on to open the App Store and Safari:

1. Press the home button to ensure you are on the home screen.
2. Flick one finger to the right until you locate the App Store app and double tap to open it. If you hear an "Update All" button, ignore it, as you won't be using the App Store for now.

The following is a list of many of the most common gestures used with VoiceOver. Note that you may find "touch" and "tap" used interchangeably in some descriptions, as are "swipe" and "flick."

One-Finger Gestures

- **One-finger touch.** Selects item under your finger.
- **One-finger double-tap.** Activates selected item. Touch the screen twice in rapid succession with the fingertip.
- **One-finger flick to the right.** Moves to next item. Touch the finger to the screen and quickly move it a short distance to the right before breaking contact with the screen.
- **One-finger flick to the left.** Touch the finger to the screen and quickly move it a short distance to the left. Moves to previous item.

Two-Finger Gestures

- **Two-finger single tap.** Pauses or continues speech. To pause speech, touch two fingers together anywhere on the screen. To continue speech, touch two fingers anywhere on the screen.
- **Two-finger double tap.** Stops or starts the current action, for example, an audio track that is playing. Tap two fingers on the screen twice in quick succession. Start or stop an action, such as stop and start an audio track that is playing.
- **Two-finger scrub.** Activates Back button if present, which will take you to the previous screen. You can always find and double tap that button, but most of the time you can accomplish the same thing more quickly with the two-finger scrub. With two fingers on the screen, move to the right, then the left, then the right again.
- **Two-finger flick up.** Reads the screen starting at the top.
- **Two-finger flick down.** Reads the screen starting at selected item.

- **Two-finger rotate.** Evokes the rotor control, which enables you to control a variety of navigation and other options. Place two fingers on the screen and twist right to move clockwise and left to move counterclockwise through rotor settings, making each twist a distinct, short movement such as turning a dial one click at a time. Once VoiceOver speaks a rotor item (Character, Word, Line, Speech Rate, Volume, Punctuation, Containers, and Headings), flick down with one finger to navigate forward by the unit just indicated on the rotor or up with one finger to move back by rotor unit. Note that rotor options are context specific. For instance, if VoiceOver is not focused on an edit field, you will not be able to alter the typing method of the keyboard. If VoiceOver is not on a web page, the rotor will not offer web elements as a means of navigation using the vertical single finger swipe. Items on the rotor can be added, removed, and reordered. You may enter the VoiceOver menu and double tap Rotor to add additional items such as speech rate, volume, or additional language options to the rotor, allowing for more options when your student uses this gesture.

Three-Finger Gestures

- **Three-finger single-tap.** Speaks page number or rows being displayed.
- **Three-finger double-tap.** Mutes or unmutes VoiceOver.
- **Three-finger flick left.** Scrolls right one page (from a lower-numbered page to the next higher-numbered page).
- **Three-finger flick right.** Scrolls left one page (from a higher-numbered page to the preceding lower-numbered page).
- **Three-finger flick up.** Scrolls down one page
- **Three-finger flick down.** Scrolls up one page.

3. Press the home button to exit the App Store. This minimizes the app without closing it.

4. Repeat the above process by flicking right until the Safari app is spoken. Double tap the screen to open it.

5. Now press the home button to return to the home screen.

Switching between Apps using App Switcher

You now have two opened and minimized apps: the App Store and Safari. Next, you will learn how to launch and use the App Switcher. As its name implies, the App Switcher enables you to switch apps without having to close an app and return to the home screen each time you want to make a switch.

1. Launch the App Switcher by pressing the home button twice. VoiceOver will say "App Switcher," followed by the word "home." If you double tap the screen when "home" is spoken, you will return to the home screen.

2. Flick left and VoiceOver will read all of the open apps starting with the app most recently accessed. Continue to flick left and listen to the open apps that VoiceOver speaks. You can select an app from this listing by double tapping anywhere on the screen after you hear VoiceOver announce the app name. For our purposes, don't open anything right now.

3. Dismiss the App Switcher by pressing the home button once, or by flicking to the right until you hear the prompt "home," then double tap the screen.

Closing Apps

As mentioned previously, when you exit an app, it is not closed, but minimized—that means it is not actively being used but is still running in the background. While there is not a direct impact on the iPad's battery when apps are minimized, the performance of the iPad may be affected by the number and type of apps running in the background. For a quick and easy way to close running apps using the App Switcher, follow these steps:

1. Press the home button twice to open the App Switcher. VoiceOver will announce the last app that was accessed.

2. Flick right or left to locate an app you wish to close. Safari will be used for this exercise.

3. When Safari is spoken, VoiceOver says, "Safari active" because Safari was opened during this current iPad section. Use one finger to flick either up or down. By default,

when the screen is double tapped, the selected item is opened or "Activate item" is spoken. If you flick up or down the default action is changed to close the current app. Double tap the screen and the app is closed. Alternatively, to close an app, swipe three fingers from the bottom toward the top of the iPad and the spoken app will automatically close.

4. Flick left with one finger and listen for VoiceOver to speak the next open app, and repeat the process.

5. Press the home button to return to the home screen, or you may double tap the screen with one finger if VoiceOver speaks, "Home."

Note: If you tap with four fingers near the top of the screen, you go straight to the first element on the screen; tap with four fingers near the bottom of the screen and go straight to the last element on the screen. In the event that these gestures don't work, go to Settings, select General, and make sure Multitasking Gestures is turned off.

Using the Notes App with VoiceOver

To become more acclimated to VoiceOver, its gestures, and interacting with the iOS onscreen keyboard, some of the pre-installed apps located on your iPad's home screen will be investigated, starting with Notes.

Creating and Editing Notes

The following steps allow you to create and edit a note using the Notes app (see Figure 2.1):

1. Press the home button to return to the home screen.

2. Flick with one finger left to right or right to left to explore the screen and locate the Notes app. You can also use explore by touch (see Chapter 1) to

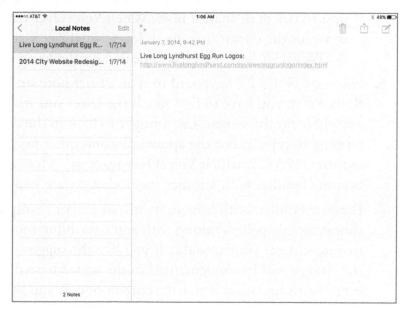

FIGURE **2.1**

The iOS Notes app showing two previously entered notes.

find the app and get a general sense of the screen layout. Whichever method you use, VoiceOver should speak the word "Notes" when the app is in focus on the screen.

3. Double tap anywhere on the screen once you touch and hear, "Notes."

4. Upon opening Notes for the first time, flick to continue and then double tap. A dialog box will appear asking if you want to turn on iCloud to share notes across multiple devices. Feel free to make either selection. iCloud will be discussed in Chapter 5. Explore the screen by either flicking or sliding your finger around the screen when a white background with a folders option for organizing notes appears.

5. Activate the edit field.

   a. If this is your first time opening the Notes app, chances are you will automatically be placed into an edit field of a new note. Edit fields are boxes that allow you to enter or change information using the keyboard. To activate the edit field using VoiceOver, double tap the edit field. Once VoiceOver says it is editing, you may begin entering text using the onscreen keyboard. VoiceOver will report, "Text field is editing," which means that you are in a text field and can begin typing.

   b. If you are not placed into an edit field and don't hear VoiceOver report, "Text field is editing," locate the Add button, which is represented by a notepad and pencil. To find it, flick right or left until you hear VoiceOver speak "New note," then double tap anywhere on the screen. Prior to this button, there are controls that allow the user to delete or share a note. When VoiceOver reports, "Body, text field is editing" it means the cursor is ready to insert whatever text you type into the notes field. A QWERTY keyboard has appeared on the lower third of the screen.

6. Use the QWERTY keyboard to type a brief note such as "Let's go shopping." Remember, you have to first touch the letter you wish to type and then double tap anywhere on the screen. Use a finger to flick to the desired letter before double tapping to type it. For the apostrophe and other punctuation marks, find and double tap the .?123 key, which VoiceOver reads as, "More numbers." In Chapter 4, you'll become familiar with another method of typing known as touch typing.

7. Become familiar with how to fix mistakes. For example, you may hear, "Let's go shopping misspelled," along with some warbling sounds. The iPad may attempt to auto-correct your mistake. If you like the suggested correction, keep typing and the change will be implemented in the text. Alternative suggestions are also given if the first suggestion is not the correct one. If you wish to delete a letter you typed by mistake, locate the Delete key on the keyboard and double tap the screen when "delete" is spoken; VoiceOver will announce the letters being deleted, and you will also hear a small audible click as you delete letters.

8. Send your note via the Messages app. You will notice four icons at the top of the screen: Back, which when double tapped will back you out of the current note, Delete Note, Share Note, and New Note. You'll also find the title of the most current note in which you are writing followed by a text field. You may double tap this text field if the onscreen keyboard has disappeared to resume editing the note.

9. Locate the Share Note button and double tap. The following sharing options will be displayed (see Figure 2.2): Mail, Message, Copy, and Print.

10. Select and double tap Mail.

11. Type an e-mail address of another iPad or iPhone user in the "To:" field if you are connected to Wi-Fi. When you activate the text field you will hear, "To: text field is editing," and the keyboard will appear on screen. Type the e-mail address, remembering to locate each letter and double tap to select it.

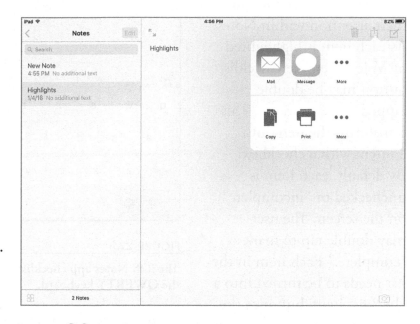

FIGURE 2.2

The iOS Notes app showing the Share Note menu.

12. Locate the Send button adjacent to the To field. Double tap the Send button to send your message. You should now be back at the note you just typed.

13. Delete your note by selecting the Delete Note button (trashcan icon). Double tap anywhere and you will be asked if you wish to delete your note. Double tap to confirm.

14. Press the home button to return to the home screen.

Checklists

The Notes app offers the ability to create a list of action items to be checked off. This is particularly helpful for task-centered, skill-building exercises pertinent to the classroom. The checklist button appears on the keyboard on a row above the QWERTY keyboard, second from left (see Figure 2.3).

The student can create a list of activities that requires their attention within Notes. As each item is highlighted by VoiceOver, the Checklist button may be double tapped to be activated. This transforms the item into an item with a checkbox. By default, each item is unchecked or "incomplete" on the screen. The user may double tap to mark as "complete." Each item in the list needs to be turned into a checklist item, but once the list is complete, the user may check off items in this list by double tapping items to mark them as complete. This is a very engaging feature that you may adapt to the student's individualized education plan.

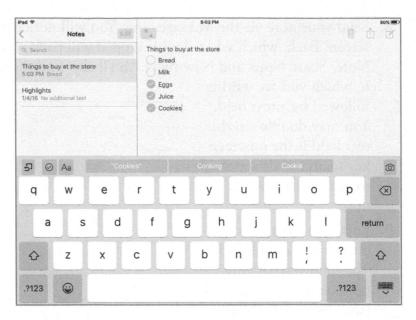

FIGURE 2.3

The iOS Notes app checklist icon appears in the top row above the QWERTY keyboard.

Using the Calendar with VoiceOver

Adding an event to your calendar is more involved than creating a note, but learning how to do so is well worth the effort, as this exercise introduces a useful VoiceOver gesture called the rotor. To make the rotor gesture, place your index finger and thumb on the screen a bit apart from each other and twist them either clockwise or counterclockwise as if you are turning a dial. The rotor allows you to change the behavior of a single vertical flick with one finger up or down. For instance, you may change your rotor to use VoiceOver to navigate by character, word, line, or by elements on a webpage. You may also change your rotor setting to adjust the volume and speed of VoiceOver's speech as well as the level of punctuation spoken. The rotor's functionality will be covered in greater detail in Chapter 6, but you will be introduced to it in this exercise. Note that the rotor gesture only works when VoiceOver is enabled. Follow these steps to add an event to your calendar:

1. Flick right to select the Calendar app on the home page and double tap. Notice in the top-middle area of the screen, you can change the view of the calendar to day, week, month, or year by locating and double tapping one of these four options (see Figure 2.4). By default, the view should be set to Day, which is fine for now. Search and Add buttons follow the calendar view options.

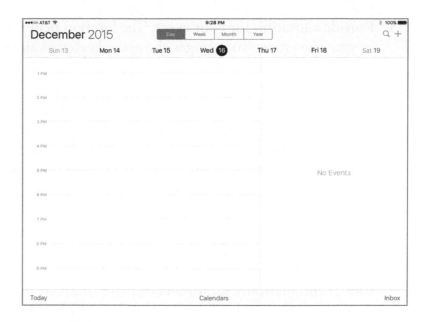

FIGURE 2.4

The iOS Calendar app in Day view.

2. Add an event to the day. The Add button (+ icon) is located at the top right of the calendar. When you hear VoiceOver say, "Add button," double tap anywhere to add a new event.

3. Enable the touch-typing mode when you hear VoiceOver say, "Text field is editing." To do so, place two fingers anywhere on the screen and rotate them right or left. An onscreen dial should appear; this is a rotor. If nothing happens, keep trying, making sure it's the pads of your fingers that are touching the screen, and that your fingers are far enough apart for the iPad to detect two fingers. While you're doing this, listen for VoiceOver to speak options such as "Containers," "Headings," "Characters," or "Words." When you hear "typing mode," lift your fingers from the screen and stop there. There's no need to double tap rotor options to confirm. Now, flick up or down with one finger to cycle through Standard, Touch, and Direct Touch options. When you hear "Touch Typing," stop flicking up or down.

4. Type your title, "Banjo Lesson," using the touch-typing mode with the onscreen keyboard. Begin by gently touching the letter *B*. VoiceOver will announce it. Then lift your finger to activate the letter. There's no need to double tap to confirm. Repeat this procedure for the remaining letters. If you touch down and hear the wrong letter, don't release your finger, but you slide your finger around the keyboard and hear the correct one. (More information about using the online keyboard appears in Chapter 7.) After typing "Banjo Lesson," the VoiceOver cursor will be stationed at the end of your title in the edit field.

5. Provide a location for your event. The location field is below the text field. To locate it, you must move your finger above the keyboard and explore by touch. Once you find the field, double tap and then type where the event will take place.

6. Provide start and end times for your event. Double tap the item below the location field to indicate that your event will last all day. Or you may go to the next field to enter start and end times. When you locate and double tap the start time field, VoiceOver will read, by default, the current date, and it will choose the top of the hour closest to the time when you are creating this appointment. Enter your own start and end times using the picker items for days, hours, minutes, and AM/PM found below the start and end time options. Picker items are fields that allow you to change the days, hours, and other options by flicking one finger up to move forward, or by flicking one finger down to move back. Calendar pickers "wrap," so if the hour is set to 1 and you need 11, you can flick down twice and you'll arrive at 11. The end time is automatically set for an hour after the start time. If that's not what you want, double tap the End button, just above the All Day header, and then adjust the pickers as necessary.

7. Set the date using the leftmost picker. If VoiceOver doesn't speak the date you want, flick up to advance the date, or down to move it backward. When this picker is set to your liking, flick right and adjust the next one. Do this until all the pickers are set properly for your event.

8. Explore additional controls. Repeat allows you to repeat this event at a frequency of your choosing. Travel Time enables you to build additional time into your event's schedule.

9. Add a timed alert for your event by swiping right with one finger and double tapping on "Alert." The default is set to None, but you can select one of the following: At time of event, 5 minutes before, 15 minutes before, 30 minutes before, 1 hour before, 2 hours before, 1 day before, 2 days before, and 1 week before.

10. To enter a URL (web address) for your event, locate the URL control, double tap, and enter the web address.

11. Locate and double tap the Notes button to tie a text note to this appointment.

12. Select and double tap the Done button in the upper-right corner to return to the Add Event screen. The Cancel button is in the upper-left corner.

Note: Every screen you access from this Event screen also has Cancel and Done buttons in the same locations. If you need to change the details of an existing event, open its event screen and flick to the Edit button in the right corner, then double tap. The form is identical to the one you used to create the event, so make whatever changes are necessary. You can also delete the event entirely using the Delete Event button that appears below the other information. You may review, edit, or delete this event by closing and reopening the Calendar app, flicking to and double tapping on the day you scheduled the event, then flicking to and double tapping the event title. Now, you can edit any of the fields of the event, or flick to and double tap the Cancel button to delete it. You'll need to flick to and double tap Delete a second time to confirm this deletion. Lastly, at the bottom of the Calendar app screen, VoiceOver provides three buttons— Today, for viewing today's events; Calendars, for viewing other calendars that may exist on other iOS devices associated with your Apple ID; and Inbox, for creating meeting invitations to invite others to an event or meeting that you are hosting.

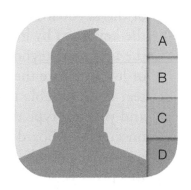

Adding a Contact Using VoiceOver

Contacts is another app, which allows you to keep an address book on your iPad (see Figure 2.5). To add a contact, follow these steps:

FIGURE 2.5

iOS Contacts app icon.

1. Flick right or left from the home screen until "Contacts" is spoken, and double tap.

2. Flick right from the upper left corner to locate the + icon near the top of the screen, which is spoken as "Add button," and double tap (see Figure 2.6).

3. Pause and listen for "Cancel" to be spoken. This button allows you to stop adding a contact, if necessary.

4. A contact's photo can be added by flicking right.

FIGURE 2.6

The Contacts app Add Contact screen.

Add Photo provides an option to associate someone's photo either saved on the iPad or one gleaned from a social network like Facebook or Twitter to be associated with an individual's contact details. By default, "First name" will be spoken, and you'll be placed in an active edit field to enter the first name of the contact. When VoiceOver speaks the prompt, "Text field is editing," type the person's first name using the onscreen QWERTY keyboard set to your preferred VoiceOver keyboard entry method.

5. Add the last name. If you flick right or left at this point, you'll only hear the letters of the keyboard because that's where the cursor is. The user may wish to remove the keyboard by locating the Hide Keyboard button on the lower right corner of the onscreen keyboard. Double tap. This may make it easier for you to flick right or left to locate the field for last name. You should hear VoiceOver say, "Last name, text field. Double tap to edit." The keyboard will reappear for you to proceed and you can type the last name. If you mistype, simply use the Delete key on the onscreen keyboard. Double tap after you type the last name, company, telephone number or numbers, and all other pertinent fields that are available by repeating this process.

6. Locate the Done button toward the top of the screen and double tap it to add the contact.

7. Review your new contact in the list of contacts by double tapping when you hear, "All Contacts." By default, VoiceOver is on a Refresh button, which, when double tapped, refreshes your list of contacts.

As you add contacts, you'll notice they are alphabetized. You can review and edit a contact by flicking right (forward) or left (backward) through the contacts, and then double tapping on any given contact. To find a contact more quickly, flick left and double tap the Search field, located at the top of the left-hand column, and type in a contact's first or last name. Exercise caution when you touch the screen to land on the keyboard near the bottom third of the screen, or you'll inadvertently select a contact instead of a letter on the keyboard. To clear the search field at any time, flick right and double tap the Clear Text button located at the end of the search field.

Note: Although many of the steps in Notes, Calendar, and Contacts can be simplified using Siri, Apple's personal assistant, this chapter focused on practicing VoiceOver gestures so that you might progress to more advanced concepts and exercises in later chapters. Also, Siri does not always do what you tell her. (Siri will be discussed in Chapter 3).

Practicing VoiceOver Gestures

Getting used to VoiceOver gestures takes practice. Apple created a VoiceOver Practice utility that lets you practice them. Once these gestures become part of your body memory, performing them becomes second nature. You won't even have to think about it. To get to the VoiceOver practice screen when using VoiceOver:

1. Press the home button.

2. Go to Settings.

3. Go to General.

4. Go to Accessibility.

5. Flick right once after you hear "Vision, heading" and you should hear, "VoiceOver on button." Double tap and you should hear, "VoiceOver on; double tap to toggle setting." Don't do it. You need more VoiceOver practice.

6. Flick right until you hear, "VoiceOver practice." Double tap. You will be taken to a blank screen where you can practice your gestures.

7. Tap anywhere on the general screen area to direct the cursor, and use the blank screen to practice some gestures while listening to VoiceOver announce what each one does. A shortcut to VoiceOver practice is to double tap four fingers on the screen at any time. To exit this utility, locate the Done button in the upper-right corner of the screen. Double tap to exit VoiceOver Practice and you should hear, "Done." You may also double tap four fingers or press the home button to exit.

You can use this practice screen with your students. VoiceOver will speak the function of the specific gesture without actually issuing the command. It's a secure way to build up your or your students' muscle memory. Of course, these gestures will mean more when they are actually employed.

There's also an app called VoiceOver Starter, available without charge from the App Store (see the Resources section at the end of this book), which guides new VoiceOver users through the various types of controls. The app provides users with a practice space for becoming more familiar with the controls.

Finally, you may encounter pop-up windows from time to time. Pop-ups vary in size, but usually don't cover the whole screen and may appear (pop up) when you select an option. The pop-up window contains a menu of commands. To dismiss pop-ups with VoiceOver on, double tap the screen with one finger.

The Zoom Screen Magnifier

Zoom is Apple's screen magnifier which, when activated, can provide magnification for any screen displayed on the device. When using magnification, only a portion of what is contained on the screen is displayed. Those who use Zoom regularly learn where certain screen elements are located, which can increase efficiency and cut down on the need to pan around the screen.

Activate Zoom by going to the Accessibility section of the General area of the Settings menu and selecting Zoom. See Chapter 3 for details on how to customize the Zoom settings you see on that screen, but note that Zoom can be set for either Window Zoom—a limited and adjustable area of magnification on the screen (see Figure 2.7)—or Full-Screen Zoom.

The Zoom gestures you'll want to familiarize yourself with include the following:

FIGURE 2.7

The Zoom Window magnifying the home screen. The handle to move the window is at the bottom center of the window's border.

- **Zoom.** Double tap three fingers to bring up the Zoom window, which magnifies the screen 200 percent.

- **Adjust zoom magnification up or down.** Double tap with three fingers and leave your fingers on the screen; don't lift them. Now drag your three fingers up to zoom or enlarge. To reduce, drag down.

- **Pan.** After adjusting the magnification to your liking, slide three fingers around the screen to pan.

- **Move the Zoom window.** If Window Zoom is enabled, rather than Full-Screen Zoom, you can drag the handle—a little bubble at the bottom center of the Zoom window's border—to move the window around the screen.

- **Bring up the Zoom menu.** Triple tap with three fingers to view the Zoom menu. (See Chapter 3 for an additional discussion of Zoom features, including the menu options.)

Alternatively, to enlarge a portion of the screen without Zoom, you can use the "pinch out" gesture, although it only works in selected apps, such as Safari. To pinch out, place your thumb and forefinger close together on the screen and spread them apart. As you do this, that portion of the screen will enlarge. To reduce, bring your thumb and forefinger closer together in the "pinch in" gesture.

There are situations where Zoom is not ideal, such as interactive educational apps that include iCalculator or anything else with multiple close-range buttons, including games. Likewise, when a student is editing text or making an appointment, depending on how large the student has made the type using Zoom, it may be difficult to access the onscreen keyboard and view what is being typed at the same time, although the new smart typing feature does minimize this issue. It can be quite frustrating to pan between the text field and onscreen keyboard. In some circumstances, Zoom users seem to need an external keyboard (see Chapter 4) as much as VoiceOver users. To experience this situation, make sure the smart type feature is not running, follow these steps to type in Notes using Zoom, and draw your own conclusion:

1. Make sure that Zoom is turned on under Accessibility Settings.

2. Press the home button to return to the home screen.

3. Double tap the screen with three fingers and without lifting your fingers from the screen, slide your three fingers up to enlarge and down to minimize. If your students require a significant degree of magnification, simulate the magnification level that they would use.

4. Lift your three fingers off the screen when you have reached the desired magnification.

5. To pan around the screen, touch down with three fingers and don't lift them. Drag the three fingers around the Zoom window to view the magnified app icons.

6. Alternately, touch the handle at the bottom center of the Zoom window's border (which looks like a little bubble) and drag it to move the Zoom window around the screen.

7. Pan or move around the screen until you locate the Notes app. Touch once to open.

8. Pan or move around the Notes screen to locate the button with the pencil and paper graphic, which adds a new note.

9. Pan down the screen by moving your three fingers in an upward motion until the keyboard shows on screen or move the Zoom window down to the keyboard.

10. Use the onscreen keyboard to type a few lines of text. Since you cannot see what you are typing, you will need to slide your three fingers to pan back to the edit field where text is displayed or alternatively move the Zoom window back up.

11. Double tap three fingers without lifting them and slide them down to reduce the level at which the screen is magnified.

12. Return to the Accessibility screen to turn Zoom off, double tap with three fingers, or use the Accessibility Shortcut to do so.

Zoom and VoiceOver Gesture Conflicts

For many students with visual impairments, Zoom alone is not enough for effective use of the iPad. However, it is possible to run VoiceOver and Zoom simultaneously. This enables large-print users to benefit from secondary speech output, while speech users may take advantage of their functional vision using Zoom.

With this good news comes bad news: gesture conflicts can arise when Zoom and VoiceOver are used simultaneously. For example, Zoom uses the three-finger double tap to change magnification, which conflicts with VoiceOver's three-finger double tap to mute speech. With Zoom, you toggle Speech with a three-finger triple tap, which conflicts with the VoiceOver gesture used to toggle Screen Curtain on and off, an option that allows the nonvisual user to black out their screen. So a user could conceivably mute their speech when wishing to turn on their screen curtain with a three finger triple tap gesture, or inadvertently change the screen's zoom by double tapping with three fingers when wishing to mute VoiceOver's speech. When Zoom is enabled, toggle speech by triple tapping three times, and turn on the VoiceOver screen curtain by tapping with three fingers four times, which will accommodate the three-finger double-tap gesture for Zoom.

Conclusion

This chapter introduced VoiceOver gestures; showed you how to open, close, and switch apps; explained how to perform a few tasks using VoiceOver; provided some resources for additional VoiceOver gesture practice; and introduced you to the Zoom screen magnifier. In the next chapter you will become even more familiar with the many accessibility options offered by your iPad, and you'll get to know Siri and how and when it can be effectively used.

CHAPTER 3

Setting Accessibility Options

IN THIS CHAPTER

- ■ Setting additional nonvisual iOS accessibility options
- ■ Identifying tools for students with some functional vision
- ■ Exploring options for customizing the VoiceOver screen reader
- ■ Introducing Siri

---

iPads are being used by more students in more classrooms than ever before, and there's no sign the trend will slow down anytime soon. The prevalence of iPads in the classroom presents both opportunities and obstacles for students with visual impairments. For its part, Apple has done a comprehensive job of devising a set of gestures that allow efficient nonvisual access to a totally visual interface.

This chapter will explain how to set accessibility options with VoiceOver turned off. While Voiceover should not be viewed as a distraction, as you begin to explore some of the features within the Accessibility Learning and Interaction options that will be described in this chapter, serious conflicts between VoiceOver's gestures and the features' intended functionality could arise. If you are a reader who is visually impaired, you can leave VoiceOver on while making the necessary gesture adjustments to follow along, but be mindful of pitfalls.

Setting Accessibility Options

Opt to turn VoiceOver off by triple clicking the home button. Now return to Settings.

From the main Settings screen you may search for any of the settings options present (see Figure 3.1) by using the onscreen keyboard to enter the word or phrase related to the setting. (If your iPad has an operating system earlier than iOS 9, you may need to tap General and then locate the Accessibility option instead of searching.) Throughout this chapter, references will be made to the location of a number of settings. You may search for all of them using the following procedure:

1. Tap Settings in the search box and the onscreen keyboard will appear.

2. Type the word "accessibility" and search results such as Accessibility and Accessibility Shortcut are presented.

3. Make the onscreen keyboard disappear, if you'd like, by selecting the Hide Keyboard button in the lower righthand corner of the keyboard.

4. Select Accessibility, which is divided into five sections: Vision, Interaction, Hearing, Media, and Learning. While this book's focus is on Vision features, the other sections are also discussed in this chapter since some students with visual impairments have additional impairments that those settings may address.

Vision Options

In the Accessibility menu, tap on VoiceOver (see Figure 3.2) to see the available options.

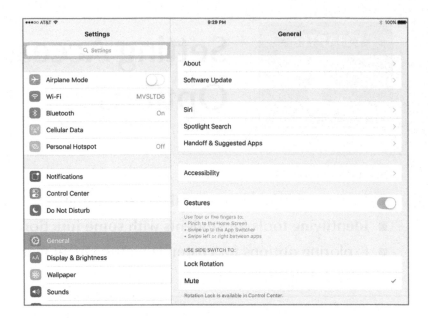

FIGURE 3.1

The Search box is located at top left of the iOS Settings menu.

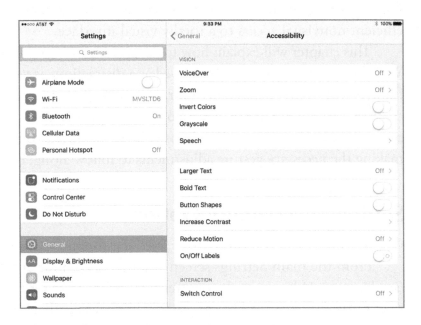

FIGURE 3.2

The Vision options in the Accessibility menu.

VoiceOver

You have been using VoiceOver until now with most of the default settings in place. Review the options on the VoiceOver menu (see Figure 3.3) and change the settings listed here to customize VoiceOver:

- **Speaking Rate.** This slider increases or decreases the speed at which VoiceOver reads the contents of the screen. Slide your finger over the bar from the tortoise icon to the hare icon to increase the rate of speech, and in the opposite direction to slow it down. (To adjust the rate with VoiceOver on, navigate to this setting and use a one-finger flick up or down to increase or decrease the rate of speech.)

- **Speak Hints.** This option is enabled by default and provides additional information on how to use a button or feature. Advanced users may wish to disable this feature.

- **Use Pitch Change.** This feature is particularly helpful when capital letters and punctuation are read.

- **Use Sound Effects.** This one is used when toggling VoiceOver on and off; it clicks when gestures are performed.

- **Speech.** This button is tied to the speech options on the main Vision menu, which are discussed later in this chapter. It allows you to view and change the default dialect and language for VoiceOver. It also allows for the addition of languages to be accessed and changed on the fly by the rotor gesture, which will be covered in greater detail as you learn how to maximize the use of VoiceOver.

- **Braille.** This setting allows you to connect and use wireless refreshable braille displays with VoiceOver. Its setup and functionality are covered in depth in Chapter 4.

- **Rotor.** The rotor function offers flexible navigation tools for accessing a website or for moving around a document, as discussed in Chapter 2. More importantly, the rotor enables you to move your cursor position by character, word, and line—essential ingredients for editing a document. The rotor also allows for changing the method of typing on the onscreen keyboard, as well as the ability to select, cut, copy, and paste text on your iPad. Finally, the rotor allows you to toggle to different languages on the fly when using a variety of multilingual apps. This important feature will be thoroughly explained in Chapter 6.

- **Typing Style.** This sets the onscreen keyboard's default method of typing to standard, touch, or direct touch. With touch typing, you touch the letter or number you want then lift your finger to enter it, while with standard you double tap each letter or number. In direct touch typing, you touch a key and immediately lift your finger to enter that character, or, you drag a finger around the keyboard to find the correct key, then lift your finger to type that key. (Using the onscreen keyboard is discussed in detail in Chapter 7.)

- **Phonetic Feedback.** This option associates a word from the phonetic alphabet with a letter. When enabled, when the letter *b* is spoken, VoiceOver will say "bravo." When *d* is spoken, VoiceOver will say "delta." This option is on by default for when the character is announced, followed by a phoenetic when one navigates by character or explores the onscreen keyboard while typing. It may be toggled off, or set to only announce phoenetics, thereby skipping the pronunciation of the character.

- **Typing Feedback.** Chooses whether VoiceOver speaks nothing, characters, words, or characters and words when either an onscreen software keyboard or an external hardware keyboard or braille display is used. Advanced students may want VoiceOver to speak only words, or nothing, when they are inputting text, especially with an external keyboard or refreshable braille display. Make your selections by tapping on the options for software and hardware.

- **Modifier Keys.** You may select the modifier keys to be used on an external keyboard to invoke VoiceOver commands from the external keyboard, as discussed in Chapter 4. By default, Ctrl + Opt are specified. You may switch this option to the Caps Lock key as an alternative.

- **Always Speak Notifications.** This feature is off by default but allows for a variety of notifications from specific apps and VoiceOver when the screen is locked or unlocked. If notifications are spoken when the screen is locked, the screen will resume its locked mode within a few seconds of the notification being spoken.

- **Navigate Images.** This is always on by default. It can be set to only announce images with descriptive text or to skip images altogether.

- **Large Cursor.** This option is off by default, but can be easily enabled by toggling this option. The large cursor provides a thicker and bolder border around selected items.

■ **Double-tap Timeout.** You can set the timeout interval for issuing a second tap on a double-tap gesture. This is a useful addition for VoiceOver users with physical motor difficulties that affect their fingers, so that the interval between taps can be greater. By default, this is set to 0.25 seconds and can be increased and decreased by 0.05 second intervals.

Zoom

Under VoiceOver in the Vision section of the Accessibility menu is Zoom. Customize the Zoom screen magnifier with these settings:

■ **Follow Focus.** When enabled, Zoom is tethered to the area of the screen that has the focus—the selected item or the insertion point in a text field.

■ **Smart Typing.** When enabled and when a keyboard and an edit field are in focus, the edit field is magnified while the keyboard is not.

■ **Show Controller.** When enabled, a round button with four arrows appears on the screen. Tapping it once will bring up the Zoom menu, which shows a list of Zoom options, including zooming in or out, toggling between full screen and window zoom, resizing the lens, choosing a filter or different colors for the window, and hiding the controller. Double tapping the Controller zooms in and out. When zoomed in, dragging the Controller pans the Zoom window.

■ **Zoom Region.** This option allows you to switch between Window Zoom and Full-Screen Zoom. By default, this option is set to zoom the contents of the Window in focus.

■ **Zoom Filter.** This provides options for inverting the colors on the screen, providing a grayscale background, or filtering for low light.

■ **Maximum Zoom Level.** This option allows you to adjust the magnification level of the screen between 1.2x to 15x.

Following are some other options in the Vision section of the Accessibility menu.

Invert Colors

This setting toggles the screen's color scheme from light to dark, and the text from black to white. You can set the Accessibility Shortcut to activate or deactivate this option. This reverse-colors feature works on all screens, and can be used with Zoom and VoiceOver. Many visually impaired students with glare sensitivities may want to use the iPad with a black background for better contrast. Invert Colors does not work well with photos; it makes them appear as negatives.

Grayscale
Converts all screens to display only black, white, and grey.

Speech
The Speech option offers a few auditory settings independent of VoiceOver usage that are preferred by some low vision users who do not wish to use all of the features of VoiceOver:

- **Speak Selection.** Enabling this setting allows you to select onscreen text using VoiceOver gestures or the corresponding braille commands and hear the text spoken. This is useful when cutting, copying, and pasting text and for selecting an article within Safari and having that content spoken—a comfortable way to review information audibly from the Internet.

- **Speak Screen.** When enabled, swiping two fingers down the screen once will read the entire contents of the screen without interruption. The Voices setting offers several options for the default voice: female voice (Samantha), or the female and male voice options of Siri. You also can select different languages to be spoken, adjust the speaking rate, and select whether you wish for spoken text to be highlighted on the screen. The latter could be effective for getting users with functional vision used to listening to text as it is being displayed and spoken.

- **Speak Auto-text.** When this option is enabled, auto-corrections and auto-capitalizations will be spoken aloud so you can decide whether to change the correction or accept it and keep typing.

Larger Text
This feature enables you to adjust the font size for any and all applications while leaving all icons and objects unmagnified and unchanged. That is, only the text is magnified. This is known as dynamic type, which provides automatic adjustments to letter spacing and line height for every font size, thereby enabling you to specify different text styles for distinct blocks of text (body, footnotes, headlines, and the like). This is a powerful feature, though it will not work with apps that do not include dynamic type. Before continuing, enable Larger Text and adjust the size of the type. Try writing a note in the Notes application to ascertain how this larger font may assist or distract your visually impaired students.

Bold Text
When enabled, fonts displayed in apps and menus will be presented in boldface. Activating this item will cause your iPad to restart.

Button Shapes

When enabled, this setting will distinguish the buttons and controls that can be activated using taps and text from those that must be activated with gestures. It creates tappable interface elements highlighted in gray. Actionable items such as menus and Send buttons will also display an underline indicating that you can tap on them to perform an action.

Increase Contrast

When enabled, this setting improves the distinction between background and text in the interest of making the text easier to read.

Reduce Motion

The Reduce Motion option reduces the movement of some screen elements.

On/Off Labels

This option applies an on/off label, where a vertical line means "on" and a circle means "off" to toggle buttons within iOS apps in addition to the color-coded toggle button (where green means "on" and white means "off").

Interaction Options

The next main section on the Accessibility menu contains Interaction Options (see Figure 3.4).

Switch Control

Apple's Switch Control setting gives people with mobility impairments greater access to their iPads by allowing them to customize how items displayed on the device are highlighted and selected. In addition to using the screen as a switch to activate items, you can connect external switches, or use head movements to

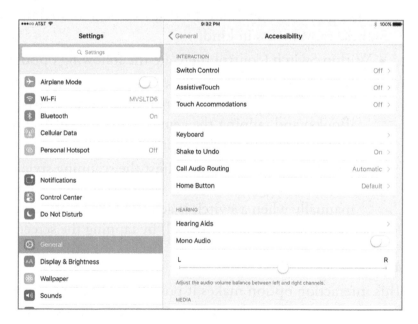

FIGURE 3.4

The Interaction options in the Accessibility menu.

navigate menus, switch between apps, and the like. When these settings are activated, iOS will sequentially cycle through all of the apps and folders on a given screen. Here are a few examples of how Switch Control might be used when enabled:

- AbleNet's Blue2 and other external switches connect to iOS devices via Bluetooth and can be used as single or dual switches. The Blue2 can toggle the onscreen keyboard on and off and can serve as a wireless transmitter when switches are connected to the two switch jacks.

- Screen taps on the device can serve as external switches. The vertical scan shows each row on the home screen. Select and single tap a row. This starts a left-to-right scan. Select and single tap a particular item.

- With head gestures enabled within the "switches" option, you may assign head movements to activate the home screen, navigate the screen, and perform various touch gestures via left and right head movements. To use head gestures, select "Switches" followed by "Add New Switch." Select "Camera" as the source that will serve as the new switch to capture the respective head movements and communicate their assigned actions to the iPad. Select "Left Head Movement" or "Right Head Movement" as the means by which your students can navigate and interact with menus and apps. You assign one of the various options to moving one's head either to the right or the left, and the iPad's camera located on the touch screen will respond to these movements in kind.

- Within Switch Control there are the following options:
  - **Recipes.** Recipes are actions that can be temporarily assigned to a switch. By default, two recipes are offered: the ability to turn pages (useful for an app such as iBooks) and tapping the center of the screen. You may create additional recipes and assign them to a specific switch.
  - **Scanning Style.** You can adjust the scanning style on the screen when a switch is in use, meaning that the focus will shift automatically within a preset time frame, or manually when a switch is activated. You may adjust scanning style and the switch mode (automatic or manual) by tapping the screen.

Assistive Touch

This interaction option makes it possible for students with motor difficulties to use the touchscreen on the iPad in a customized fashion. By enabling Assistive Touch, you can customize specific menus and controls on your iPad, create specific gestures for these students, and save the gestures as Favorites. It's best to leave this option turned off when it's not needed, since it can interfere with some VoiceOver controls.

Touch Accommodations

Touch Accommodations allows the user to set the duration for how long to hold a finger down on the screen to activate a gesture and to determine whether a repeated touch should be ignored. Tap Assistance allows for using the initial touch or final touch to execute a gesture.

Keyboard

You can customize onscreen and external keyboards and sticky keys in this section. *(Sticky keys allow users to use keyboard shortcuts or type capital letters by pressing certain keys one at a time. For example, the Shift, Ctrl, and Alt keys will remain active until the next key in the command is pressed.)*

Shake to Undo

When this option is enabled, an Undo prompt will appear when the device is shaken. You may want to turn this feature off if a student tends to inadvertently shake his or her iPad.

Call Audio Routing

When enabled, audio may be routed through a Bluetooth headset or external speaker when a FaceTime call is made.

Home Button

Because clicking the home button at the default speed required to invoke the Accessibility Shortcut can be problematic for some students, you have the option to slow the required speed down here.

Hearing Options

The following are the Hearing options on the main Accessibility menu (see Figure 3.5).

Hearing Aids

You can pair your iPad (4th generation or later) to a

FIGURE 3.5

The Hearing options in the Accessibility menu, also showing the Media and Learning options.

hearing aid designed to accept audio output via a Bluetooth connection by enabling the Hearing Aids setting. The iPad will search for hearing aids within range when this option is enabled. Select the hearing aid and enter the pairing code to complete the connection.

Mono Audio
Here you may toggle Mono Audio on and off. By default, the iPad is set to play audio in stereo, which is obvious when headphones are used.

Balance
Using the provided slider, you can adjust the volume balance of the stereo output between left and right ears. The default setting for the hearing option is set to 50 percent, but if you move the button along the spectrum with your finger, you can adjust the volume balance between left and right channels. This is particularly useful for students with hearing loss in one ear.

Media Options
The Media options section of the accessibility menu (also shown in Figure 3.5) allows you to control options when playing videos on the iPad.

Subtitles and Captioning
Here you can indicate a preference for subtitles or closed captioning on video playback (if available). The style setting allows you to customize typeface, font size, background color, and the like.

Audio Descriptions
Audio description for video may be enabled for people with visual impairments. When this setting is enabled, videos with audio description tracks will play the description automatically to let people with visual impairments know what is occurring visually within the video.

Learning Options
The final group in the Accessibility menu is Learning, and it has only one menu item, Guided Access (see Figure 3.5). Guided Access allows a parent, teacher, or administrator to limit the iOS device to a single app by disabling the home button, as well as to restrict certain areas of the screen to touch input. By default, this option is disabled.

Tap on Guided Access to turn on this feature. You will be asked to set a passcode. This prevents a student who is restricted to a single app from returning to the home screen to access other apps. After Guided Access has been turned on and you have provided a passcode, return to the home screen and select an app to open it. Triple click the home button, and you will be taken to a screen where you can disable or configure these settings:

- **Touch.** Use when you don't want users to be able to use the touch screen. There may be times you wish to prevent the student from issuing gestures to activate features on the iPad.
- **Motion.** Renders the iPad unresponsive if the user moves it. Triple click the home button and enter the passcode again to return to the home screen.
- **Hardware buttons.** Hardware buttons can be switched off while Guided Access is on, which means that nothing will happen when the user presses the home, power, or volume buttons.

Accessibility Shortcut

The Accessibility Shortcut is the last item on the Accessibility menu in Settings. As noted in Chapter 1, this menu item provides the options that can be activated when the Home button is pressed three times. In Chapter 1, this shortcut was set to turn VoiceOver on and off.

Activating Siri on Your iPad

If you have a third- or fourth-generation iPad with iOS 6 or later, you can take advantage of the iOS personal assistant, Siri. If you haven't done so already, turn Siri on via the General Settings Siri screen.

To use Siri you must have Internet access. Press and hold the home button until Siri opens. It shows up onscreen directly above the home button, and speaks in a voice that is diferent from that of the synthesizer used by VoiceOver. Siri responds to spoken commands. Upon opening, it will ask, "What can I help you with?" If your students do not wish, or are unable, to press and hold the home button to activate Siri, you may enable the Hey Siri option in the Siri settings menu, which allows you to say "Hey Siri" to open the assistant. VoiceOver will say, "Listen button. Double tap and then speak to use Siri." You may also wait for the two short, successive tones after Siri speaks and then speak your question or command. You can say something as simple as, "Open App Store," or you may ask something more complex such as, "What is the capital of Arkansas?" Siri can even "tweet," provided you have downloaded and set up the Twitter app. To find out more about what Siri can do, press and hold the home button and after Siri asks, "What can I help you with?" you can ask Siri, "What can you do?"

Although Siri isn't always reliable, it continues to improve. Siri currently provides access to Messages, Reminders, Calendar, Maps, Mail, Clock, Contacts, Notes, and Safari. You may also change the dialect of Siri and its default language, and associate the Siri app with the contact details that you entered into your iPad's Contacts App with the Siri app to personalize the Siri experience.

Conclusion

There are a host of other settings available to you under Settings on the home screen. Information about these options can be found in the *iPad User's Guide,* which can be found online and through iTunes (see the Resources section at the end of this book for more information). iTunes will be covered in more detail in Chapter 5.

Now that you are more familiar with the plethora of accessibility settings available on the iPad, it's time to become acquainted with external keyboards and refreshable braille displays.

CHAPTER
4

External Keyboards and Refreshable Braille Displays

IN THIS CHAPTER

- Using an external Bluetooth QWERTY keyboard
- Reviewing wireless keyboard commands
- Using a refreshable braille display
- Reviewing common braille display commands for the iPad

---

iOS devices utilize Bluetooth, a wireless service that allows you to connect your iPad to any number of external devices, such as a keyboard or refreshable braille display. When watching proficient iPad users who are blind at work, notice how much more efficiently and accurately they move around an iPad using commands from an external keyboard or refreshable braille display, or both, than using the screen commands that have been discussed in previous chapters. In fact, such users will rarely touch the actual screen. And, for the most part, they will use the same braille and screen reader commands they are accustomed to using with braille notetakers and computers with screen readers. This is therefore a key option meeting the needs of students who are blind or visually impaired.

This chapter will show you how to connect an external keyboard and a refreshable braille device to an iPad. In both cases, you must activate Bluetooth first, and then pair the iPad with your preferred device.

Bluetooth Keyboards

The exercises covered in Chapter 2 show how challenging an onscreen keyboard can be for typing lengthy assignments requiring robust word processing, which is why many sighted iPad users often rely on external keyboards. For this reason, and with prices averaging about $70, buying an Apple keyboard or another iOS-compatible keyboard is a sound investment.

You might also consider Apple's iPad Keyboard Dock combination: a full-size keyboard that sits atop a charging dock so you can charge the device while you type. This option is a bit large for transporting in a backpack, so it may be best used at home or in a classroom setting.

Pairing a Bluetooth Keyboard to the iPad

You can pair only one wireless keyboard with any iPad at a time (see Figure 4.1). To pair an external keyboard with your iPad, follow these steps:

1. Turn on the external keyboard.
2. Open Settings on the iPad.
3. Click on Bluetooth and activate it by tapping once with one finger (see Figure 4.2); if VoiceOver is active, double tap. This will toggle Bluetooth services on and off.
4. Once Bluetooth is on, your iPad will display the name of your iPad and a message that your device is now "discoverable." This means that your iPad may be discovered by other Bluetooth devices, and, conversely, that your iPad may discover or find other devices.
5. The iPad will now begin to scan or search for other devices. Allow the iPad to search for the QWERTY

FIGURE 4.1

An iPad with a wireless QWERTY keyboard. The Bluetooth wireless symbol indicates that they are connected.

FIGURE 4.2

The iOS Settings menu showing the Bluetooth option.

keyboard. Consult your keyboard's documentation to ensure that your keyboard is discoverable to other Bluetooth devices that are searching for it.

6. Select and tap the keyboard once iPad has found it.

7. Enter the pairing code that came with your keyboard (typically 0000, 1111, or 1234). Once you are informed that the keyboard is connected, the two devices will communicate with each other whenever both are turned on and within approximately 30 to 45 feet of each other. The only time you would need to repeat this process is if your keyboard's battery goes dead.

Note: To pair a different keyboard, you must first "unpair" the current one.

Once the keyboard is connected, your students can navigate and enter text much like they would on a computer. To explore what the keyboard can do, press Ctrl + Opt + K to access the practice gestures screen, where keystrokes are not acted on, and where VoiceOver announces what the keystrokes do.

Using the external keyboard will be much easier than panning between edit fields and the onscreen keyboard. Productivity will increase, frustration will decrease, and you and your students can concentrate on completing the tasks at hand.

Wireless Keyboard Commands on the iPad

Table 4.1 shows the keystrokes you can use for navigating and editing your iPad from an Apple wireless keyboard, many of which do not have Escape or Backspace keys. This may be confusing at first for some students familiar with Windows-style keyboards. Also worth noting is that Apple keyboards have two Command (Cmd) keys and two Option (Opt) keys. The Command keys are located closest to the spacebar one on either side. The Option keys are next to the command keys. In the keystroke commands shown in the table, these keys are used in conjunction with others to provide enhanced functionality.

Refreshable Braille Displays

For VoiceOver users, refreshable braille displays provide an intuitive alternative to using the onscreen keyboard, especially for extended writing tasks when time and accuracy are critical (see Figure 4.3). The commands used with braille displays within VoiceOver were taken from three decades of braille note-taking know-how from leading manufacturers of refreshable braille devices.

VoiceOver supports braille displays that range in price from $995 on the low end to $6,000 on the high end (for a list of refreshable braille displays currently supported by

TABLE **4.1**   Wireless Keyboard Commands

Commands for General Editing

Command	Keystroke
Show or hide the onscreen keyboard	Eject (if present)
Move to the next/previous text field (when using apps like Mail)	Shift + Tab
Undo	Cmd + Z
Redo	Shift + Cmd + Z
Cut	Cmd + X
Copy	Cmd + C
Paste	Cmd + V
Select all	Cmd + A
Delete backward one character	Del
Delete backward one word	Opt + Del
Delete to the end of the line	Ctrl + K
Stop and restart VoiceOver speaking	Ctrl
Change to next language keyboard (when you have more than one language selected)	Cmd + Space Bar
Change to previous language keyboard	Shift + Cmd + Space Bar

Commands for General Movement and Text Selection

Add Shift to the following keystrokes to initiate the corresponding commands below for selecting text.

Command	Keystroke
Move left/right by character	Left/Right Arrow
Move left/right by word	Opt + Left/Right Arrow
Move to the beginning or end of the line	Cmd + Left/Right Arrow or Ctrl + Left/Right Arrow

Command	Keystroke
Move up/down by line	Up/Down Arrow
Move up/down by paragraph	Opt + Up/Down Arrow
Move to the beginning/end of the document	Cmd + Up/Down Arrow

Commands for Typing Special Characters

If you want to type accented characters while using the English keyboard layout, employ one of the following key combinations followed by the letter to be accented. If you use one of the key combinations followed by pressing the Space Bar, the accent mark is displayed without a letter. The only exception is the cedilla, which is always placed under the letter *C*, and therefore is created by simply pressing the Option and C characters together.

Accent Mark	Keystroke
Acute accent (´)	Opt + E
Grave accent (`)	Opt + Accent key (the leftmost key below Esc and above Tab on most keyboards)
Circumflex (^)	Opt + I
Dieresis (¨)	Opt + U
Tilde (~)	Opt + N
Cedilla (ç)	Opt + C

Commands for Navigating

You can use your keyboard to go to the home screen, open apps, and perform most other functions available on the iPad. Often, touching the screen is more convenient, but if you're using the keyboard for typing and need to perform other functions, it's useful to be able to do so without taking your hands off the keyboard. Here are the navigation commands for an Apple wireless keyboard; most apply to other keyboards as well.

Note: Almost all the keyboard commands include the VoiceOver keys Ctrl + Opt. Ctrl + Opt activates VoiceOver commands by using keystrokes on the keyboard in place of gestures you would use when touching the iPad.

(continued)

TABLE **4.1** *(Continued)*

Command	Keystroke
VoiceOver	Ctrl + Opt
Read all, starting from the current position	Ctrl + Opt + A
Read from the top	Ctrl + Opt + B
Pause or resume speech	Ctrl
Move to the status bar	Ctrl + Opt + M
Press the home button	Ctrl + Opt + H
Select the next/previous item	Ctrl + Opt + Right/Left Arrow
Tap an item	Ctrl + Opt + Space Bar
Open the Item Chooser (an alphabetic list of all the items on your device's screen, which can be browsed or searched)	Ctrl + Opt + I
Find text (open a search field)	Ctrl + Opt + F (opens a search field)
Find next	Ctrl + Opt + G
Find previous	Ctrl + Opt + Shift + G
Label the current item	Ctrl + Opt + Slash
Choose the next/previous rotor item	Ctrl + Opt + Up/Down
Choose the next/previous speech rotor item such as speech rate	Ctrl + Opt + Cmd + Left/Right Arrow
Adjust speech rotor item	Ctrl + Opt + Cmd + Up/Down Arrow
Mute or unmute VoiceOver	Ctrl + Opt + S
Turn the screen curtain on or off	Ctrl + Opt + Shift + S
Turn on VoiceOver Help (announces what keys do as you press them)	Ctrl + Opt + K
Return to the previous screen, or turn off VoiceOver help	Esc
Move to the next app on App Switcher	Cmd + Tab
Move to the previous app on App Switcher	Cmd + Shift + Tab

Quick Nav is a feature that allows you to perform a variety of commands without pressing the Control and Option keys. For example, when in the Safari web browser, with Quick Nav enabled, you can use single letters to navigate by web elements. Quick Nav is disabled by default. Toggle Quick Nav on and off by pressing the left and right arrow simultaneously.

Command	Keystroke
Turn Quick Nav on/off	Left Arrow + Right Arrow
Turn single letter Quick Nav on or off	Ctrl + Option + Q
Select the next/previous item	Right/Left Arrow
Change the Rotor setting	Up Arrow + Left/Right Arrow
Select the next/previous item specified by the rotor setting	Up/Down Arrow
Select the first/last item	Ctrl + Up/Down Arrow
Double tap an item	Up Arrow + Down Arrow
Scroll up/down/left/right	Option + Up/Down/Left/Right Arrow

The following commands work on web pages when Quick Nav is on. Add Shift to move back to the previous item of the same type.

Command	Keystroke (Add Shift to move to the previous item)
Next heading	H
Next heading at level 1–6	1 to 6
Next link	L
Next text element	S
Next landmark	W
Next text field	R
Next list	X
Next table	T

(continued)

TABLE **4.1**   *(Continued)*

Command	Keystroke (Add Shift to move to the previous item)
Next element of same type	M
Next image	I
Next button	B
Next form element	C

Source: Adapted from Dresner, A. (2012). *A quick guide to iMessages with VoiceOver.* Boston: National Braille Press.

iOS, visit www.apple.com/accessibility/ios/braille
-display.html). The price difference correlates to
the number of refreshable braille cells the particular
device provides. For example, a 12-cell device
is going to cost much less than a 40-cell one.
In addition, electronic braille notetakers, which
include proprietary internal applications, cost
considerably more than stand-alone braille displays,
because notetakers offer more functionality.

Pairing Your Braille Display to the iPad

As a rule, iOS allows users to pair Bluetooth
devices through its Bluetooth Manager, but
because all the braille display drivers and
functionality are located in the VoiceOver control
panel, Apple insists that you pair your braille
display through VoiceOver's braille settings.

Follow these steps to pair your refreshable braille display to your iPad:

FIGURE **4.3**

**An iPad with a 40-cell braille display
alongside the Bluetooth wireless symbol.**

1. Turn on the braille display; consult the device's documentation if necessary.

2. Navigate to the VoiceOver section of the Accessibility Settings, and tap on VoiceOver.
   If VoiceOver is off, you may leave it off and use standard gestures, or toggle it on and
   utilize VoiceOver gestures.

3. Tap or double tap on the Braille option to activate it (see Figure 4.4). If Bluetooth is not currently active, you will be prompted to turn it on.

4. Choose a braille display under the last option on the Braille settings screen (see Figure 4.5); your iPad will scan the immediate vicinity and identify any braille devices that are powered on and are in range (it is recommended to have only one braille device powered on within range).

5. Activate the appropriate braille display listed on the screen.

6. Enter the device's pairing code using the onscreen keyboard when asked. You will be asked this if this is the first time that you've connected your display.

7. Activate by selecting the Pair or Done button when completed.

Your display should now be connected, and braille should appear on the display when VoiceOver is turned on. The iPad will make an audible

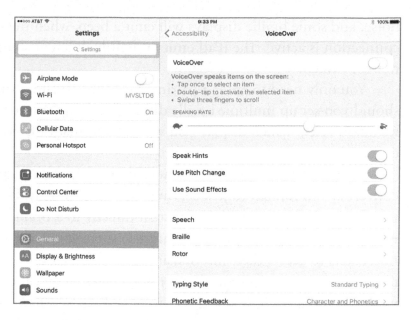

FIGURE 4.4

The VoiceOver menu in Settings showing the Braille option.

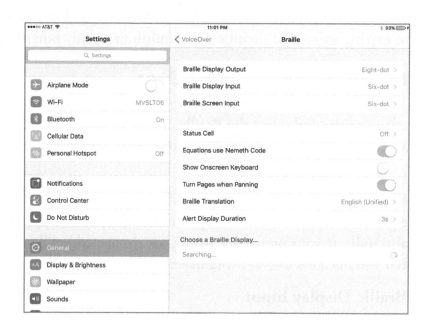

FIGURE 4.5

The options in the Braille settings menu.

noise, and some braille displays will emit a beep, when the pairing is successful and the connection is active. The iPad emits a slightly different sounding tone when the devices are not connected.

You only need to enter a pairing code the first time you connect the devices. However, should you set up multiple braille displays to connect to the iPad, you will have to manually select which display you wish to automatically connect to for each subsequent connection.

When a refreshable braille notetaker is connected to an iPad, its functionality is converted and limited to just serving as a braille display. For example, you can't copy text from a website and save or paste it directly to a BrailleNote file present within the notetaker's word processor. There are also some conflicts between the keystrokes used by notetakers to access their internal apps and those used by Apple to allow the notetaker to access iOS devices. Consult your notetaker's technical documentation, which should provide alternative iOS keystrokes to remedy these conflicts.

Users continue to experience difficulties from time to time in pairing notetaking devices to iOS devices; the devices sometimes become unpaired. These instances require assistance from technical support specialists employed by the notetaker's manufacturer. If a student's primary goal is to first connect the iPad using a refreshable braille display, select a braille display with few or no onboard applications. Such displays primarily serve as braille input/output devices for mainstream products such as the iPad and are less likely to experience such difficulties, thus minimizing any potential technical support hurdles.

Braille Settings in VoiceOver

There are a variety of braille settings available within VoiceOver. Return to the VoiceOver settings page and select the Braille option to have a look. VoiceOver must be turned on and the braille display connected for the key combinations mentioned here to work.

Braille Display Output

From this menu item (see Figure 4.5) you can select uncontracted six-dot, uncontracted eight-dot, and contracted computer braille as your output on the braille display. You can also indicate your preference from your connected braille display's keyboard. Press Space Bar + braille keys 1-2-4-5 (braille letter *G*) to toggle this feature from anywhere within iOS.

Braille Display Input

The Braille Display Input setting allows you to select the type of braille you prefer for input. You can toggle between your set output and input preferences by pressing Space Bar + braille keys 2-3-6. This makes it easier for a student to read contracted braille and then toggle from a contracted braille keyboard input to eight-dot computer braille for writing an e-mail address or entering a website URL. The student may wish to read contracted braille using the Space + G toggle, but independently toggle their mode of braille input using this command.

Braille Screen Input (iOS 8 and Later)

This menu option allows you to set your preference for the type of braille used in the onscreen braille keyboard. The onscreen braille keyboard can be activated via the rotor (discussed in Chapter 6). If you are feeling adventurous, back out of the Braille settings, select the Rotor option, and activate the Braille Screen Input option (see Figure 4.6).

You will see within all edit fields and the Safari web browser (discussed in Chapter 6), that Braille Screen Input is now offered as an

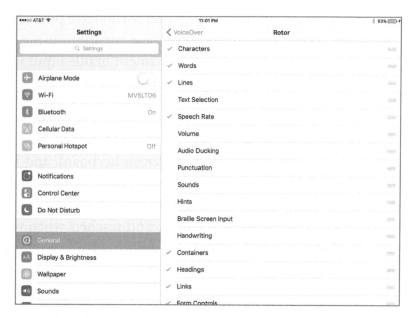

FIGURE **4.6**

The Rotor options in the VoiceOver menu showing the Braille Screen Input option.

option on the rotor. Once you select Braille Screen Input from the rotor options, place both index fingers, both middle fingers, and both ring fingers on the screen as if you were typing on a braille keyboard to begin entering braille characters directly into an active field. This feature allows for the searching of apps from the home screen by typing the braille letters of the specific app; the entering of text within edit fields when a keyboard is present; and the efficient browsing of the Internet using braille-oriented gestures when tapping the screen. When searching for an app from the home screen, there will not be a QWERTY keyboard on the screen, and this does not behave like a typical edit field. Just start brailling characters, and when the app you want is spoken, flick two fingers to the right to launch it.

Status Cell

This option places a single dot in the left-most or right-most cell on a refreshable braille line, which may be helpful for locating either end of a braille display. It is recommended, however, that this option remain in the default off position, as giving up space on a braille display is usually inadvisable.

Equations use Nemeth Code (iOS 7 and Later)

When enabled, this setting provides support for Nemeth braille output when equations are encountered within text. For instance, if you have purchased a math book that includes equations, VoiceOver will translate these equations using Nemeth Braille Code for Mathematics rules. As of iOS 9.2, Nemeth braille input is not yet supported by iOS.

Show Onscreen Keyboard (iOS 7 and Later)

When enabled, this option allows an onscreen keyboard to appear within edit fields as an input option for sighted individuals to interact with users of braille displays. The sighted keyboard user enters text on the onscreen keyboard, and the information is shown on the braille display; the braille user may enter braille characters that are then displayed on the screen. While it's not a perfect method of interaction, this solution can serve as a handy instructional tool for sighted parents and teachers when working with blind students who are reading and writing braille. Also, such a feature begins to lay the groundwork for improved face-to-face communication between sighted and deafblind braille users.

Turn Pages When Panning

While reading a book using an iOS-supported e-book reader (see Chapter 7), this option will automatically turn the page when the reader pans to the bottom of the current page, thus eliminating the need for the reader to manually turn the page.

Braille Translation

This feature's primary role is to establish the default contracted braille translation table when contracted braille is enabled. By default, Apple has set this to be the Unified English Braille (UEB), which provides a unified, consistent braille standard for English-speaking countries in North America. Since this is the adopted braille standard for all of North America, it's best to use UEB as the default contracted braille option for your iPad.

Alert Display Duration

Here you can adjust the duration that iOS alerts are displayed on screen before they disappear. Some braille users may need a little more time to read these messages before they disappear from the display.

Choose a Braille Display . . .

As described earlier in this chapter, here is where you pair your braille display to the iPad.

Using a Braille Display with the iPad

Students using braille displays with their iPads will rarely touch the actual screens. They will use many of the same mnemonic braille screen reading commands they are accustomed to using with braille notetakers and braille displays connected to Windows computers. See Table 4.2 for a summary of common commands.

Because each display's command set is different, your display may offer additional key combinations than those listed in Table 4.2. To explore what your display can do with VoiceOver, press Space Bar + K. This puts you into the practice gestures screen, where keystrokes are not acted on, and where VoiceOver announces what the keystrokes do. Press the Space Bar in combination with all the letters and symbols and try your display's special keys. VoiceOver will tell you what, if any, action the keystroke performs. Not all key combinations are used. Exit this keyboard help mode with Space Bar + B as the back command.

TABLE **4.2** **Braille Display Commands for the iPad**

The following is a generic list of iPad braille display commands for displays that have braille keyboards. Note that the term "chord command" means to press the Space Bar with the dots listed; thus the keys listed below should be pressed in conjunction with the Space Bar.

Action/Function	Chord Command (Space Bar + Braille Keys Indicated)
Move to previous item	Braille key 1
Move to next item	Braille key 4
Pan braille left	Braille key 2
Pan braille right	Braille key 5
Move to the first element	L (braille keys 1-2-3)
Move to the last element	Braille keys 4-5-6
Scroll right one page	O (braille keys 1-3-5)
Scroll left one page	OW sign (braille keys 2-4-6)
Scroll up one page	Braille keys 3-4-5-6

(continued)

TABLE **4.2** *(Continued)*

Action/Function	Chord Command (Space Bar + Braille Keys Indicated)
Scroll down one page	Braille keys 1-4-5-6
Speak page number or rows being displayed	ST sign (braille keys 3-4)
Select previous rotor setting	Braille keys 2-3
Select next rotor setting	Braille keys 5-6
Move to previous item using rotor setting	Braille key 3
Move to next item using rotor setting	Braille key 6
Activate current item	Braille keys 3-6
Move to the status bar	S (braille keys 2-3-4)
Press home button	H (braille keys 1-2-5)
Launch the App Switcher	H (braille keys 1-2-5) twice quickly
Turn on keyboard help	K (braille keys 1-3)
Exit keyboard help	B (braille keys 1-2)
Read all, starting at selected item	R (braille keys 1-2-3-5)
Read all, starting from the top	W (braille keys 2-4-5-6)
Pause or continue speech	P (braille keys 1-2-3-4)
Toggle speech on and off	M (braille keys 1-3-4)
Volume up	AR sign (braille keys 3-4-5)
Volume down	GH sign (braille keys 1-2-6)
Toggle screen curtain on/off	Braille keys 1-2-3-4-5-6
Activate the Back button, cancel, or close pop-up menu	B (braille keys 1-2)
Activate the Delete key	D (braille keys 1-4-5) or braille key 7
Activate the Return key	E (braille keys 1-5) or braille key 8
Activate the Tab key	T (braille keys 2-3-4-5)

Action/Function	Chord Command (Space Bar + Braille Keys Indicated)
Activate the Shift + Tab key combination	OU sign (braille keys 1-2-5-6)
Switch between contracted and uncontracted braille output	G (braille keys 1-2-4-5)
Switch between contracted and uncontracted braille input	Braille keys 2-3-6
Automatically translate to contracted braille	Braille keys 4-5
Quick Nav key toggle	Q (braille keys 1-2-3-4-5)
Single letter Quick Nav key toggle	Braille keys 1-2-3-4-5-7
Select text	Braille keys 2-5-6
Deselect text	Braille keys 2-3-5
Select all	Braille keys 2-3-5-6
Cut text	X (braille keys 1-3-4-6)
Copy text	C (braille keys 1-4)
Paste text	V (braille keys 1-2-3-6)
Undo	Z (braille keys 1-3-5-6)
Redo	Braille keys 2-3-4-6
Create custom label	Braille keys 1-2-3-4-6
Eject key (shows/hides onscreen keyboard)	SH sign (braille keys 1-4-6)

Conclusion

This chapter discussed pairing keyboards and refreshable braille displays to the iPad, and helped you become familiar with the VoiceOver braille settings. Next, you will learn about finding and using apps to assist your students in completing tasks.

CHAPTER 5

Finding and Managing Content

This chapter focuses on using the iPad to complete different tasks. You will want to work intently with your students to ensure that they know where items are located on the home screen and that they are familiar with the screen layouts for their apps.

You will also want to ensure that your students have a working knowledge of the VoiceOver gestures described in Chapter 2, Sidebar 2.1. As for entering data such as e-mail addresses, passwords, and the like, students may rely on either a refreshable braille display with a braille keyboard or a wireless QWERTY keyboard to enter this information, as described in Chapter 4. Some students may surprise you and instead take to either standard or touch typing via the onscreen keyboard, described in detail in Chapter 7.

Setting Up an Apple ID

You may recall that when you booted up your iPad earlier in this book, you were prompted to set up an Apple ID and password—the gateway to your Apple account. If your iPad was purchased by a school district, a technician may have set up an account already. If this is the case, or if you have already set up an Apple ID, you can skip this section. Always check with the school's information technology staff before you set up an account, or log in or out—especially if certain apps have already been purchased by the school district.

Ensuring e-mail accessibility can be tricky. While you will want your students to be able to open messages from the e-mail address associated with your Apple account, the student won't be able to do that if the parent decides to use his or her own e-mail address, along with his or her credit card because by default, obtaining an Apple ID requires you to tie a method of payment to your Apple account to purchase content and apps. In such instances, the parent's e-mail address cancels the student's e-mail address.

However, there is a way for both e-mail addresses to co-exist. Since you may be dealing primarily with *free* content or content that has already been purchased, Apple lets you set up an Apple ID without a method of payment. This can be particularly useful for students who are not in the position to use accounts tied to credit cards. Setting up an account without a method of payment avoids the possibility of any unauthorized purchases made by a student that could be billed to the parent's or school district's primary method of payment.

Note: For simplicity's sake, the following instructions are presented as implemented with VoiceOver off and are subject to change by Apple. (See the Resources section for links to Apple's instructions.) If you are a visually impaired educator or parent, feel free to use VoiceOver with the alternative gestures you have learned.

Without an Associated Payment Method

To set up your Apple ID (for free apps and free or already purchased content) *without* a credit card, follow these steps:

- Tap on the App Store icon (see Figure 5.1) from the home screen. The App Store will be explored in greater detail later in this chapter.
- Find a free app and select it; it doesn't matter which one. There are lots of them, but if you can't find any, skip to the App Store Overview section of this chapter for guidance.
- Tap on the Get button, followed by the Install button.
- Follow the prompts to Create an Apple ID.
- Select None when you are asked for a payment method.

FIGURE 5.1

The iOS App Store icon.

- Enter the rest of the required information and select Done. You will be asked to verify your account before being able to use your ID.
- Verify your account via e-mail: Open the Mail app to find the e-mail sent from Apple. (Chapter 6 covers how to set up and use e-mail.) Tap the Verify Now link to activate your account. You'll be taken to a secure page to enter your Apple ID and password to complete your account verification.

With an Associated Payment Method

To set up an Apple ID (for paid apps and content) *with* an associated credit card, follow these steps:

- Select Settings from the home screen.

- Choose iTunes & App Store (see Figure 5.2).

- Tap Sign In. If an Apple ID is already associated with this iPad, you will see an Apple ID button near the top of the screen that displays the e-mail address for that ID. If you need to set up a new ID, tap this button and then choose Sign Out on the pop-up screen that appears. Then tap Sign In.

- Tap on Create an Apple ID and follow the prompts.

- Choose your region for purchasing content. The default is the country you chose when setting up your device. Then choose Next.

FIGURE 5.2

The options in the iTunes & App Store settings menu.

- Opt to have the Terms and Conditions e-mailed to you for easier reading by tapping Send by E-mail when the screen displays the iTunes Store Terms and Conditions. To do this, enter your e-mail address and tap Send.

- Agree to the Terms and Conditions by tapping the Agree button located in the bottom-right corner of the screen. Tap Agree again when the confirmation appears.

- Enter your e-mail address and password, security questions and answers, and your date of birth. You also can enter an optional rescue e-mail address and decide whether to subscribe to e-mail newsletters from Apple. When you provide a rescue e-mail address, all future security e-mails, such as password resets, will be sent to the rescue e-mail address. The rescue e-mail address must be different from your Apple ID e-mail address, which you will use for logging into Apple's various retail storefronts and services.

- Enter the rest of the required information, and then tap Next.
- Enter your billing information. To change the default card type, select the Credit Card field. Select your card type, and tap Done. You will not be charged until you make a purchase.
- Select Next upon completion of the billing information fields. You'll see a screen that says, "Verify your e-mail address."
- Tap Done, and check your e-mail for a verification message from Apple.
- Open the e-mail and tap the Verify Now link to activate your account. You'll be taken to a secure page to enter your Apple ID and password to complete your account verification.
- Tap Verify Address once you've entered your e-mail address and password.

Note: See the Resources section at the back of this book for links to the Apple ID instructions that these steps were based on.

Apps, iBooks, and iTunes

Once you've established your Apple ID and password, you can begin the process of finding and downloading content to your iPad. Three primary apps deliver content to your iPad:

1. The App Store, which delivers apps.
2. iBooks, which delivers eBooks.
3. iTunes, which delivers multimedia content, such as music, TV shows, and movies.

App Store Overview

The App Store allows you to search for, download, install, and update apps for your iPad, as well as other iOS devices. Downloaded apps can be used on up to five devices. Educational institutions wishing to share an app with more than five devices can purchase volume licenses through the Apple Education Volume Purchase Program (see the Resources section at the back of this book).

The App Store is organized by five tabs displayed at the bottom of the landing screen.

- **Featured.** This tab (see Figure 5.3) presents a list of featured apps available for download. Selecting the Categories button at the top left of the screen displays the featured apps organized by categories such as games, education, and entertainment.

Tapping on See All on the upper right of each category section takes you to a new page containing all of the featured apps in that category. Select an app here and you'll be presented with details and the opportunity to purchase and download the selection.

- **Top Charts.** This tab (see Figure 5.4) lists the current top-selling apps. The apps are listed using three criteria at the top of the page: Paid, Free, or Top Grossing.

- **Explore.** If you enable location services for the App Store (Settings, then Privacy, then Location Services), this tab will show apps that are popular near your location if available (see Figure 5.5). In the left side of the screen are a variety of categories for browsing.

- **Purchased.** This tab (see Figure 5.6) provides a record of apps downloaded and purchased using your Apple ID. You may also review a list of apps that have been purchased via

FIGURE 5.3

The App Store with the Featured tab selected.

FIGURE 5.4

The App Store with the Top Charts tab selected.

another iOS device, but which are not installed on your iPad. You can select these uninstalled apps and install them from this tab.

- **Updates.** When selected, this tab (see Figure 5.7) displays the installed apps that have updates available for download. By default, updates to apps are automatically downloaded. You may toggle this feature on and off within the iTunes and App Stores section under Settings. Find the Updates toggle under Automatic Downloads and adjust it to your preference.

If you have turned off automatic updating, when you navigate to the App Store on your home screen, VoiceOver will notify you of available updates by saying, App Store, followed by a number that indicates how many updates are ready to install (this number also appears in a red circle on the top right corner of the App Store icon on your home screen). At the top left of the Update tab's screen in the App Store is an Update

FIGURE 5.5

The App Store with the Explore tab selected.

FIGURE 5.6

The App Store with the Purchased tab selected.

All button (see Figure 5.7) that you can press to install all available updates, or you can choose to review each individual update, including a detailed accounting of new features and bug fixes in that version. Some seasoned users prefer to update applications one at a time, after careful review, to avoid the inadvertent introduction of new bugs or an accidental accessibility issue with VoiceOver. Whatever method you choose, it is important to keep your apps up to date.

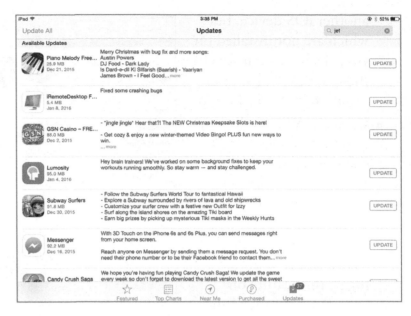

FIGURE 5.7

The App Store with the Updates tab selected.

Searching for Apps with VoiceOver

There will be times when you and your students won't want to sift through a list of apps. For example, you may have a specific app in mind, or at least a few key search phrases. The five tabs just described include search functionality located at the top right of each page.

The following exercise will guide you through using the search field to find and download an app, specifically the free ViA (Visually Impaired Apps) app (see Figure 5.8).

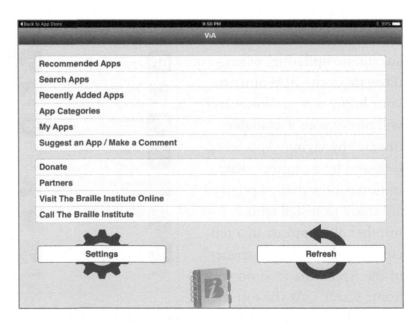

FIGURE 5.8

The ViA app by the Braille Institute of America.

The ViA app, developed at the Braille Institute of America, is designed to help anybody, especially educators, keep up-to-date with apps that are optimal for users with visual impairments. You can also use ViA to search for apps by their ratings or prices. The content for ViA is updated regularly and can be a valuable addition to your and your students' iOS toolkit. With the ViA app you can do the following:

- View a list of apps recommended by the Braille Institute of America and its partners.
- Review recently added apps.
- Review and search for apps by categories: Accessibility, Education, Entertainment, Health & Medical, Navigation & Mobility, News & Reference, Productivity & Life Management, Reading & Magnification, and Social Networking.
- Set up personalized app categories via the My Apps option.
- Comment on how well an app is working for your students.
- Review a list of ViA partners and consider the option to donate to the ViA effort.
- Choose which apps for which specific devices you want displayed using the Settings menu.

It is necessary to set up an ViA Account on the Braille Institute's website to take advantage of all of the functionality within the Settings portion of this App (see the Resources section of this book for more information).

Note: It is advisable to regularly activate the ViA Refresh button in order to download current information. This download may take several minutes, during which time the app's functionality will be limited.

The following exercise is effective for engaging your students in the app-searching process.

1. Make sure VoiceOver is enabled on the iPad.
2. Locate the App Store on the home screen and double tap.
3. Locate the Search text edit field. Typically, you may navigate to the top of the screen using the four-finger, single-tap VoiceOver gesture near the top of the screen or Space Bar + braille keys 1-2-3, if a braille display is being used.
4. Locate the search field either by flicking right until Search is spoken, or by pressing Space Bar + braille key 4.
5. Double tap the screen or press Space Bar + braille keys 3-6 until VoiceOver says, "Search field is editing." A cursor will be present on the braille display where you may now enter text.

6. Enter the name of the app, ViA, in the text field. Remember, most text edit fields on the iPad have clear text buttons that will clear the edit fields of content. If when you begin entering text, text is already present, the iPad will append the text to the already existing text.

7. On the search results page, one of the first few options that will be suggested is the ViA app from the Braille Institute of America. Select this and more information about the app will appear on the screen, such as release date, size, customer ratings, and system requirements.

8. Return to the previous screen listing the search results. To the right of the ViA app, select Get, then select Install, and then enter your Apple password when prompted, after which installation of the app should begin.

The app's location on the home screen depends on the number of apps currently installed on your iPad. The iPad fills screens with apps from left to right, starting with the top row on the screen. It will put the new app in the first empty spot. If your home screen is full, a new screen will be created and the app will appear in the upper-left corner.

Navigating Multiple App Screens

A single iPad home screen can hold up to 20 apps, plus up to 6 additional apps in the dock area. As more apps are added, additional app screens are added. The apps in the Dock area remain the same at the bottom of every home screen. You might end up having four or six or more screens of apps. Here are three important gestures for navigating multiple app screens.

1. Press the home button twice to switch among open apps using the App Switcher (more on this feature in a moment).

2. With VoiceOver turned on, tap three fingers anywhere on the home screen to hear how many app screens there are and which one you are on. VoiceOver will announce the row, column, and page or screen number of the app that has been identified by the three-finger gesture.

3. Touch three fingers down on the screen and lightly and quickly flick your fingers across the screen, either to the right or the left, to scroll through app screens. Flick three fingers to the left, and you will move forward by one screen. Flick three fingers to the right, and you will move back one screen. If nothing happens, it could be that your cursor was left up in the status bar area or down in the Dock. You can redirect it by touching any part of the home screen with one finger and then try flicking with three fingers again.

Searching for Apps

To search for apps on your iPad, flick three fingers down on any app screen to perform a "spotlight search." You will be placed in an edit field. An onscreen keyboard will appear in the bottom third of the screen. Type in the name or partial name of the app you're searching for and hit the Search button. You can also use this function to search for specific content on the iPad. You will notice that the search results also include individual items in your Mail, Calendar, iBooks, and any other apps that are installed.

To bring up a list of currently open apps, quickly press the home button twice. This brings up the App Switcher, which lists recently used apps that may be accessed using VoiceOver gestures and braille equivalents. You can navigate through these open apps by flicking right to move across them, and then double tapping any app you wish to use. Flicking left allows you to navigate back through these apps in the opposite direction. To dismiss App Switcher, double tap the home button.

Moving Apps

Moving apps around the screen of an iPad with VoiceOver is complex, but with practice, you'll find it's worth the effort to be able to locate your favorite apps right where you want them. Remember, the iPad arranges apps on the screen in either a 4 x 5 grid in portrait mode or a 5 x 4 grid in landscape mode, with 4 to 6 additional apps along the bottom in the dock area and the ability to accommodate an additional two apps. To move an app, follow these steps:

1. Find the app you wish to move and locate its screen position by using the three-finger, single-tap gesture. VoiceOver will say, for example, "Row 3, column 1, page 1 of 3, middle-left side."
2. Double tap the app you wish to move, but hold your finger on the screen until you hear VoiceOver announce, "Moving," followed by the app's name.
3. Slide your finger—keeping it on the screen—to where you'd like the app to be located.
4. Lift your finger.

Note: If you move an app all the way to the edge of the right side of the screen, you will jump onto the next screen of apps. If you move to the left edge of the screen, you will jump to the previous screen. When VoiceOver announces, "Pause for page change," you will hear a whirring noise as the screen changes forward or backward. When changing screens, it is imperative to move your finger directly left or right, not at an angle. This will move you to the same row as the one you were located on the original page, and you will be placed at either column 1 of the new page, if you're moving forward, or column 4 of the new page, if you're moving backwards. You can then navigate left, right, up or down. Lift your finger when you've moved the app to the desired location.

If you do move an app to a different page, you will have to double tap and hold it to resume moving it, should you wish to put it in another location on this screen.

To move an app to the Dock, while holding the app with your finger, slide your finger to the bottom of the screen until your hear, "In Dock," and then the position number. For example, "In Dock, position 3," indicating it is now the third app in the Dock. Lift your finger when you have placed the app in the desired position in the Dock.

Organizing Apps with Folders

The iPad lets you organize apps in folders. This task is pretty straightforward. After you decide which apps you would like to put into a folder, and where you'd like the folder to be located, simply drag one app on top of another app. To create a folder:

1. Find two apps you'd like to organize into a single folder.
2. Double tap and drag the first app on top of the second app and wait for an announcement from VoiceOver that the first app is on top of the second app.
3. Lift your finger and you will hear VoiceOver announce that it is creating a folder. It will provide a generic name based on the apps you are putting into the folder. To rename the folder, VoiceOver will indicate, "Double tap to edit text field." You can then type the name you would like to give this folder.
4. Find the folder VoiceOver created and where your two apps now reside. You may drag more apps on top of the new folder to add them to the folder.

Deleting Apps

When you no longer want an app on your iPad, you may get rid of it by doing the following:

1. Locate the app you want to delete.
2. Double tap the app, but keep your finger touching down on the screen after the second tap. You will hear a tone and VoiceOver will announce, "Moving," followed by the app's name.
3. Double tap the item again.

4. Double tap the Delete button when VoiceOver asks if you are sure you want to delete your app. If you've changed your mind, double tap the Cancel button.

Note: Certain preinstalled apps cannot be deleted. However, if you wish to restrict specific apps or types of apps from your students, open Restrictions in the General area of Settings (see Figure 5.9). This option allows you to disable specific preinstalled apps and the Safari web browser, and it allows you to specify what types of content are not allowed on your iPad. When you select Enable Restrictions, you will be asked to set up a 4-digit PIN, and to select the options you wish to be restricted on this particular device.

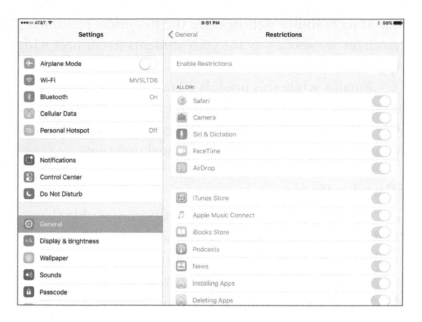

FIGURE 5.9

The Restrictions settings menu.

Finding the Right Apps for Your Students

With tens of thousands of apps to choose from, how do you decide which apps are best for your students? First and foremost, involve your students in the process of selection. Then, create a chart with a Tasks column, a Search column, and an Apps column.

Under Tasks, list all of the classroom-related tasks that the student is expected to complete. Under Search, associate key phrases that come to mind for each task as potential search criteria. For example, "note taking," "book reading," or "money identification." Next, perform searches in the App Store and identify a minimum of three possible apps for each task. Write these apps in the Apps column of your chart.

Once you have a list of potential apps, do some research to determine whether they are accessible for Zoom and VoiceOver users. For this you may use the ViA app that you downloaded earlier. Keep in mind that just because an app exists in the App Store doesn't mean it works well with iOS accessibility tools.

Another effective means for selecting apps is to ask your peers what apps their students and children are using. Also, you can find specific reviews on apps at the AppleVis and Maccessibility websites (see the Resources section at the end of this book). These resources are also a way for your students to connect with other visually impaired users of Apple products.

Finally, while this book is a great starting point, lots of questions will invariably arise as you and your students begin to explore iOS devices. Getting connected to one of the iOS online forums or blogs, such as AppleVis or Maccessibility, is an effective way to network and get answers to individual questions.

iBooks Basics

The iBooks app is a storefront for iOS-compatible electronic books (see Figure 5.10). It also organizes your downloaded books and readable PDFs into a library. If your iPad does not have the iBooks app pre-installed, you can download it from the App Store. You will learn how to actually search for and download iBooks in the next chapter.

FIGURE 5.10

The iBooks app icon.

iBooks can contain electronic books, PDF files, and audiobooks. VoiceOver can read aloud the e-books and PDFs stored in iBooks, as long as the PDF includes electronic text. (You cannot simply scan a hardcopy handout and save the resulting image as a PDF file, as doing so presents the scanned data as an image, not as recognizable and readable text.)

It is also possible to create PDF files from a variety of file formats, with Microsoft Word the preferred format for best conversion into electronic text. It is even possible to use commercial optical character recognition (OCR) software to extract electronic text from a scanned image and then save that text as a PDF. When shared with students (either via e-mail attachment or a cloud-based service—discussed later in this chapter), the student can opt to open the PDF with iBooks, which will save a copy of the file under the PDF section of the iBooks bookshelf. The PDF file format is a secure way of delivering materials such as class handouts to students because its content cannot be easily altered by the end user.

Another point of discussion is how pictures and other images are handled in iBooks. When e-books are created, the images can be labeled with descriptions, known as "alt tags" (a place in which to put "alternate text"), which VoiceOver reads aloud, although they are invisible to readers when VoiceOver is turned off. Some images are beautifully described, but more often a picture or graphic is described simply as "image" with no attendant description, or perhaps the image isn't denoted audibly at all. Parents and teachers can usually download sample versions of e-books to see how accessible they might be.

Finally, if you have a promising writer in your class, Apple offers an authoring tool, called iBooks Author (see the Resources section at the end of this book for more information), for individuals who wish to deliver content via the iBooks app. That means a student can use a Mac computer (not an iPad) to create and publish content that can be read as an e-book and downloaded from the iBooks store. In order to sell an e-book, the writer must enter into an agreement with Apple that permits the corporation to keep part of the revenues. iBooks Author can also be used to provide students with syllabi and other class-related materials, provided you have access to the content in an electronic format.

iTunes

The iTunes Store app (see Figure 5.11) facilitates the purchase and delivery of multimedia content. The app comes preinstalled on all Apple products and has six tabs that organize the store: Music, Movies, TV Shows, Top Charts, Genius, and Purchased. It enables the user to search for, purchase and download, and re-download past purchases of music, movies, TV shows, and podcasts. As in the App Store, these categories let you search for, locate, and buy multimedia. Genius makes suggestions for purchases based on what you've bought previously.

Windows and Mac versions of iTunes can be downloaded from http://www.apple .com/itunes/download. The Windows version of iTunes lets you back up the iPad's contents to a PC and synchronize Microsoft Outlook contacts, notes, appointments, and Internet Explorer Favorites with the iPad's Calendar, Contacts, Notes, Mail, and Safari apps.

Storing, Syncing, and Sharing Content with iCloud

When Steve Jobs, co-founder of Apple, introduced the

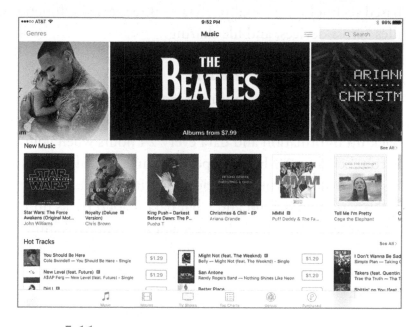

FIGURE 5.11

The iTunes store.

company's free iCloud service just months before he passed away in 2011, people found it so confusing that Jobs finally came up with a pat response: "It just works."

Indeed it does, but the confusion remains. Many people imagine it's a great big hard drive in the sky. It's not. It's a collection of services running on Apple's servers to which you can connect. Whereas before, people backed up content to their computers or other physical devices, content was now going to be stored in a "cloud" and transferred automatically when their devices connected to Wi-Fi.

The main thing you need to know is that, when enabled, iCloud (see Figure 5.12) automatically backs up certain types of data and syncs that data across all of your iOS devices in real time. Two caveats: (1) iCloud doesn't back up everything, and (2) it offers limited free storage space (5 gigabytes at this writing), although you can pay for more. iCloud, does however, offer unlimited free storage for music, apps, and iBooks purchased through the iTunes and App Stores (see Chapter 6), provided those items are still available on those sites.

FIGURE 5.12

The iCloud icon.

A chief advantage of storing information in the cloud is that it is less likely to be lost, damaged, or stolen, and can be restored if needed. Cloud-based technology generally refers to three separate functions: back-up and storage, syncing files across devices, and file sharing.

Backup within iCloud

To activate iCloud on your iPad, go to Settings, then iCloud, and log in with your Apple ID. Then go to Backup to activate iCloud Backup, the service that will automatically back up information and data every 24 hours when your iPad is locked and the device is connected to Wi-Fi and a power source. Should you drop or lose your iPad, you won't lose the data that you have backed up in iCloud. (See the Resources section for more information on iCloud and what data iCloud backs up.)

Note: Some school districts employ various Volume Purchase Program app deployment and management tools and may also back up the iPads they provide students using the school's Apple ID. In that case, you would not want to change the ID used for iCloud.

Notice that iCloud backup of your Word documents, Excel spreadsheets, podcasts, audiobooks, or music purchased elsewhere has not been mentioned. That's because iCloud is Apple-centric; it only works with Apple's products. Another misconception is that you no longer have to worry about storage space. Not so. The data and information from your iOS device may be stored in iCloud, but the apps themselves still reside on your iPad. To see how much storage space each of these items is using, go to Manage Storage under Storage under the iCloud setting.

Syncing Content in iCloud

iCloud was initially designed to sync and store media purchased through iTunes across iOS devices. Any new music, movies or shows you purchased through iTunes was automatically and wirelessly pushed to all your iOS devices. And you could access any of these files whether or not you were connected to the Internet, as long as you had a Wi-Fi connection.

This sync feature now extends to apps built into every iOS device, such as Notes, Calendar, or Contacts, as well as iTunes and App Store purchases. So, for example, when you enter an appointment in Calendars on your iPad, you can set iCloud to sync with your iPhone, where it will also appear. All this can be done by signing into iCloud with your respective iOS devices, and selecting the information you wish to sync via iCloud services.

However, things get complicated when attempting to sync files from non-Apple-based programs, such as Word and Excel, between a PC and an iOS device. While it's possible to sync certain files through iTunes or via Apple's new iCloud Drive, it's fairly complicated to connect an iOS device to a PC, open up iTunes, navigate using the desktop screen reader, and synchronize information. Most people simply e-mail files from their PCs to their iPads when they make changes or updates, but that's not the same as syncing information, which implies automatic, real-time updates. Now, however, there are cloud-based file sharing services available that aim to solve this obstacle. Dropbox, one such service, is discussed later in this chapter.

Also, most students cannot sync school-owned iPads to anything. Typically, they don't even have Apple IDs that they're allowed to use on the iPads. School districts are working hard to develop policies and procedures for installing apps; backing up data; figuring out which e-mail accounts they'll allow; and determining whether to use cloud services, and if so, which ones. Even the Apple ID to be used in the App Store is important because the district may be using apps purchased through the Volume Purchase Program, and you wouldn't want your students to miss out on benefiting from any apps that could be at their disposal, nor would you want to donate any apps that you or your students' family have personally purchased to an institution's iPad. Such confusion creates unnecessary headaches for those persons who are employed to support and maintain their institution's iOS devices.

One last word about iCloud and synchronization: As a general rule, when you delete information from one device, it is deleted from the iCloud as well, and will not be there the next time you access the device or iCloud. This means that when other devices connect to iCloud to synchronize your latest updates, these updates also include deletions that you made on other devices. Therefore, use extreme care when deciding to delete a contact, appointment, note, or important bookmarked website from any of your devices.

Sharing Content with iCloud

iCloud is better suited to sharing data and information with oneself across devices than it is for sharing with others. Consequently, the iCloud app built into your iPad is not a good option if collaboration or file sharing with other people is a priority, especially if they use a non-Apple product. (See Using Dropbox later in this chapter for a better alternative.)

As noted previously, at this point, it's probably easiest to share Windows-based data files as attachments to e-mails. Or, if you do want to take advantage of iCloud to share documents and data files, switch to an Apple-based app such as Pages (discussed in Chapter 7) or PaperPort Notes, which allow you to create text documents and presentations while iCloud syncs these files across your devices. When you use one of these Apple-developed apps to create a document, you can use iCloud to store, sync, and share it with other iOS-device users.

Using Dropbox

Dropbox (see the Resources section at the back of this book), a cloud-based file sharing and storage service, is an optimal solution for students because it works across platforms. That is, a student can access files stored in his or her Dropbox whether he or she is using a Windows PC, Mac, iPhone, Android phone, or iPad. Think about it this way: Dropbox is a box you can place files into. You can open the box anytime, from any device connected to Wi-Fi or the Internet, and all your contents will be in the box. And you get 2 gigabytes of space for free at present. You can purchase additional space for a monthly fee, or acquire additional space by taking advantage of some of Dropbox's marketing opportunities, like inviting friends and colleagues to use its services.

In addition to storing your files and accessing them on multiple devices, you can also share Dropbox files and folders with other users. To do so, you need to grant access to specific files or folders within your Dropbox account to other users. Then, regardless of who updates a file in the shared folder, everyone who shares the folder has access to the updated version. For example, you could place an assignment in a Dropbox folder and grant access to a student. The student would complete the assignment, you would grade it, and the student would have access to the graded version. (See Chapter 7 for some specific applications of Dropbox.)

Installing Dropbox on a Mac or PC

To install Dropbox on your computer, follow these steps:

1. Visit www.dropbox.com to sign up for a Dropbox account. Your e-mail address will serve as your user name, and you will need to select a password.

2. Follow download instructions and install the Dropbox utility on your Mac or PC. Note: Installing on a PC is accessible; installing it on a Mac is not.

3. Open the Dropbox folder that is added after download and installation. On a PC, the Dropbox folder will be in your Documents folder; on a Mac, it will be in your Home folder (location may vary depending on the settings within your operating system). When you open this folder, you'll notice that it contains a Getting Started file and a few folders. From now on, any file or folder that you place within this Dropbox folder will be available to you on any other computer or portable device, such as an iPad, on which you install Dropbox.

Note: You need to install Dropbox on every device from which you wish to access folders in Dropbox.

Installing Dropbox on the iPad

To install the Dropbox app on your iPad (see Figure 5.13), follow these steps:

1. Search for Dropbox in the App Store, select, and install it.

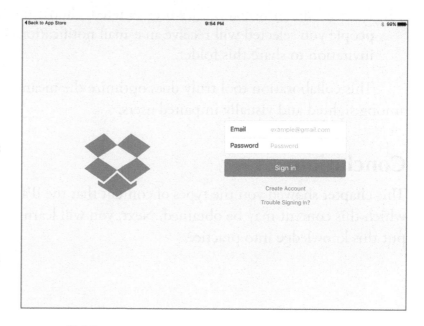

FIGURE 5.13

The Dropbox app login screen on an iPad after downloading from the App Store.

2. Select the Dropbox app when it appears on your iPad's home screen.

3. When you open the app, you will be asked either to sign in to your account or sign up for a new account if you don't already have one.

4. Enter your Dropbox e-mail and password when prompted.

Sharing a Folder in Dropbox

Here's how to share a folder in your Dropbox account with someone else:

1. Find the folder you want to share; be sure it's in your Dropbox account.

2. To the right of the folder name will be a circle with a downward-pointing arrow. Click on the circle and you will see a list of options pop up.

3. Click on the first option, Invite People to Collaborate. (You will also see an option to send a link to the folder, move the folder, or view the Shared Folder Settings, which lists the individuals who have access to the folder.)

4. On the screen that appears, type in the e-mail address or addresses of the person or people with whom you want to share the folder. There is also a field for including a message along with your invitation. The last field you will see, These People, allows you to choose whether you want the person to be able to edit the folder or just view it.

5. Once all the information has been entered, choose the Invite button. The person or people you selected will receive an e-mail notification inviting them to accept your invitation to share this folder.

This collaboration tool truly does optimize the means by which information is shared among sighted and visually impaired users.

Conclusion

This chapter showed you the types of content that the iPad can access and the means by which this content may be obtained. Next, you will learn how you and your students can put this knowledge into practice.

CHAPTER 6

The iPad Online

IN THIS CHAPTER

- Browsing the Internet
- Using the rotor
- Using E-mail and instant messaging

This chapter provides practical advice and exercises for performing five essential online tasks on the iPad: searching, retrieving, reviewing, interacting, and sharing. For braille readers, the emphasis will be on using a refreshable braille display.

Before trying out these exercises with a student, be sure that you and your student are connected to a wireless or cellular network; that Zoom and/or VoiceOver are enabled; and that a wireless QWERTY keyboard or braille display is connected to the iPad. Although some visually impaired students can perform the following exercises without these external peripherals, using them will be better in the long term, as iPad tasks become more complicated and involved.

Safari: Web Browsing Made Easy

To access the Safari web browser (see Figure 6.1), return to the home screen, and with VoiceOver and Wi-Fi enabled, double tap the Safari button located in the Dock at the bottom of the home screen.

Along the very top of the Safari screen, moving from left to right, are eight items (see Figure 6.2):

1. **Back button.** Use this button to return to the previous webpage. VoiceOver will report this button as "dimmed" if you are just starting a web browsing session and haven't yet

FIGURE 6.1

iOS Safari icon.

navigated to more than one page.

2. **Forward button.** Use this button to move ahead to the next visited webpage in your browsing session. Again, this option is dimmed if there is no page to which you may navigate forward.

3. **Show Bookmarks.** Bookmarks (see Figure 6.2) allows you to save and organize your favorite websites, view your saved reading lists, and access feeds from supported social networks.

4. **Address Bar.** Entering a website URL, commonly referred to as an "address," into this edit field (see Figure 6.3) will take you to that website. A search term may also be entered into this edit field to search for a webpage or topic. To enter a URL using VoiceOver, flick to the edit field and double tap, type in the address using the onscreen keyboard, and activate the address by locating and double tapping the Go key from the onscreen

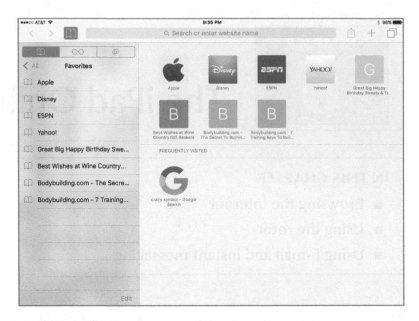

FIGURE **6.2**

The Safari browser with the Bookmarks tab open.

FIGURE **6.3**

Safari browser showing a URL in the Address Bar, with the keyboard up.

keyboard. To enter a URL using a braille display, press Space Bar + braille keys 3-6 to edit the address field. Type in the address from the braille display. Activate the address by pressing Space Bar + braille keys 1-5 or, for devices with an eight-key braille keyboard, press Space Bar + braille key 8.

When using a braille display to enter a URL, be aware of whether the display is employing contracted or uncontracted braille. To toggle between contracted and uncontracted braille input, press Space Bar + braille keys 2-3-6. Your students may find it more efficient to enter website addresses using eight-dot computer braille as the preferred method of input.

After typing a URL, double tap Go from the onscreen keyboard. As with most edit fields, there's a Clear Text or X button in the Address Bar if you need to start over. If you find it's taking a long time for a website to open, you may touch the address field at any time with one finger and VoiceOver will announce what percentage of the webpage has been loaded.

5. **Reload.** Once a webpage has been rendered onscreen (see Figure 6.3), the reload, or circular arrow, button appears. If the page does not load correctly or you wish to refresh the contents of the webpage, activate the reload button to refresh the page.

6. **Share.** This option (see Figure 6.4) allows you to share the webpage you are on via AirDrop (which allows sharing with nearby people who have enabled AirDrop on their iOS devices), messages, e-mail, and social media, or to save the page as a PDF file (iOS 9 and later) to be read in iBooks. From the Share screen you also may copy the URL to your

FIGURE 6.4

Safari with Share option activated.

iPad's clipboard so it can be pasted into any other edit field on your device; bookmark the site or add it to your list of favorite websites; add it to your reading list to view the page's contents in Safari Reader, an offline means of accessing website content; or add a link to the website to your home screen. You can also print the webpage if you have access to wireless printers in range of your iPad.

In addition to saving the page as a PDF, two more options that are new as of iOS 9 are Find on Page and Request Desktop Site. Find on Page provides a quick means for quickly locating text on the current webpage. Request Desktop Site provides users with the equivalent desktop address for the current website. Many sites are optimized for viewing and interaction based on the device being used to access the site (known as *responsive web design*). Some sites optimized for mobile devices may not offer as much functionality as the desktop version of the site. Selecting Request Desktop Site will present the desktop computer version of the website on your iPad.

7. **New Tab.** This allows you to open another webpage within Safari without closing the current webpage.

8. **Pages.** Selecting this option will show you which pages are open within Safari (see Figure 6.5). To use the Pages option, flick to the right with one finger and review the webpages that are open on your device. Double tap the desired website to open it, or flick down once with one finger and double tap to close the webpage. These steps are similar to those used for activating and deleting apps within the App Switcher.

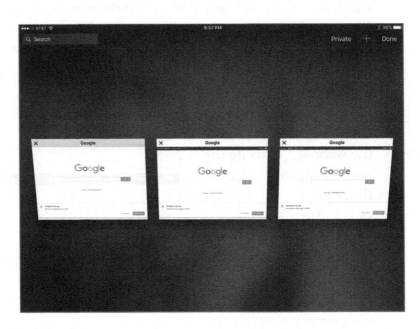

FIGURE **6.5**

Safari Pages view with three pages open.

Navigating a Website Using Web Elements

When your students go to a website using VoiceOver, they can flick down with two fingers to hear the entire page, touch down on the screen to hear specific text, or flick around with one finger to the right or left to quickly scan the page. Students who want to move around websites more efficiently can do so by learning to use web elements with Apple's rotor function.

Before proceeding, it's important to understand what web elements are, and what they enable the user to do. "Web elements" are components of a webpage that organize the information presented to a visitor so that specific content can be quickly located. Navigating via web elements is an efficient means for visually impaired users to surf the web. Specific web elements include headings, tables, links, form controls, edit fields, radio buttons, and check and combo boxes.

When your students navigate through apps, screens, and webpages, they will employ different techniques depending on the screen layout and the purpose of the search. A student may use links to visit content within a website or to surf other websites. Headings may be used to quickly navigate through a webpage in order to find desired information. Form controls can enable the user to log on to a website, shop online, make purchases, fill out surveys, and so forth. In order to navigate by web elements, the student will want to learn how to use the rotor function, introduced in Chapter 2.

The Rotor

Apple's unique rotor function is useful for navigating websites and documents. When a student with a visual impairment has Safari open to a webpage the he or she wants to explore, the rotor can provide a brief, yet comprehensive snapshot of the page.

To activate the rotor, use the two-finger rotate gesture described in Chapter 2, Sidebar 2.1. Place two fingers on the screen as if you were turning an actual dial. When you turn the dial clockwise, you will hear VoiceOver move forward through the available web elements; if you move counterclockwise, you move backward. This means that if you go too far, you can simply move your fingers in the other direction to back up.

Now turn the rotor dial until you hear "Headings." Then, flick one finger up or down to move forward or backward by headings. This is a new concept that will become clearer when you actually use it to perform specific exercises designed for your students. Web elements available for navigation are Characters, Words, Lines, Containers, Headings, Links, Form Controls, and Tables, among others. (The next section will cover how to customize the elements that appear in the rotor.)

For refreshable braille display users, Space Bar + braille key 6 moves forward by element; Space Bar + braille key 3 moves backward.

As you navigate through web elements, VoiceOver reports how many of each element are present on the current webpage. For example, there may be 4 headings, 39 links, 6 form controls, and 0 tables.

To turn the rotor dial and set the rotor to the desired option, Space Bar + braille keys 5-6 will move it clockwise, while Space Bar + braille keys 2-3 will move it counterclockwise.

Customizing or Selecting Rotor Options

To customize what options are offered on the rotor dial, do the following with VoiceOver on:

1. Press the home button.
2. Go to the Settings menu and then to General, Accessibility, and VoiceOver menus.
3. Locate the Rotor option and double tap it to open a screen that will allow you to customize what is available on the rotor when you twist your fingers (see Figure 6.6).

The Rotor screen includes 31 items. Most of them involve ways to move around a screen, while some are for controlling VoiceOver

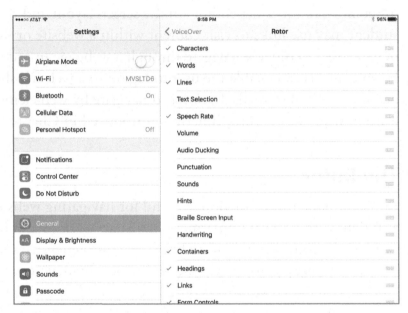

FIGURE 6.6

The Rotor options in the VoiceOver settings menu.

in typing mode. You can customize which items appear on the rotor and in what order. Note that the rotor will only display items when the items are present in the context of the way the iPad is being used at that moment. For example, web elements will only appear as active rotor options when you are on an active webpage or within an app that contains web elements.

As you explore the list of rotor items, VoiceOver will announce "Selected" before some. This means that they already appear on the rotor by default or have been previously selected. If you want to add an item to the rotor, flick to the item, double tap it, and

VoiceOver will say "Selected." Flicking to and double tapping any item that is already selected will deselect the item and remove it from the rotor.

The order in which these options appear on this list is the order in which the elements will appear on your rotor dial when you turn it. To the right of each item on the list is a button to reorder the text fields (symbolized by three parallel lines) that you can use to shift around the order. Let's say, for example, you want to be able to find Search Fields very quickly, but it is way down on the list. Following these steps, you can move it up:

1. Flick to Search Fields, then flick right, double tap, and hold your finger on the Reorder button until a series of audible tones is emitted by the iPad. Please note that there are currently no QWERTY or braille equivalents to this double-tap-and-hold gesture.

2. Slide your finger up or down until "Moved above" or "Moved below" is spoken, followed by each rotor element.

3. Double tap the screen when the desired position is reached.

Practice Exercises Using the Rotor Function

The two practice exercises here are designed to familiarize you and your student to Safari and the versatility of the rotor function.

Rotor Exercise 1

1. Flick to the Address Bar edit field within Safari and double tap the screen or press Space Bar+braille keys 3-6. VoiceOver will speak the phrase "is editing," which means you can enter text into the field.

2. Enter the web address www.afb.org and select the Go key from the onscreen keyboard. You will be taken to the home page of the American Foundation for the Blind (AFB). VoiceOver will provide the status of the page being loaded; you may hear a repeated clicking as it loads. When the page is loaded, VoiceOver will announce, "Skip to content," which, if selected using a single-finger double tap, will take you directly to the main content on the webpage. This is an example of an "in-page link"—one that points to another place on the same website.

3. Activate the rotor by placing two fingers on the screen and rotating them as if you were turning an actual dial. Use the rotor settings to explore the page by various web elements. Stop and listen as each web element is spoken, and have the student write down or braille how many of each web element currently exist on the page. As of this writing, there are 23 headings, 93 links, 17 form controls, 11 buttons, and 3 text fields on the AFB homepage.

4. Navigate the rotor setting to Headings.

5. Flick one finger up to move backward by heading, or flick down to navigate forward by heading. When using an external braille display, use Space Bar + braille key 6 to move forward, and Space Bar + braille key 3 to move backward by headings. And if you wish to navigate by heading using the onscreen braille keyboard discussed in Chapter 4, you can activate it using the rotor, then braille the letter *h* using the onscreen keyboard, and then flick up or down with one finger to navigate by headings.

6. Find a heading that interests you. To read through the contents under that heading, flick one finger to the right. You can perform the same task using a refreshable braille display by pressing Space Bar + braille key 4 to simulate a single finger flick right or Space Bar + braille key 1 to flick to the left.

This exercise may be repeated using other web elements present on the rotor. Remember, when performing this activity with links or form controls, you will need to double tap the screen to activate a link or form control that is selected. The refreshable braille keyboard equivalents for double tapping are either Space Bar + braille keys 3-6 pressed simultaneously, or you can select the cursor routing button on the braille display above the highlighted web element.

Rotor Exercise 2

1. Flick to the Address Bar edit field in Safari and double tap the screen. From a braille display, press Space Bar + braille keys 3-6 or the routing button over the edit field, until "is editing" is spoken.

2. Type in the question: "What is the distance between Boston and San Francisco?" Then, press Go from the onscreen keyboard or press Space Bar + braille keys 1-5, or Space Bar + braille key 8 to activate the Enter key, which will render the search results within Google.

3. Set the rotor to navigate by headings. Remember, flick one finger up to move backward through headings, or flick down to move forward. Since Google organizes its search results by headings, it should be relatively easy to find your answer.

4. Once you have located the desired heading, use a single finger flick right or left to obtain your answer.

These two exercises also can be modified for other websites and search criteria to improve your students' Safari web-browsing skills.

Finding and Downloading Books

It's fair to say that there are now more books available to readers with visual impairments than most of us will ever read—thanks to digital books and the Internet. Still, more is better. In this section, we will explore a few excellent e-book solutions currently available for the iPad: iBooks, Read2Go, and BARD. These apps offer great access for readers who are blind or visually impaired using large print, speech, braille, or some combination thereof. Other iOS book readers exist, but they don't offer the breadth of adaptive access you get with these three.

As mentioned in Chapter 5, the iBooks app is free, and the iBooks Store offers many free books, particularly those in the public domain; others you will need to purchase. The app also enables users to read documents in an ePUB format if the document is not rights-protected. iBooks offers other functions too, but for our purposes we'll stick to its book offerings.

The second app, Read2Go, from Bookshare and available in the App Store, lets users read books from Bookshare if they are members (see the Resources section at the back of this book for more information), as well as unprotected DAISY books available elsewhere, such as training materials produced by Freedom Scientific or DAISY books from National Braille Press. (DAISY, which stands for Digital Accessible Information System, is a digital format designed to be accessible to people with "print disabilities," including those who are visually impaired.) This file format allows authors and publishers to produce content that can be accessed audibly, via e-text, or by refreshable braille. It also provides an intuitive and efficient vehicle for readers to read and navigate large amounts of text. Bookshare membership is free to students with print disabilities who live in the United States; otherwise there is a small yearly membership fee. Your students can visit the Bookshare website, www.bookshare.org, to become a member.

In 2013 the National Library Service for the Blind and Physically Handicapped (NLS) released the BARD Mobile app, a mobile means of downloading and reading braille and audio books from the Braille and Audio Reading Download (BARD) website of the NLS. Users of this app must have an account to access the BARD service, which they can obtain from their local NLS library or online (see the Resources section for more information). Simply fill out the necessary paperwork and provide proof that the applicant is print impaired, and you will receive login credentials to access this service. Once this app is downloaded and you've used it to log into the service, you will be able to download, listen to, and read in braille your favorite NLS book or magazine. The app's user manual also can be accessed through its help option.

Now it's time to search for some books to download and try out these apps.

Using iBooks to Find and Download Books

Open the iBook app (see Figure 6.7). Make sure the My Books tab at the bottom of the screen is selected. This screen, also referred to as the Library, displays all the books that you have downloaded. The buttons located at the top of the screen in this view are List View/ Grid View at left, Collections at center, and Select at right. The List View button can be toggled to display books in a list (likely optimal for students who are blind) or grid, which visually displays only the book covers (may be preferred by students with some functional vision). The Collections button allows users to toggle between different collections of materials. By default, this is set to view All. In the Collections menu, you can opt

FIGURE 6.7

The iBooks library.

to display only the books, audiobooks, or PDF files in your iBooks library; create a new collection; or hide books stored in iCloud. The Select button allows you to select, delete, or move a selected book to another collection.

Note that there are six tabs on the bottom of the iBooks screen: My Books, Featured Books, NY Times Best Sellers, Top Charts, Top Authors, and Purchased, which brings up a history of the books purchased and associated with your Apple ID, and iCloud, where you may access books downloaded by your other iCloud-connected iOS devices. On the Purchased tab, you may view most recent purchases, all your purchases, or purchases not made on this device. The latter enables you to download onto your current device any books purchased on your Apple account via another iOS device. Selecting Featured Books, NY Times Best Sellers, Top Charts, or Top Authors will take you to the iBooks Store, where you may browse books displayed based on which tab you've selected. If you'd rather search for a particular book, use the search field near the top right of the screen of any of these tabs.

Downloading Books Using iBooks

Follow these steps to download a book using the iBooks app.

1. Use the iBooks tabs along the bottom of the screen to browse the iBook Store to find a book you would like to download. If you select one that requires a purchase, don't feel obliged to buy it right now; simply select the Sample button, which will download a free sample to your iBooks library bookshelf. If you select a free book or purchase one, the complete book will download to your bookshelf. (If a Read button is present, select it to read the downloaded book or sample.)

2. This book is now stored in your iBooks bookshelf. Return to the My Books screen by selecting that tab at the bottom of the screen.

3. Navigate to the book you just downloaded; it will be displayed at the top of your books list or as the first item in the grid view. If a book is a sample or a new book, the book cover will have a colored triangle in the upper right corner indicating whether it is a sample or new. (When VoiceOver is on, the title will be preceded by the words "Sample" or "New.")

4. Select the title, and you will be able to read it, as described in the next section.

5. If you have downloaded and are reading a sample, a "Buy" button is prominently displayed among the buttons at the top of the screen. You can select this button to buy the book at any time.

iBooks Reading Controls

Several controls appear near the top of the screen when reading a book. To the right of the Library button is the Table of Contents button, and to the right of that is the Buy button, if the download is a sample. The title of the book appears in the center of the row. Next is the Appearance button, which opens a screen and enables changes to the brightness of the screen, font size, font type, and color theme (setting a background color or enabling reverse colors), as well as setting auto-night theme and scrolling view (either page view or continuous scrolling). To the right of the Appearance button is a Search button where you can search by word or by page number to quickly navigate to a specific place within the book. The final control, Page Bookmark, is for marking your place in the book.

The book's onscreen content can be read aloud or with a braille display. When reading with VoiceOver, by flicking down with two fingers, VoiceOver will read the entire page, and will automatically turn to the next page and continue reading. If you are using a refreshable braille display and press Space Bar + braille keys 1-2-3-5, VoiceOver will read the book continuously, automatically turning the pages. This is due to the automatic page turning feature within VoiceOver's braille settings, which may be toggled on/off by the user. The same page navigation commands for moving forward and backward on the home screen—Space Bar + braille keys 1-3-5 to move forward by page; Space Bar + braille keys 2-4-6 to move back—can be used to manually turn pages in an iBook. Note that the rotor can be used to change the way VoiceOver navigates through and reads the text on a given page, as described in more detail in Chapter 7.

Near the bottom of every book page there is a page chooser control that provides an alternative means of turning pages by flicking down with one finger or using Space Bar + braille key 6 to move forward by page or flicking up with one finger or Space Bar + braille key 3 to move backward by page. You also can swipe three fingers left to move forward by page, and three fingers right to turn back by page when using VoiceOver. Below the page chooser in the center of the page is an item that reads your current page number and lets you know how many pages are in the publication. For example, you might be on page "5 of 53" pages. If you flick to the left, you will find a link to the page on which the last link you have activated, if any, appears. This is a handy "back" button if you follow a link in the text to a reference or a sidebar, for example, and want to go back where you started from. If you flick to the right, VoiceOver will announce the number of pages left in the chapter. If you're in the table of contents of a book, you may select links to specific chapters and activate them to navigate more quickly to specific pages in a book.

The Read2Go App

If you have not done so already, purchase and download the Read2Go app (see Figure 6.8) from the App Store. Remember, in order to use Read2Go you need to be a Bookshare member.

Open the app and look for the four tabs along the bottom of the main Read2Go screen:

FIGURE 6.8

The Bookshare Read2Go app icon.

- **My Books.** Your downloaded books reside here, where books may be organized by title, author, or date downloaded. The Edit button allows you to edit and delete books from your Bookshelf.
- **Search Bookshare.** This tab lets you browse and search for specific titles.
- **Settings.** Here you can make adjustments to print and audio settings. Please note that Read2Go's built-in audio speech engine must be disabled before a refreshable braille display will display the text of a Bookshare book. This is also where you sign into Bookshare.

- **Help.** This feature provides easy-to-follow assistance with using the app, as well as version information.

Using Read2Go to Find and Download Books

Follow these steps to find and download books from Bookshare directly onto your iPad using VoiceOver:

1. Open the Read2Go app.
2. Double tap on the Search Bookshare tab.
3. To search for a specific book, you must select the search criteria, either Title, Author, or ISBN number, before entering your search term. Or, simply browse the Latest or Most Popular lists, or browse by Categories.
4. Find a book, select it, and then select the Download button. When the download is complete, you'll be asked if you would like to read the book. Select Yes to read the book.

Reading with Read2Go

When reading a book with Read2Go, you can choose to navigate by Section, Page, or Bookmarks via the Navigation button. Bookmarks can be set while reading. To the right of the Navigation button are the Set Bookmark and Settings buttons. The Settings button is used to change the font size; foreground and background colors; and highlight, word highlight, and bookmark colors. Settings is also where you go to select whether book images will be shown and modify audio options.

It's a good idea to practice reading, navigating, and bookmarking. When finished practicing, select the My Books button at the top of the app, and select the Edit button if you wish to delete books from your bookshelf.

Using the BARD App to Find and Download Books

BARD Mobile (see Figure 6.9) may be the most intuitive of the reading apps covered here. It provides high-quality audio and refreshable braille access to a variety of books and magazines made available by NLS.

BARD Mobile has four tabs along the bottom of the screen: Bookshelf, Get Books, Settings, and Now Reading. The Bookshelf tab provides easy-to-navigate sections to select and read previously downloaded audiobooks and braille books

FIGURE **6.9**

The BARD Mobile app icon.

and magazines. The Get Books tab offers the same options for browsing or searching for specific books or magazines available through NLS. The Settings tab provides a means of adjusting third-party audio settings when content is read by a recorded human voice. You may also adjust visual settings or user account settings for logging into the app. Finally, the Now Reading option takes you to the most recent audio or braille content accessed via the app.

There's a lot to cover when using the BARD app. Audio content is rendered in a VoiceOver-friendly player that has labeled controls to play, pause, rewind, go forward, and adjust reading speed—a similar approach to using a traditional Talking Book Recorder from the Library of Congress. Braille content is displayed as a hard-copy braille book or magazine would be displayed using a refreshable braille display. If your student has an account with the National Library Service, you'll want to focus on downloading and accessing a variety of audio and braille reading material via the Bookshelf tab. As stated earlier, the BARD app is an intuitive and robust e-book reader that's effective for a range of visually impaired users and skill levels, so fewer details for using the app are provided here. For more instructions, the BARD App, provides an Bard online user manual under the Help tab.

Sending and Receiving E-Mail and Messages

The iPad offers two distinct means of sending and receiving electronic communications: the built-in Mail app, which sends and receives e-mail, and the built-in Messages app, which sends and receives messages.

Mail App

Here are some quick facts about the Mail app, which appears in the Dock station along the bottom of the screen (if it hasn't been moved):

- You must have an e-mail account to use it.
- To send and receive e-mail, it is necessary to be connected to the Internet via either Wi-Fi or cellular service.
- You may need the assistance of your information technology specialist to set up your iPad to send and receive e-mail through the school's server.

Setting Up Your E-Mail Account

To set up your e-mail account on your iPad, select the Mail, Contacts, Calendars option (see Figure 6.10) under Settings.

From here, select Add Account, select your e-mail client (see Figure 6.11), and follow the instructions for setting up your e-mail account. Depending on your e-mail type, you may be able to set up your iPad to automatically search for your provider's e-mail settings, or you may have to manually enter these options. Please consult with your provider to ensure that you have the right incoming and outgoing e-mail settings. If you are setting this up for one or more students you'll need to have their usernames and passwords on hand to complete the setup.

Once your e-mail account is set up, open the Mail app.

Receiving and Sending E-mail

Once you set up your e-mail account, you may read, write, and send e-mails. When first opened, the Mail app shows a list of Mailboxes at the left and a larger area for messages on the right (see Figure 6.12). The layout of screens in the Mail app will vary slightly, depending on whether you are holding the iPad horizontally

FIGURE 6.10

The Mail, Contacts, Calendars options in the Settings menu.

FIGURE 6.11

The Add Account options in the Mail, Contacts, Calendars settings menu.

or vertically. The top of the screen contains an Inbox button (or Mailboxes button if you have more than one e-mail account set up) followed by a number in parentheses that represents the number of unread e-mails present within the inbox. Other subsequent mail folders displaying sent items and deleted items (or Trash) follow, and new folders can be created to organize e-mails that have been received. If your student sets up multiple e-mail accounts on the iPad, he or she will be able to toggle to different accounts to check each respective inbox.

To use the Mail app with VoiceOver, first select the account you wish to use. Tap on the Inbox you want to open and check for mail. The Inbox (see Figure 6.13) is composed of a search field for locating e-mails within the Mail app, above a listing of all e-mails. For each e-mail in the list, the sender's name, time sent, subject line, and a few lines of the message are displayed. You can flick right with one finger to quickly read through the list or press Space Bar + braille

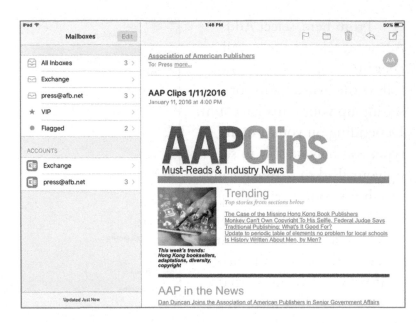

FIGURE **6.12**

The Mail app showing a list of mailboxes on the left and an open message on the right.

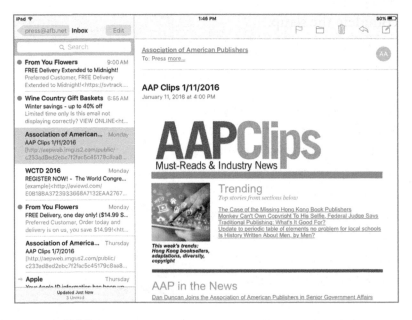

FIGURE **6.13**

A Mail app Inbox showing a list of messages on the left and an open message on the right.

key 1 or 4. To open any message, flick to the message in the Inbox and double tap or press Space Bar + braille keys 3-6 on your braille display. You can read through the message by flicking one finger to the right or by pressing Space Bar + braille key 4.

There are a series of buttons at the top of the screen when an e-mail message is open. A Back button takes you out of the current message and back to the Inbox. Previous and Next buttons navigate to previous and next messages without exiting the current message. You may flag a message, mark it as unread, move it to Junk, or select the Mark Message button, or you may move a message to another folder by selecting the Move button. You may also eliminate a message by selecting the Delete button. If you accidentally delete a message, simply exit your Inbox, return to the list of Mailboxes, open the Trash folder, find and open the desired deleted message, double tap on Move, flick one finger to the right, and double tap on Inbox. The deleted message is now restored to its rightful place within the Inbox.

Select the Reply button to reply to the sender of the e-mail, reply to all participants in the e-mail, forward the e-mail, save images in the e-mail, or print the e-mail. The last button is Compose. Composing an e-mail on an iPad is similar to doing so on a desktop computer. To compose a new message, flick to the Compose button in the upper-right corner of the screen and double tap. A new message window will open with the cursor focused on the To: field and the onscreen keyboard in place. A word of caution involving the subject line: after entering the text in the subject line, remember to flick to and double tap the message body before you begin composing the actual e-mail—or you will have a very long subject. In other words, you need to refocus the cursor in the message area before you begin to type the body of your e-mail. When you have finished composing your message, return to the top of the screen. At the far left is a Cancel button, and at the far right a Send button, which you can locate and double tap or select by pressing Space Bar + braille keys 3-6. You'll hear a brief whooshing sound to signify that the message is traveling to the recipient, and a copy of the message will be placed in your Sent folder.

Other Actions in E-Mail

Apple makes it easy to delete items in a list such as e-mails or messages (discussed in the next section) without opening them. Simply flick to the desired unread e-mail or message. You'll hear or read the subject and VoiceOver will say "Actions available." When you flick up or down to select an action, the first item you should hear is, "Delete." Double tap to delete the selected message. In the case of e-mails, there will be a More option that, when selected, allows you to reply, forward, flag, mark as "read," set a notification, or move the message to a selected folder. The default action when double tapping an e-mail or message is to open and read it, but you may also delete messages fairly quickly using the aforementioned method.

The e-mail app works in conjunction with the Contacts app (discussed in Chapter 2) for sending e-mail. If an individual's e-mail address is listed in your Contacts app, you can select that contact's e-mail address to automatically launch the Compose screen in the Mail app.

Also, many word-processing apps let you e-mail directly by activating a button within that app, which avoids the necessity of going into your e-mail account through Mail (see Chapter 7 for a discussion of word processing on the iPad). In fact, this is an excellent method of submitting assignments, such as sending homework to instructors. With the file open in the app you've used to create the file, or in Dropbox, select the Share option. Mail Recipient is usually one of the first options you may select. The file will appear attached in a new e-mail message ready for you to compose. Another method of attaching files is to begin within the body of an e-mail message. With VoiceOver activated, double tap and hold until a menu appears allowing you to attach a file or insert a photo or video. Conversely, a student can read a file attachment in an e-mail through the Mail app by locating the attachment and double tapping, or by selecting the attachment to have it open in their preferred word-processing app.

Messages App

The pre-installed Messages app, which sends and receives text messages, works over Wi-Fi, 4G, or 3G connections. These messages are free to send and receive between iOS devices and Mac computers (iMessages) when using Wi-Fi. When sending messages over the cellular network or to non-iOS devices, cellular text messaging rates may apply. These messages are also distinguished by color. iMessages (those sent to other iOS users) are blue, while messages sent to non-iOS users are green.

To use Messages with VoiceOver on, first make sure that the iMessage toggle is turned on in the Messages area of Settings. On that same screen, select the Send & Receive setting to select the e-mail account or accounts at which you would like to be able to receive iMessages. This should be set up automatically based on your Apple ID.

Now, open the Messages app (see Figure 6.14). Here you'll find a Compose button, a search field, and a list of received text messages, organized by conversation. Open a conversation to see all of the messages that have been sent and received between or

FIGURE 6.14

The Messages app icon.

among the participants. You may also compose a new message by typing an email address, phone number, or contact name from your Contacts app. You can send a group message by selecting multiple recipients. Media, such as photos or videos from your iPad photo library or camera, can also be attached to a message. And you can type or dictate a message within the message body. (Dictating text is covered in Chapter 7.) The Send button follows the edit field. VoiceOver also audibly indicates when the message's recipient is typing a response to you.

To delete a message from the list of received messages, select the message and flick down until the Delete option is presented.

Conclusion

In this chapter you learned about a number of tasks pertinent to online access, becoming more familiar with Safari, using the rotor, downloading books, and sending and receiving e-mails and messages. It's time to move on and become more familiar with word-processing apps that you can use with your students to complete writing and editing tasks.

Strategies for Completing Tasks in the Classroom

IN THIS CHAPTER

- Using the onscreen keyboard
- Manipulating text
- Using voice input of text
- Understanding specific apps for classroom tasks

This chapter focuses on using the iPad to work on assignments in the classroom, mainly on specific word-processing tasks such as entering, editing, and manipulating text as well as sharing it with others by printing and e-mailing it. Math apps are also considered. While there's a great deal that can be accomplished using Bluetooth keyboards and refreshable braille displays, you will find that some students prefer to use the onscreen keyboard along with their preferred mode of keyboard entry to perform these tasks.

Using the Onscreen Keyboards

As discussed in Chapters 2 and 4, using the onscreen keyboard for tasks beyond writing e-mails and notes can be time-consuming and cumbersome. For more complex word-processing tasks, you can maximize your students' efficiency and reduce stress by attaching to the iPad a Bluetooth keyboard, braille display, or both. However, there are times when a Bluetooth external keyboard or braille display isn't handy, and your students will be pressed into using the onscreen keyboard to enter text. Here are some suggestions for such times.

Screen Orientation and Typing Style

In Chapter 1, you locked the screen into the portrait orientation to provide stability and consistency while exploring the iPad. But some apps require a landscape orientation, and some visually impaired students prefer to type in landscape mode, which more closely approximates the size of a standard keyboard. It's best to allow students to try typing using both orientations, and then let them choose the orientation they prefer.

When in portrait orientation, with the side switch pushed down toward the bottom of the iPad, the screen is locked. To move from portrait to landscape orientation, first unlock the iPad's screen orientation by pushing the side switch on the right edge toward the top of the iPad. VoiceOver will say, "Orientation unlocked;" Now, turn the iPad 90 degrees clockwise until "Landscape" is spoken. If you then turn it 90 degrees counterclockwise (back to its original position), VoiceOver will say, "Portrait." Turn it 90 degrees clockwise again to return to landscape, and then one more 90-degree turn clockwise to accomplish a "portrait flip," which means the screen is back in portrait mode but the orientation has been flipped—that is, the top of the iPad is now at the bottom, although the screen is still viewed right side up. When you find the orientation the student prefers (some students may be better oriented with the home button located at the top of the screen), slide the side switch to lock the orientation. VoiceOver will say, "Orientation locked."

Another decision for your students to make when using the onscreen keyboard is which typing method to use: touch, standard, or direct touch typing. This is set in the "Settings" menu, under Accessibility, then VoiceOver, and Typing Style. Remember that direct touch typing is often used by students with quite a bit of functional vision or sighted users who have Voiceover enabled; this method of keyboard entry allows for keys to be touched and characters automatically insert much as if VoiceOver were not active. With touch typing, you touch the letter or number you want and then lift your finger to enter it. With standard typing, you locate the desired character and then double tap. In addition to the double tap method used with standard typing, there's another gesture that can be employed: split tap. With this gesture, instead of double tapping, you enter a character by touching a key and, while holding the key with one finger, tap the screen with another finger to enter the character. This method can also be used when deleting text for more efficient editing.

Keyboard Settings

Go to Settings and select General, then Keyboard (see Figure 7.1), which is located toward the bottom of the screen. The Keyboard screen contains a button for customizing both standard and emoji keyboards. (Emojis are digital icons used to express an idea or emotion visually.) You can toggle between these two keyboards by selecting the key with the smiley face icon on it (VoiceOver will state, "Next keyboard: emoji"), located to the left of the Space Bar and adjacent to the Microphone key (which allows for text to be dictated into text fields).

For now, let's focus on the functionality and key features of the standard keyboard that can be enabled in the Keyboard settings menu:

- **Text Replacement.** Text replacement is a shorthand way to write text. Combinations of letters can be designated here to represent specific, frequently typed words. When those letters are typed anywhere on the iPad, they automatically expand into the indicated words. For example, "OMW" expands into "on my way" (see Figure 7.2).

- **Auto-Capitalization.** When Auto-Capitalization is enabled, the iPad will capitalize the first words of sentences and first and last names in certain fields.

- **Auto-Correction.** When enabled, Auto-Correction compensates for some of the limitations of the onscreen touch keyboard. An auto-correct function predicts the way you want to complete certain words and automatically makes the correction, which can

FIGURE 7.1

The Keyboard options in the General settings menu.

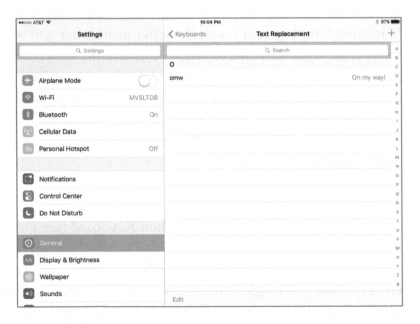

FIGURE 7.2

The Text Replacement screen in the Keyboard settings menu.

save keystrokes and correct typical errors. It's handy for those who use gestures, but is less significant for those using braille displays or QWERTY keyboards.

- **Check Spelling.** Check Spelling enables the iPad to give you alternate suggestions for words you've typed that aren't in its spelling dictionary.

- **Enable Caps Lock.** When enabled along with VoiceOver, you can toggle Caps Lock on and off by tapping the Shift key three times with one finger. VoiceOver announces the Caps Lock status when you toggle. If you're using touch typing, enable all caps by touching the Shift key with one finger and, while holding the Shift key down, triple tap anywhere with another finger. Double tap the screen to disable caps lock functionality.

- **Shortcuts.** Enables the text replacements you may create.

- **Predictive.** This feature provides three suggestions for how you wish to complete words as you type. The predictive options appear on the keyboard just above the top letters. VoiceOver speaks the suggestions, which may be selected and inserted at the cursor position by double tapping the desired suggestions. They can be selected or ignored. Though the predictions may initially confuse users who are new to interacting with screen readers, they can be useful.

- **Split Keyboard.** When this setting is enabled, the keyboard can be literally split in half so that each half is closer to the side of the screen and there is a space in the middle. This keyboard version is preferred by some people who do most of their typing with their thumbs. To enable the split keyboard, tap and hold on the keyboard with two fingers—one on each side of the keyboard—and spread your fingertips apart. As you do, the keyboard will split in half. Another option is to tap and hold the Keyboard key in the bottom-right corner of the keypad, then select Split. To merge the keyboard back, tap and hold each half of the keyboard with two fingers and push them back together, or tap and hold the Keyboard key and select "Merge" with VoiceOver on, the split keyboard is enabled by using the two-finger scrub gesture (see Sidebar 2.1) in an active edit field on the iPad, and the gesture will toggle between the split and merged keyboards.

- **Period Shortcut.** When this setting is enabled, double tapping the Space Bar inserts a period and a space at the end of a sentence. It also capitalizes the first letter in the next sentence. When touch typing, press the Space Bar twice. If using standard typing, perform a split double tap, mentioned earlier (touch and hold the Space Bar while tapping the screen twice with another finger). If the setting is off, switch to the numbers screen and choose the period. This, of course, takes longer, so your students may want this enabled.

- **Enable Dictation.** This setting allows the user to dictate text aloud when an edit field is active.

Hidden Onscreen Keyboards

The default onscreen keyboard is a standard QWERTY keyboard, but without the numbers and symbols and with only limited punctuation showing. Tapping the ".?123" keys on either side of the spacebar (read by VoiceOver as "More: numbers") will display a numbers and symbols keyboard. On that keyboard, you will see a "#+=" key (read as "More: symbols"), which displays a third keyboard that includes even more additional symbols. Tap the "ABC" key to return to the alphabet.

The numbers keyboard also contains an "Undo" button. If you make a mistake such as deleting or cutting out a big chunk of text, or accidentally paste something where it should not be in a document, and want to undo this action, tap the ".?123" key and the "Undo" button. This will reverse the last action you have taken such as cutting, deleting, or pasting text.

Tracking the iPad Cursor

Tracking the Cursor with VoiceOver

The position of the cursor is particularly important when editing text. VoiceOver makes a sound when the cursor or insertion point moves on the screen, and it speaks the character that the insertion point moves across. Flick up or down with one finger to move the insertion point forward or backward in the text, by the unit set on the rotor. If you set the rotor to Characters, Words, or Lines, and flick down to move forward, the insertion point appears after the character, word, or line that VoiceOver speaks. If you move backward by flicking up, the insertion point now appears before the item that VoiceOver speaks.

The following practice exercise can help clarify this important concept. (Note: only type the words and letters that appear within the quotation marks in the steps that follow, not the quotation marks themselves.)

1. Enable VoiceOver if you haven't already.
2. From the home screen, activate the Notes app.
3. Type the word "bold" followed by a space.
4. Set the rotor control to Characters.
5. Flick up with one finger. When you hear "l" that means the insertion point is positioned before the "l," since you were moving backward.
6. Type "u."

7. Flick down with one finger to move forward. When you hear "d," it means the insertion point is after the "d" and you can type "er."

8. Touch or flick to the word and hear VoiceOver say "boulder."

Tracking the Cursor with a Braille Display

For braille display users, VoiceOver says, "is editing" to indicate that you are in an edit field and can begin typing. If you're in an edit field and do not hear VoiceOver say "is editing," you need to press Space Bar + braille keys 3-6 to move the cursor to the correct spot, or simply press the cursor routing button on the braille display to where you desire the cursor to be moved. You must repeat the Space Bar + braille keys 3-6 combination whenever you switch text fields—such as when moving from the document name text field to the document contents text field. Otherwise, when you type you will be adding text within the previous text field.

Selecting Text on the iPad

The iPad has a "clipboard" feature that you can use to copy, cut, and paste text as you would on a laptop or desktop computer. You can also select a word in order to check for spelling suggestions, or to look it up in the iPad's built-in dictionary.

Selecting Text using VoiceOver

Select All

The Select All option of the rotor setting will select the entire contents of a document so that you can cut or copy and paste it to another document within that same app, or to an edit field in a completely different app. To select all text, copy or cut to the clipboard, and then paste from the clipboard to the desired location using VoiceOver, follow these steps:

1. Type a sentence, then double tap anywhere above the keyboard. VoiceOver should read what you typed.

2. Activate the rotor by rotating two fingers on the screen until VoiceOver speaks, "Edit."

3. Flick up or down to Select All, and double tap.

4. Continue to flick up or down through the choices—Cut, Copy, and Paste—until you find the one you want.

5. Double tap the desired choice.

Select a Word

To select a word to copy or cut to the clipboard, follow these steps:

1. Move the insertion point to the word you want to select. The cursor can be positioned at either end of the word, but there should be no spaces between the cursor and the word.

2. Set the rotor to Text Selection if your iPad is running iOS 9. Make sure that Text Selection has been enabled in the VoiceOver Rotor settings.

3. Flick down until you hear VoiceOver say, "Word."

4. Ensure that the cursor is located on the first letter of the desired word and flick right with one finger to select the word at the position of the cursor. Subsequent flicks will select additional words. Flicking left will deselect the desired element. (You may also select text by spreading your index finger and thumb apart to select by element and pinching your thumb and index finger to deselect it.)

5. Use the rotor to return to the edit option and flick up or down to the cut or copy option. Double tapping either option will cut or copy your selection to the clipboard. Remember, when you "cut" text, you chop it out of the edit field altogether, so only cut if you truly wish to remove this text and paste it elsewhere.

6. Place your cursor at the desired location for placing the text now stored on the clipboard. Use the rotor to return to the edit option and flick up or down. Selecting paste will paste the contents of the clipboard in the current cursor location.

Selecting Text with a Braille Display

If you are using a braille display, you can bypass these VoiceOver gestures by using the following procedure and keyboard commands:

1. Make sure you are in an edit field where there is a cursor present.

2. Move to the beginning of the text you want to select. Set the rotor to the element by which you want to select text: character, word, or line. Use Space Bar + braille keys 5-6 to move the rotor clockwise; use Space Bar + braille keys 2-3 to move counterclockwise.

3. When you've reached the desired setting, use one of the following commands:
    a. Select text: Space Bar + braille keys 2-5-6
    b. Deselect text: Space Bar + braille keys 2-3-5
    c. Select all: Space Bar + braille keys 2-3-5-6
    Note: Because of Apple's gestures and keyboard equivalents, coupled with the manner in which the cursor moves, it is only possible to select moving forward through a

document by characters, lines, or words. When you use these commands to move backward through a document, it deselects the text.

4. Here are the braille keyboard commands for Copy, Cut, and Paste:
   a. Copy: Space Bar + braille keys 1-4 (braille letter *c*)
   b. Cut: Space Bar + braille keys 1-3-4-6 (braille letter *x*)
   c. Paste: Space Bar + braille keys 1-2-3-6 (braille letter *v*)

Entering Text by Voice
Using VoiceOver for Voice Input

The newer versions of iOS devices have built-in dictation applications. Before proceeding, please note that voice input is best used for quick messaging or web searches. While dictation can be an effective tool for using an iPad, it is critical that students learn actual reading and writing skills and avoid becoming dependent on voice input.

The iOS Dictation function is accessible via the onscreen keyboard, but only when the iPad is connected to the Internet. With VoiceOver enabled, on the onscreen keyboard find the key with the microphone icon—adjacent to the Space Bar (see Figure 7.3)—double tap, wait until you hear the tone, then begin speaking. To add punctuation, just say the name of the punctuation you'd like to use (such as "comma," "period," or "question mark"). Say, "new paragraph" when you need one. The text will appear onscreen in the active edit field as you dictate. Double tap the "Done" button and another tone will sound to indicate the dictation session has terminated. Dictation is most accurate when you speak clearly in an environment with minimal to no background noise.

An alternative to using the Dictation key is to perform

FIGURE 7.3

The onscreen keyboard showing the Dictation (microphone) button.

a two-finger double tap within an edit field to start the dictation function, speak your text, and then perform a two-finger double tap to turn the feature off. VoiceOver will say, "thinking," and then repeat what you have said, entering this text into the desired edit field. Note that if you perform this two-finger double tap outside of an edit field, or when the keyboard is not active within the edit field, you will start and stop the iPad's last multimedia session. More times than not, this is music, and the iPad will revert to the last musical selection that was recently accessed. Make sure the onscreen keyboard is present and within VoiceOver's focus before performing this two-finger double tap shortcut.

Using Siri for Voice Input

Siri (the iOS personal assistant present on third-generation and later iPads running iOS 6 or later) takes the dictation feature one step further. When you enable Siri within Settings, your home button becomes the hotkey for interacting with your iOS device. Hold down the home button for a couple of seconds and you will hear two beeps to indicate that Siri is now active. You may then ask Siri a question, look up or e-mail a contact, query your next appointment, dictate an e-mail, browse the Internet, and the like (see Chapter 3 for more on Siri). Speak clearly at a steady pace. All in all, Siri works fairly well.

Word-Processing Apps

While word processing—creating and editing substantial written documents—is possible on an iPad, the iPad generally lacks the functionality and features available on a traditional desktop computer with a program like Microsoft Word. There are three apps—AccessNote, iA Writer, and Pages—that offer word-processing capabilities robust enough to be used for tasks such as creating and editing a document for a class assignment.

These apps have buttons that allow files to be shared, stored in the cloud, e-mailed, and printed. The apps work in conjunction with Dropbox and other file-sharing services such as iCloud Drive, which is used to house the files. For example, you can e-mail a link via the cloud service or manually through the Mail app to a student for a file stored in Dropbox. Within Dropbox is an action button, which, when selected, enables the recipient to open the selected file in their preferred app. It's also easy to print using these word-processing apps. Select the file, and the iPad scans for any iOS-enabled printers within range. Select the printer you wish to send the file to, and it wirelessly prints the document.

AccessNote

Developed by the American Foundation for the Blind, Access Note (see Figure 7.4 and the Resources section at the back of this book) is a free, basic notetaker available in the App Store. This app incorporates external keyboard and specific braille key commands into the user interface and is well suited for searching for text globally across all notes and within a note.

FIGURE 7.4

The AccessNote app.

AccessNote comes preset to work in conjunction with Dropbox and automatically creates an AccessNote folder in your Dropbox account. (Syncing with Dropbox can be enabled under Settings in the AccessNote app.) The text files you place in that folder can be edited and shared across platforms. For classes, you can create folders for specific class subjects within AccessNote, and then create files specific to classes on specific days within these various folders. For example, you could create Social Studies, Biology, World Literature, and History folders within AccessNote. Your students could create documents for each class within these specific folders and name them by the dates on which the class occurs. They could then take notes within these files, edit the notes on either their iPads or PCs, and then share, e-mail, and print the notes, all via buttons within the app.

iA Writer

iA Writer is a more robust text editor with similar functionality to AccessNote (see Figure 7.5 and the Resources section at the back of this book). It features an Export Text option that makes it easy to e-mail the file as a text attachment, copy the file contents to the clipboard, print the file, or open the file in another app. iA Writer also makes it easy to rename and move

FIGURE 7.5

The iA Writer app icon.

files out of iCloud via its File Browser button. Files may be deleted by selecting the Edit option under File Browser, or by just following the prompts.

Pages

Pages is the word-processing app of the Apple iWork suite of productivity apps (see Figure 7.6 and the Resources section at the back of this book). Pages is one of the more commonly used iOS word-processing apps, plus it's compatible with Microsoft's Word files, which means you can provide a Word document to your students—either as an e-mail attachment or through Dropbox—and they can open it, export the document into a Pages file, make all of the necessary edits, and then send the file back to you.

FIGURE 7.6

The Pages app icon.

Pages now allows users to save files to Dropbox. The following instructions for uploading documents from the Pages app to Dropbox show how you can save documents in different formats:

1. With the Pages doc open, select the tools icon in the upper-right corner.
2. Single finger swipe, locate, and select Share and Print.
3. Scroll down and select Open in Another App.
4. Scroll down and select the format you want to use. The first option is Pages; the second option is PDF; and the third is Word. Note: VoiceOver will read the icons first—"Pages, PDF, Word." Then, if you keep swiping, it will read the labels "Pages, PDF, Word" again. You need to select your option when the icons, not the labels, are announced. Select your preferred format, and you will hear "Open in another app; cancel."
5. Scroll down to Choose App. From here, the various apps to which you can save will appear. These will depend on the particular apps installed on your iOS device. Let's say Open in Dropbox appears first. When you select it, you will hear "Dropbox: save to Dropbox; cancel."
6. Scroll down to Name, and you can rename your document, if you choose.
7. Open Dropbox, which comes right after Destination. You will hear: "Choose a Destination." Scroll down until you find the Dropbox folder where you want to place your document. Select that folder.
8. Scroll down and select Choose at the bottom-right corner of this field. You will hear "Save to Dropbox; cancel."
9. Swipe over to the Save button in the upper-right corner and select.

If your students are not using Dropbox, you can simply e-mail the file as a Microsoft Word or Pages document. Pages gives you that option from within the app itself.

Printing and E-Mailing from Your iPad

When it comes to printing from your iPad, very little setup is required. Most of today's newer printers are able to receive print jobs wirelessly from iOS devices on the same Wi-Fi network. Wireless printing is a desirable function to have as there will be instances where your students' instructors still require hardcopy print versions of assignments.

Math on Your iPad

Several apps are available that enable your students to perform accessible scientific calculations and to create and read spreadsheets on the iPad.

Calculators

While the preinstalled calculator on the iPad is accessible for VoiceOver users, your students may find the Talking Scientific Calculator app somewhat more intuitive to use (see Figure 7.7 and the Resources section at the back of this book). This app, available from the App Store, has its own talking calculator, which does not interfere with VoiceOver and allows for all of the functionality present in today's online and physical scientific calculators.

Students can use either a QWERTY or braille keyboard to enter numbers, which will also be spoken, to perform calculations from the easiest to the most complex. VoiceOver's braille settings allow for the Nemeth braille code to be used when equations are encountered, which is

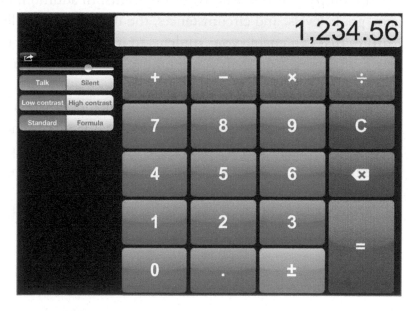

FIGURE 7.7

The Talking Scientific Calculator app.

the default setting. Be sure that this option is toggled on in the Braille section of the VoiceOver menu under Settings if the student will be accessing Nemeth equations within iPad apps such as iBooks.

Spreadsheets

The Numbers app (see Figure 7.8 and the Resources section at the back of this book), available via the App Store, lets you create a spreadsheet or open, read, and edit an Excel or Numbers spreadsheet. You can share spreadsheets through Dropbox, or e-mail them as attachments. This app does not offer the same functionality as the desktop version of Microsoft Excel, but it is somewhat more accessible and does give your students a way to review and edit numerical data portably.

FIGURE 7.8

The Numbers app icon.

Conclusion

In this chapter you have gleaned some helpful strategies for teaching your students how to complete tasks independently in the classroom. While not all iPad features have been covered, this book should prove to be an effective blueprint for you as you present the iPad to your students. In addition, depending on your students' ages, grade levels, and circumstances, the iPad and its smaller counterparts have additional features that can enable your students to interact more inclusively beyond the walls of your classroom and within their communities. These features are covered in the appendix to this book, Beyond the Classroom.

Moving forward, it is important to remember that technology is ever changing, with more features coming as the proliferation of iOS services and applications continues. The accessibility offered by the iPad is truly leveling the playing field for visually impaired students who are striving to keep pace with their sighted peers in the classroom and workplace.

The challenges will continue to be great, but so will the technology. These are exciting times, for sure. Stay tuned.

APPENDIX · # Beyond the Classroom

The iPad offers a range of functionality that blind and visually impaired students will find useful for everyday tasks outside of the classroom.

Uses for the Camera
Capturing Images
Most iOS devices have two cameras: a forward-facing camera on the front of the device, opposite the home button, and a rear-facing one on the back surface of the device. Within the Camera app you may choose which of these cameras to use as well whether the selected camera will take a still image or a video. Lining up the camera with the intended target or subject can be challenging when the tablet is being used to snap a picture. However, VoiceOver does a respectable job of reporting to the user the status of the photo that has been taken and saved. For instance, if a photo is blurry and dimly lit, VoiceOver will announce this. It will also attempt to distinguish how many faces are in the photo. Aside from lining up the camera, the camera app is completely accessible when taking, saving, deleting, and sharing pictures and videos. VoiceOver announces all of the camera controls and provides detailed access within the Photos apps, where users may display, share, or delete stored photos and videos.

Identifying Colors
The camera also can be used to identify the colors of objects in a photo using the free Color Identifier app, available in the App Store (see the Resources section at the back of this book for more information). Color Identifier provides real-time feedback as to which colors are viewed by the camera. There's a basic color mode and a mode that provides more descriptive color names. Examples of these descriptive color names include Lavender Rose and Moon Mist. What better way to teach students how to identify objects by their colors while making it fun with these descriptors!

Keeping Track of Money

Another need of people who are visually impaired is being able to identify paper currency. The Looktel Money Reader app (see the Resources section at the back of this book for more information) provides an accurate means for meeting that need. When the app is activated, the user simply holds the currency in front of the camera to hear VoiceOver announce the denomination.

Getting Help

Another use for the camera is as a means for soliciting help. iOS's built-in FaceTime app (see Figure A.1) provides free audio and video calling between users of iOS devices. Open the FaceTime app, select Video before initiating a call, and then enter the name, e-mail address, or mobile number of another iOS user and you will have instant, face-to-face access to the recipient. If the person called is sighted, he or she can provide visual help in situations where a student with a visual impairment is not yet oriented in his or her physical surroundings or when the student needs to locate or identify something of importance. In the same vein as FaceTime, the Be My Eyes app (see the Resources section at the back of this book) is a free service that links registered people with visual impairments to registered sighted volunteers. One minor downside of the Be My Eyes app is that there can be a wait when connecting with a volunteer.

FIGURE **A.1**

iOS FaceTime app icon.

Reading Printed Text via OCR

Finally, the camera can be used for optical character recognition (OCR) of printed materials, in which software can be used to recognize text within an image and convert it to recognizable digital characters. While there are a number of free and low-priced OCR options currently on the market, the KNFB Reader (see the Resources section at the back of this book) provides stability and accuracy for users who would like to point the iPad camera at printed text to have it read aloud. This pocket-sized option provides clear, intelligible auditory readings.

Location Services
Using GPS
The built-in iOS Maps app allows the user to answer three questions via GPS:

1. Where am I?
2. What is around me?
3. How do I get to my destination?

When used in conjunction with Siri, the Maps app is a useful and free tool for determining where you are, while even providing feedback on street names and approximate addresses. You may ask Siri for directions to a specific address or establishment, and the Maps app will provide auditory directions for reaching the destination from your current location. Orientation and mobility instructors can use this free resource to augment their students' travel lessons.

For more intensive GPS usage with an emphasis on nonvisual pedestrian travel, two apps—Seeing Eye GPS and Blind Square (see the Resources section at the back of this book)—provide an extremely useful and accessible means for identifying your current location, creating routes, and for following routes either on foot or in a vehicle. Both apps even provide an emphasis on public transit considerations. While each has expenses associated with usage, they offer different perspectives and user interfaces for visually impaired students who must master independent travel in order to successfully transition to either a post-secondary educational environment or the competitive workplace.

Accessing Real-Time Information
Enabling your iPad's Location Services (in the Privacy menu under Settings) also supports real-time sharing of information among different apps. Apps can send "push notifications" or updated bits of information to you. These notifications often pertain to where you are located. For instance, a news app may provide you with local weather updates, local breaking news, or significant points of interest in the vicinity; or a social networking app can alert you to friends who are nearby (if they have also enabled Location Services for the same app).

Interacting with Social Networks
What Your Students Need to Know
While it is unlikely that your blind and visually impaired students will be interacting with social networks such as Facebook and Twitter in the classroom, you may want to call their

attention to the following points so they can interact independently and safely with their classmates and take advantage of the other uses of social media:

- Social network apps such as Facebook, LinkedIn, and Twitter are designed similarly, with feature tabs found at the bottom of the screen. When a tab is selected, the app screen presents choices and interaction options pertinent to the tab selected. For instance, a News Feed tab may display the latest tweets, Facebook posts, or news stories. A Notifications tab may be used to draw your attention to activities directly related to you (such as friend requests, tweets that mention you, and the like).

- Some social networking apps such as Facebook and Twitter can be set up within Settings. Other social networking apps such as LinkedIn must be downloaded from the App Store.

- The process for taking a photo and then posting it on either Facebook or Twitter is accessible.

- Students are able to view the location of their nearby friends as well as have their approximate location viewed by others, if they so desire.

- Social networks can be a positive, concise means for students to gain quick access to information pertinent to their interests and academic areas of study.

- Social networks such as LinkedIn can be a springboard for a student's career development and can even provide a path to gainful employment.

Growing Phenomenon

There are many other social networks beyond Facebook, Twitter, and LinkedIn, such as Instagram, Flipboard, and Tumblr. The number of social networks continues to grow, and students who are blind or visually impaired now have practical access to these social networks. It is critical, therefore, that teachers, in conjunction with parents, educate students about the benefits and possible drawbacks and dangers of using social networks. The reality is that while social media can be a great resource for gaining and sharing useful information, it can also cause a host of problems if used inappropriately.

As with the innumerable uses of the iPad within the classroom and for schoolwork at home, the uses of iPads and other iOS devices for everyday tasks continues to grow. When you help your students with visual impairments learn to use these devices, their independence will likewise grow, both in and outside of the classroom.

Resources

App Reviews and Advice on Accessibility

Access World: Technology News for People Who Are Blind or Visually Impaired
www.afb.org/aw

A free online magazine providing information on assistive technology and product reviews from the American Foundation for the Blind.

AppleVis
www.applevis.com

An information-sharing website for blind and low vision users of Apple's range of products, including iOS devices. Includes sections on getting started with your iOS device, setting it up, and becoming familiar with it, as well as a forum, guides, blogs, podcasts, and product reviews.

Maccessibility
www.maccessibility.net

A website for compiling and providing access to resources for blind, visually impaired, and other disability groups using Apple products. Provides news and commentary, podcasts, and online communities.

WonderBaby iPad Articles and App Reviews
www.wonderbaby.org/articles/ipad-apps-and-accessibility

Articles about accessibility features in the iPad and reviews of apps for use with children who are visually impaired on the WonderBaby.org blog for parents from the Perkins School for the Blind.

Apple Resources

Apple Education Volume Purchase Program
www.apple.com/education/it/vpp/

Site for purchasing volume licenses for educational institutions wishing to share apps with more than five devices.

Apple ID
Setting up an Apple ID with a credit card
https://support.apple.com/en-us/HT204316

Setting up an Apple ID without a credit card
https://support.apple.com/en-us/HT204034

Apple ID for students program
www.apple.com/education/it/appleid/

Apple Special Education
www.apple.com/education/special-education/

Website for teachers with suggestions for using Apple iOS products with students who have special needs.

iBooks Author
www.apple.com/ibooks-author/

iPad User Guide
https://itunes.apple.com/us/book/ipad-user-guide-for-ios-9.2/id1035374126?mt=11

Online iPad User Guide
http://help.apple.com/ipad/9/

File Sharing and Cloud Storage

Dropbox
www.dropbox.com

iCloud
www.apple.com/support/icloud/

General Information

Financing the iPad (for Parents)

5 Ways to Get a Free iPad for Your Special Needs Child! by Amber Bobnar
www.wonderbaby.org/articles/ipad-funding-special-needs

Third-Party Apps
Accessible App Advice
ViA app (free)

https://itunes.apple.com/us/app/via-by-braille-institute/id528499232?mt=8

An app developed at the Braille Institute of America to help educators and consumers find apps for users with visual impairments. Sorts apps by category, price, and rating. Provides a forum for discussion with other iOS users and links to external reviews, podcasts, and blogs about specific apps. Full functionality requires setting up a ViA account with Braille Institute at http://www.brailleinstitute.org/digital/mobile-applications.html.

Identification
Be My Eyes (free)

https://itunes.apple.com/us/app/be-my-eyes-helping-blind-see/id905177575?mt=8

An identification app that links people with visual impairments to sighted volunteers via live video chat. The visually impaired user points the rear-facing camera to show the sighted user whatever needs to be identified.

Color Identifier (free)

https://itunes.apple.com/us/app/color-identifier/id363346987?mt=8

A color identification app that uses the camera on an iOS device to speak the names of colors in real time.

Looktel Money Reader

https://itunes.apple.com/us/app/looktel-money-reader/id417476558?mt=8

A money identification app that recognizes currency, using the camera, and speaks the denomination, enabling people with visual impairments or blindness to identify and count bills in real time, without an Internet connection. Displays the denomination on the screen in large, high-contrast numerals. Supports 21 currencies.

Math/Spreadsheets

Numbers

https://itunes.apple.com/us/app/numbers/id361304891?mt=8

An accessible spreadsheet app that also creates as interactive charts, tables, and images of data. Works between Mac and iOS devices and Microsoft Excel.

Talking Calculator

https://itunes.apple.com/us/app/talking-calculator/id424464284?mt=8

A comprehensive calculator with features such as large colorful buttons, optional high contrast, full VoiceOver support, and the option to use speech for answers, button names, and formulas.

Orientation/GPS

BlindSquare

https://itunes.apple.com/us/app/blindsquare/id500557255?mt=8

Describes the environment and announces points of interest, street intersections, and user-defined points as you travel.

Seeing Eye GPS

https://itunes.apple.com/us/app/seeing-eye-gps/id668624446?mt=8

A fully accessible turn-by-turn GPS app that contains features unique to blind users.

Reading

BARD (Braille and Audio Reading Download) Mobile (free)

https://itunes.apple.com/us/app/bard-mobile/id705229586

A service of the National Library Service for the Blind and Physically Handicapped (NLS) that provides access to the huge library of braille and talking books, as well as magazines and audio files. Requires registration with the NLS; for instructions go to www.loc.gov/nls /bardnls.

KNFB Reader

https://itunes.apple.com/us/app/knfbreader/id849732663?mt=8

A reading app that converts printed text into high-quality speech. Captures pictures of any type of printed text, uses document analysis technology to determine the words, and reads them aloud with text-to-speech and braille access. Provides synchronized speech and text highlighting. Syncs with and exports files to Dropbox.

Read2Go

https://itunes.apple.com/us/app/read2go/id425585903?mt=8

An accessible e-book reader that provides access to the library of books in DAISY format for people with print disabilities from Bookshare as well as other DAISY books. Requires membership with Bookshare at www.bookshare.org; free to students with verified print disabilities and schools in the United States and available for a fee to others.

Text Editing/Word Processing

AccessNote (free)

https://itunes.apple.com/us/app/accessnote/id591287188?mt=8

An accessible basic notetaker designed specifically for VoiceOver users from the American Foundation for the Blind. Incorporates external keyboard and specific braille key commands into the user interface. Comes preset to work in conjunction with Dropbox and automatically creates an AccessNote folder in an existing Dropbox account, if there is one. The text files placed in that folder can be edited and shared across platforms.

iA Writer

https://itunes.apple.com/us/app/ia-writer/id775737172?mt=8

A text editor that optimizes plain-text writing while making it easy to export files into e-mail as a text attachment, copy the contents to the clipboard, print the file, or open it in another app. Syncs with Dropbox and iCloud.

Pages

https://itunes.apple.com/us/app/pages/id361309726?mt=8

A powerful word processor, part of the Apple iWork suite of productivity apps that helps create reports, resumes, and documents. Is compatible with Microsoft's Word files.

VoiceOver

VO Starter (free)

https://itunes.apple.com/us/app/vo-starter/id586844936?mt=8

Guide for new VoiceOver users, with practice space for becoming more familiar with VoiceOver gestures and controls.

Index

Page references followed by 't' and 'f' indicate tables and figures respectively.

About the Author

Larry L. Lewis, Jr., M.A., M.S., is the founder and president of Flying Blind, an assistive technology consulting and sales company. He has over 20 years of experience serving the adaptive technology industry in domestic and international product and sales management roles at companies such as HumanWare and Optelec as well as an extensive background in assessing, training, and recommending adaptive technology solutions for people who require adaptive speech or braille. Mr. Lewis is the author of *iOS Success: Making the iPad Accessible: A Guide for Teachers and Parents,* which covered iOS 6, has published articles on accessible technology in *Access World* magazine, and served as the subject matter expert for online courses from the Hadley School for the Blind on topics such as applying adaptive strategies to web browsing, developing listening skills in the workplace, building professional word-processing skills, and the utilization of social networks by individuals who are visually impaired.

I (NORMAL CONTROLS)		II (NONDIALYZED PATIENTS)		III (DIALYZED PATIENTS)	
206.9 (14)	143.8 (2)	194.6 (11)	143.0 (1)	288.0 (21)	249.0 (19)
150.0 (5)	192.6 (10)	145.6 (3)	170.0 (6)	269.2 (20)	346.1 (23)
197.3 (12)		174.9 (8)		288.3 (22)	216.6 (16)
173.2 (7)		187.5 (9)		357.5 (24)	202.6 (13)
147.2 (4)		223.4 (17)		229.2 (18)	213.5 (15)

The rank sums are

$$R_1 = 14 + 5 + 12 + \cdots + 10 = 54$$
$$R_2 = 11 + 3 + 8 + \cdots + 6 = 55$$
$$R_3 = 21 + 20 + 22 + \cdots + 15 = 191$$

Note that $n_1 = n_2 = 7$, $n_3 = 10$, and $N = 24$. The observed value of the Kruskal-Wallis statistic for these data is

$$H = \frac{12}{N(N+1)} \sum_{i=1}^{3} \frac{R_i^2}{n_i} - 3(N+1)$$

$$= \frac{12}{24(25)} \left(\frac{54^2}{7} + \frac{55^2}{7} + \frac{191^2}{10} \right) - 3(25) = 14.94$$

From Table VI, the critical point is 10.6 for a size .005 test based on the chi-square distribution with $k - 1 = 2$ degrees of freedom. Since 14.94 exceeds this value, we may conclude that differences in liver size do exist among the three populations. The P value of the test is less than .005.

The Kruskal-Wallis test does assume continuous populations. However, the test can be safely applied to data that originally consist of ranks. If the sampled populations are normal with equal variances, then the hypothesis being tested is the same as that of the one-way classification, completely random design in analysis of variance.

EXERCISES 13.4

1. Vitamin A deficiency is a well-recognized public health problem in many areas. Inadequate dietary intake of vitamin A is the most important factor responsible for this deficiency. A chief source of vitamin A is β carotene, which is derived from vegetables. It has been shown that adding green leafy vegetables to the diet results in an increase in serum vitamin A concentrations. A study is run to determine whether adding fat to the diet has any benefits. A group of 30 children, each of whose serum

vitamin A concentration is less than 20 mg vitamin A/100 ml blood serum is randomly split into three subgroups. Each group receives 40 g spinach daily, but the fat in the diet varies. At the end of the experiment, these data on the serum vitamin A concentration are obtained:

I (NO ADDED FAT)	II (5 g FAT ADDED)	III (10 g FAT ADDED)
18.1	29.1	26.6
16.5	15.8	16.1
21.0	20.4	18.8
18.7	23.5	25.0
7.4	18.5	21.8
12.4	21.3	15.4
16.1	23.1	19.9
17.9	23.8	15.5
	20.1	21.1
	11.9	25.5

   a. Compute the rank sum for each group.
   b. Test the null hypothesis that the fat content of the diet has no effect on serum A concentration at the $\alpha = .1$ level.

2. Urease is an enzyme known to produce ammonia in the gastrointestinal tract. Ammonia is known to be detrimental to patients with liver disease. A study is conducted to compare the urease concentration in the gastric juices in five populations: normal controls, I; patients with extrahepatic portal vein obstruction, II; patients with amoebic liver abscess, III; patients with viral hepatitis, IV; and patients with idiopathic portal hypertension, V, respectively. These data (in milligrams per milliliter) are obtained:

I	II	III	IV	V
261.1	221.9	201.4	600.9	160.6
186.2	188.7	146.1	301.2	135.0
239.1	167.6	96.8	607.9	455.1
243.3	224.9	173.9	283.3	402.3
296.8	178.8	280.8	193.3	457.9
270.5	147.9	100.3	159.4	559.6

Based on these data and the Kruskal-Wallis test, can you claim at the $\alpha = .05$ level that these populations differ with respect to the gastric urease concentration?

3. Poisonings may occur owing to extensive contact with pesticide residue on crops. Pesticide absorption through the skin varies with the anatomic region of the body. The palm of the hand is especially sensitive. A study is run to compare the exposure time of the right hand in five different types of agricultural workers. The data are collected by filming the workers for a 17-minute period and determining, for each, how long the right hand is in contact with the crop. These data result:

TOBACCO HARVESTERS	COTTON SCOUTS	PEACH THINNERS	BLUEBERRY PICKERS	SWEET CORN PACKERS
14.4	11.7	15.8	16.1	14.3
12.9	13.8	16.2	16.0	14.5
12.0	14.2	15.9	15.9	14.8
13.9	10.3	16.7	16.4	14.9
13.3	7.0	16.4	16.6	14.0

Based on the Kruskal-Wallis test, can you claim that the exposure time of the right hand differs among these groups of workers? Explain your answer based on the P value of the test.

4. Since the liver is the major site of drug metabolism, it is expected that patients with liver disease may have defects in the elimination of drugs metabolized by the liver. One such drug is phenylbutazone. A study is conducted of the response of the system to this drug. Three groups are studied: normal controls, patients with cirrhosis of the liver, and patients with chronic active hepatitis. Each subject is given orally 19 mg phenylbutazone/kg body weight. Based on blood analysis, the time of peak plasma concentration (in hours) is determined for each. These data result:

NORMAL	CIRRHOSIS	HEPATITIS
4.0	22.6	16.6
30.6	14.4	12.1
26.8	26.3	7.2
37.9	13.8	6.6
13.7	17.4	12.5
49.0		15.1
		6.7
		20.0

Based on the Kruskal-Wallis test, can you conclude that the three populations differ with respect to the time of peak plasma concentration of phenylbutazone? Explain your answer on the basis of the P value of the test.

5. The supraorbital nasal glands (salt glands) have an important function in marine birds. These glands help to excrete sodium chloride when environmental conditions force the bird to consume more salt than normal. A study is conducted to determine the role of

these glands in the excretion of lead, a common environmental pollutant. Three groups of ducks are studied: normal controls, I; ducks force-fed with a dose of commercial lead shot, II; and ducks fed with lead shot and $CaNa_2EDTA$, III. These data are found on the lead concentration (in micrograms of lead per gram of tissue) in the nasal glands:

I	II	III
1.4	11.1	5.0
1.0	10.3	8.2
.9	10.2	4.9
.7	9.7	3.2
.5	7.7	4.4
1.2	10.1	3.1
3.4	11.6	5.1
1.3	13.3	2.9

Use the Kruskal-Wallis test to determine whether differences in the lead concentration in the nasal glands exist among the three populations.

FRIEDMAN k-SAMPLE TEST FOR LOCATION: MATCHED DATA

13.5 □ In this section we present a distribution-free test for k identical populations when the observations from the k populations are matched. The test, developed by M. Friedman in 1937, is especially sensitive to differences in location.

Friedman Test

Assume that we are interested in comparing the effects of k treatments. It is felt that there is a variable which, although not of direct interest, might interfere with our ability to detect real differences among the k treatments. We want to control this extraneous variable by blocking. That is, we split the experimental units into b groups, or "blocks," each of size k, with members within a block being as nearly alike as possible relative to the extraneous variable. Then we randomly assign the k treatments to units within each block. To test the null hypothesis of identical treatment effects, we rank the observations within each block from 1 to k (smallest to largest), giving tied scores the average group rank. Next we compute R_i, $i = 1, 2, \ldots, k$, the sum of the ranks associated with each of the k treatments. If H_0 is true, each of these rank sums should be moderate in size; otherwise, there should be substantial differences among them. It can be shown that the expected value of each rank sum under H_0 is $b(k + 1)/2$.

The *Friedman statistic S* is designed to compare the observed rank sums with this expected value:

$$S = \sum_{i=1}^{k} \left[R_i - \frac{b(k + 1)}{2} \right]^2$$

Note that if H_0 is true, each of the differences $R_i - b(k + 1)/2$ should be small, yielding a small value of S; otherwise, S will be inflated. The probability distribution for S has been tabulated for a limited number of choices for k (number of treatments) and b (number of blocks). However, it has been found that the statistic

$$\frac{12S}{bk(k + 1)}$$

follows an approximate chi-square distribution with $k - 1$ degrees of freedom if H_0 is true. Thus this statistic serves as our test statistic with rejection of H_0 occurring for large values of the statistic. The P values are read from Table VI of Appendix B.

We illustrate the use of the Friedman test in Example 13.5.1.

EXAMPLE 13.5.1 □ Recent studies have shown that even microliter amounts of crude oil, when applied to the surface of fertile eggs of several avian species, may result in damage to the embryo. In addition to a high aromatic hydrocarbon content, certain crude oils contain high concentrations of nickel and vanadium. The effects of these elements on the embryonic development of mallards are studied. Since ducks from various clutches (nests) have different genetic backgrounds, this factor is controlled by blocking. Six clutches are used in the experiment. Four eggs are randomly selected from each clutch and assigned at random to one of four treatments:

   I. No crude oil applied (control)

  II. Treated with 1 μL crude oil

 III. Treated with 1 μL crude oil with 700 ppm vanadium

  IV. Treated with 1 μL crude oil with 700 ppm nickel

The eggs are allowed to develop for 18 days, at which time the weight, in grams, of each egg is determined. These data result (the rank of each observation *within its block* is given in parentheses):

		Treatment			
		I	II	III	IV
B	1	16.77 (4)	14.34 (2)	16.08 (3)	14.29 (1)
l	2	15.61 (4)	11.92 (1)	13.22 (2)	13.95 (3)
o	3	14.46 (4)	14.45 (3)	11.72 (1)	13.59 (2)
c	4	13.08 (3)	16.11 (4)	10.18 (1)	12.22 (2)
k	5	14.47 4)	12.85 (1)	13.52 (3)	13.22 (2)
(clutch)	6	12.01 (2)	16.13 (4)	12.68 (3)	10.73 (1)

The treatment rank sums are

$$R_1 = 4 + 4 + 4 + 3 + 4 + 2 = 21$$
$$R_2 = 2 + 1 + 3 + 4 + 1 + 4 = 15$$
$$R_3 = 3 + 2 + 1 + 1 + 3 + 3 = 13$$
$$R_4 = 1 + 3 + 2 + 2 + 2 + 1 = 11$$

Note that if H_0 is true, these rank sums should all be close to the expected value of

$$\frac{b(k + 1)}{2} = \frac{6(4 + 1)}{2} = 15$$

There does seem to be some deviation from this value. Is the deviation enough to conclude that there are differences among the four treatments? To answer, we compute the value of the Friedman statistic S, and use it to find the value of the test statistic

$$X_{k-1}^2 = \frac{12S}{bk(k + 1)}$$

For these data,

$$S = \sum_{i=1}^{k} \left[R_i - \frac{b(k + 1)}{2} \right]^2$$

$$= \sum_{i=1}^{4} \left[R_i - \frac{6(4 + 1)}{2} \right]^2$$

$$= (21 - 15)^2 + (15 - 15)^2 + (13 - 15)^2 + (11 - 15)^2$$

$$= 36 + 0 + 4 + 16 = 56$$

The observed value of the $X_{k-1}^2 = X_3^2$ statistic is

$$\frac{12S}{bk(k + 1)} = \frac{12(56)}{6(4)(5)} = 5.6$$

From Table VI in Appendix B, we see that the P value for this test is between .25 (critical point, 4.11) and .1 (critical point, 6.25). Since this is large, we cannot conclude that there are differences among the treatments.

The Friedman test does assume continuous populations. However, it can be used to analyze data that originally consist of ranks. It is the distribution-free analog of the normal theory randomized complete block design.

EXERCISES 13.5

1. During the last few years, an increasing number of cases of suspected pentachlorophenol (PCP) poisoning of farm animals have been brought to the attention of veterinarians. A study is conducted to consider the effects of varying amounts of PCP on the total weight gain (in kilograms) in pigs. Litter mates are used as blocks to control the effects of natural differences among animals of different parentage. These treatments are used:

   I. Fed lactose (controls)

   II. Fed lactose and 5 mg purified PCP/kg body weight

   III. Fed lactose and 10 mg purified PCP/kg body weight

   IV. Fed lactose and 15 mg purified PCP/kg body weight

   These data are obtained on the total weight gained by the end of the experimental period:

		Treatment			
		I	II	III	IV
B	1	8.9	6.6	5.6	4.2
l	2	7.2	6.9	7.3	6.9
o	3	3.1	6.2	7.2	4.1
c	4	7.1	8.3	6.3	5.8
k	5	6.7	6.4	5.9	9.4
	6	5.3	6.7	8.0	7.9
(litter)	7	2.4	5.5	6.1	3.1
	8	5.7	9.2	9.6	4.2

   If the PCP level does not affect total weight gain, each rank sum should lie close to what value? Use the Friedman test to compare the effects of these four treatments on total weight gain.

2. A study is conducted to compare the mercury concentration in the brain, muscle, and eye tissues of trout exposed to a sublethal dose (.3 toxic unit) of methyl mercury. Twelve trout are used in the experiment; each is considered a block. These data on the concentration (in micrograms of mercury per gram of tissue) result:

			Tissue	
		BRAIN	MUSCLE	EYE
	1	1.65	.98	.49
	2	1.37	1.17	.40
	3	1.48	1.05	.44
B	4	1.40	1.45	.55
l	5	1.61	.96	.43
o	6	1.59	1.00	.39
c	7	1.22	1.24	.43
k	8	1.66	1.01	.57
(trout)	9	1.49	.86	.87
	10	1.67	1.13	.52
	11	1.31	1.18	.46
	12	1.55	1.17	.45

If there are no differences in the mercury concentrations in these three tissue types, each rank sum should be close to what value? Use the Friedman test to compare the effects of a .3-toxic-unit dose of methyl mercury on the mercury concentration in the brain, muscle, and eye tissues of trout.

3. A laboratory administrator is considering purchasing a machine to analyze blood samples. Five such machines are on the market. After trial use, each of eight medical technicians is asked to rank the machines in order of preference, with a rank of 1 being assigned to the machine most preferred. These data result:

				Machine		
		I	II	III	IV	V
	1	1	3	4	2	5
B	2	4	5	1	2	3
l	3	4	1	3	5	2
o	4	4	1	5	2	3
c	5	1	3	2	5	4
k	6	1	2	3	4	5
(technician)	7	5	1	3	2	4
	8	5	1	4	3	2

If there is no clear preference, each of the rank sums should be close to what value? Use the Friedman test to determine whether technicians perceive differences among the machines.

CORRELATION

13.6 □ In Chapter 11 we discuss the problem of measuring the degree of linear association between two random variables X and Y. This is done by means of the Pearson product-moment coefficient of correlation. Now we introduce a measure of linear association that is particularly useful when either the data consist of ranks or the data set is small enough to be ranked easily. The method was introduced in 1904 by C. Spearman.

Spearman's Rank Correlation Coefficient

Consider a set (x_1, y_1), (x_2, y_2), (x_3, y_3), ..., (x_n, y_n) of n paired observations on the random variables X and Y. To estimate the correlation between X and Y, we first rank the observations on X from 1 to n, smallest to largest. We then do the same for the observations on Y. We thus generate a set of n paired ranks, which we denote by (r_{x_1}, r_{y_1}), (r_{x_2}, r_{y_2}), (r_{x_3}, r_{y_3}), ..., (r_{x_n}, r_{y_n}). Again, we assign tied scores the average group rank. The estimated correlation between X and Y is found by calculating the Pearson coefficient for the set of paired ranks. That is, we define the *Spearman rank correlation coefficient* r_s by

$$r_s = \frac{n \Sigma r_x r_y - \Sigma r_x \Sigma r_y}{\sqrt{[n \Sigma r_x^2 - (\Sigma r_x)^2][n \Sigma r_y^2 - (\Sigma r_y)^2]}}$$

This procedure yields results that are slightly different from those of the Pearson method. However, for large sample sizes, there is close agreement. Furthermore, if there are *no ties*, the Spearman coefficient is given by

$$r_s = 1 - \frac{6 \Sigma d_i^2}{n(n^2 - 1)}$$

where $d_i = r_{x_i} - r_{y_i}$, the difference between the X and Y ranks. Thus if there are no ties, the Spearman coefficient is easier to compute than the Pearson. The interpretations of the two are the same. Namely, values near 1 indicate a strong positive correlation; large values of X tend to be associated with large values of Y. Values near -1 indicate a strong negative correlation; large values of X tend to be associated with small values of Y. Values near 0 indicate no linear association. It is suggested that the Spearman procedure not be used if there are a large number of ties.

We illustrate the Spearman procedure in Example 13.6.1.

EXAMPLE 13.6.1 □ A study is run to determine the association between an individual's blood nicotine concentration and the nicotine yield of the cigarette smoked. These data are obtained (ranks are in parentheses):

X (BLOOD NICOTINE CONCENTRATION, nmol/liter)	Y (NICOTINE CONTENT PER CIGARETTE, mg)
185.7 (2)	1.51 (8)
197.3 (5)	.96 (3)
204.2 (8)	1.21 (6)
199.9 (7)	1.66 (10)
199.1 (6)	1.11 (4)
192.8 (3)	.84 (2)
207.4 (9)	1.14 (5)
183.0 (1)	1.28 (7)
234.1 (10)	1.53 (9)
196.5 (4)	.76 (1)

For these data,

$$\Sigma r_x = \Sigma r_y = 55 \qquad \Sigma r_x^2 = \Sigma r_y^2 = 385$$
$$\Sigma r_x r_y = 2(8) + 5(3) + 8(6) + \cdots + 4(1) = 325$$

Computing r_s directly, we obtain

$$r_s = \frac{n\Sigma r_x r_y - \Sigma r_x \Sigma r_y}{\sqrt{[n\Sigma r_x^2 - (\Sigma r_x)^2][n\Sigma r_y^2 - (\Sigma r_y)^2]}}$$

$$= \frac{10(325) - 55(55)}{\sqrt{[10(385) - 55^2][10(385) - 55^2]}}$$

$$= .27$$

Since there are no ties, r_s can be computed by the shortcut formula:

$$r_s = 1 - \frac{6\Sigma d_i^2}{n(n^2 - 1)}$$

$$= 1 - \frac{6[(2 - 8)^2 + (5 - 3)^2 + (8 - 6)^2 + \cdots + (4 - 1)^2]}{10(10^2 - 1)}$$

$$= 1 - \frac{6(120)}{10(99)} = .27$$

Since the Spearman coefficient of correlation does not differ greatly from the Pearson, we may approximate the coefficient of determination r^2 by

r_s^2. In this case, $r_s^2 = .07$. Thus approximately 7% of the variation in the blood nicotine concentration can be attributed to a linear association with the nicotine yield of the cigarette smoked. Since this value is small, we interpret r_s as indicating a very slight positive correlation between X and Y.

EXERCISES 13.6

1. Continuous infusion of a drug at a constant rate is supposed to maintain its serum concentration at a constant and predictable level. This does appear to be the case within an individual patient. However, there is a problem in that the same drug dosage does not necessarily produce the same serum concentration in different patients. To study this phenomenon in patients treated with ampicillin for severe purulent meningitis, 24 patients are subjected to a constant-rate infusion of the drug. It is felt that there is a relationship between the serum ampicillin concentration and the patient's rate of creatinine clearance. These data are obtained:

x (CREATININE CLEARANCE, ml/min)	y (SERUM AMPICILLIN CONCENTRATION, mg/liter)
69.0	60.0
70.0	38.5
81.0	92.0
85.0	19.2
85.1	41.0
84.0	69.2
95.0	42.7
96.1	78.1
100.0	50.0
107.0	20.0
107.5	28.3
110.0	15.0
112.6	12.8
116.5	35.0
120.2	13.3
120.0	59.6
122.5	47.8
130.1	24.6
135.0	18.0
132.3	48.5
155.7	21.2
170.0	23.0
121.0	7.4
125.0	10.0

   a. Rank each of the sets of observations from 1 to 24.

   b. Find Σr_x, Σr_y, Σr_x^2, Σr_y^2, and $\Sigma r_x r_y$. Use these values to find r_s from its definition.

   c. Since there are no ties, the shortcut formula can be used. Verify your answer to part **b** by computing r_s from this formula.

   d. The estimated correlation for the Pearson coefficient is $-.49$. Compare this value to that of Spearman.

   e. Does there appear to be a strong linear association between X and Y? Explain your answer on the basis of the estimated value of r^2.

2. Patients with osteoporosis, a disease of the bone that produces a decrease in bone mass, are studied. The patients are treated with human parathyroid hormone fragment. It is hoped that a strong relationship exists between the calcium accretion rate during treatment and the final bone volume, so that this variable can be utilized in the future to predict final bone volume. These data result:

x (CALCIUM ACCRETION RATE, mmol/24 hr)	y (FINAL TRABECULAR BONE VOLUME, %)
2.5	8.0
3.0	12.1
4.0	9.1
4.6	10.0
6.1	11.0
7.5	5.2
11.0	10.1
12.3	18.0
15.0	14.9
15.2	9.7
17.0	15.0
20.5	17.0
24.6	12.2
28.3	47.2
30.0	31.4

Find r_s. Does there appear to be a strong positive correlation between X and Y? Explain on the basis of the approximate value of r^2.

3. One characteristic of vision is "smooth pursuit" eye movements, or the capacity of the eyes to track objects moving slowly across visual fields. A study is run to explore the relationship between the maximum velocity reached by the eyes during smooth pursuit and blood alcohol content. Twelve subjects are used. The maximum smooth-pursuit velocity is determined for each. Then the subjects are asked to drink either whiskey and water or gin and tonic until they consider themselves unfit to drive. At this point, the maximum velocity of smooth pursuit is measured again, and the subject's blood alcohol content is determined. These data result:

x (BLOOD ALCOHOL CONTENT, mg/dl)	y (SMOOTH-PURSUIT VELOCITY, % DECREASE)
20	2
45	11
68	30
68	50
70	4
75	6
85	19
86	30
108	38
110	10
120	51
150	60

Find r_s and interpret this value in a practical sense.

4. To tag baboons for future study, the animals must be immobilized temporarily. One drug used for this purpose is phencyclidine hydrochloride. A study is conducted to determine (1) the relationship between the dose administered and the time to complete immobilization and (2) the relationship between the dose administered and the elapsed time from complete immobilization until large movements are seen. These data result:

x (DOSE, mg drug/kg body weight)	y (TIME TO IMMOBILIZATION, min)	z (TIME TO RECOVERY, min)
1.21	7.6	100.2
1.36	8.2	100.1
1.78	8.7	100.5
1.10	7.9	90.4
1.57	8.0	97.7
1.49	7.4	87.8
1.59	7.7	79.5
1.02	8.5	119.8

a. Find and interpret the Spearman coefficient of correlation between X and Y.
b. Find and interpret the Spearman coefficient of correlation between X and Z.

APPENDIXES

APPENDIX A

SUMMATION NOTATION

In many statistical procedures it is necessary to manipulate sets of numerical observations. A shorthand notation has been developed to help simplify these operations. The notation uses the Greek letter sigma (Σ) to indicate addition. The use of this notation is illustrated below.

EXAMPLE A.1 $\square$ Consider the following set of observations:

$$x_1 = 4 \qquad x_3 = 2 \qquad x_5 = -3$$
$$x_2 = 1 \qquad x_4 = 5$$

$$\sum_{i=1}^{5} x_i = x_1 + x_2 + x_3 + x_4 + x_5$$
$$= 4 + 1 + 2 + 5 + (-3) = 9$$

(add the x's)

$$\sum_{i=1}^{5} x_i^2 = x_1^2 + x_2^2 + x_3^2 + x_4^2 + x_5^2$$
$$= 4^2 + 1^2 + 2^2 + 5^2 + (-3)^2$$
$$= 16 + 1 + 4 + 25 + 9 = 55$$

(add the squares of x's)

$$\sum_{i=1}^{5} 2x_i = 2x_1 + 2x_2 + 2x_3 + 2x_4 + 2x_5$$
$$= 2(4) + 2(1) + 2(2) + 2(5) + 2(-3)$$
$$= 8 + 2 + 4 + 10 + (-6) = 18$$

(multiply each x by 2, then add)

$$\sum_{i=1}^{5} (x_i - 1) = (4 - 1) + (1 - 1) + (2 - 1)$$
$$+ (5 - 1) + (-3 - 1)$$
$$= 3 + 0 + 1 + 4 - 4 = 4$$

(subtract 1 from each observation, then add)

$$\sum_{i=1}^{3} x_i = x_1 + x_2 + x_3$$
$$= 4 + 1 + 2 = 7$$

(add first three observations)

$$\sum_{i=3}^{5} x_i^3 = x_3^3 + x_4^3 + x_5^3$$
$$= 2^3 + 5^3 + (-3)^3$$
$$= 8 + 125 - 27 = 106$$

(add cubes of last three observations)

In most statistical applications, all the observations are used in the computations. When this is true, the limits of summation and the subscripts may be omitted. In this case, we could write $\Sigma x = 9$, $\Sigma x^2 = 55$, $\Sigma 2x = 18$, and $\Sigma(x - 1) = 4$. The limits of summation and the subscripts cannot be dropped in the last two calculations.

PRACTICE 1 ☐ Consider this set of observations:

$$y_1 = 3 \qquad y_3 = 1 \qquad y_5 = 2$$
$$y_2 = 6 \qquad y_4 = -1 \qquad y_6 = -4$$

Find Σy, Σy^2, $\Sigma 3y$, $\Sigma(y + 2)$, $\Sigma_{i=1}^{3} y_i$, $\Sigma_{i=3}^{6} y_i^2$, $\Sigma_{i=2}^{5} 2y_i$. (Answers are given at the end of Appendix A.)

Rules for Summation

The following rules allow us to simplify complex expressions so they can be evaluated quickly:

Rule 1
$$\sum_{i=1}^{n} c = nc$$
(c is any real number)

Rule 2
$$\sum_{i=1}^{n} cx_i = c \sum_{i=1}^{n} x_i$$
(constants can be factored out of summation expressions)

Rule 3
$$\sum_{i=1}^{n} (x_i + y_i) = \sum_{i=1}^{n} x_i + \sum_{i=1}^{n} y_i$$
(sums can be split and evaluated separately)

EXAMPLE A.2 ☐ Consider these two data sets:

$$x_1 = 2 \qquad y_1 = 2$$
$$x_2 = 3 \qquad y_2 = -1$$
$$x_3 = 5 \qquad y_3 = 4$$
$$x_4 = 2 \qquad y_4 = 6$$

$$\sum_{i=1}^{4} x_i = 12 \qquad \sum_{i=1}^{4} y_i = 11$$

Consider the expression

$$\sum_{i=1}^{4} (2x_i - 3y_i + 3)$$

The rules for summation can be used to simplify this expression as follows:

$$\sum_{i=1}^{4} (2x_i - 3y_i + 3) = \sum_{i=1}^{4} 2x_i + \sum_{i=1}^{4} (-3)y_i + \sum_{i=1}^{4} 3 \qquad \text{rule 3}$$

$$= 2\sum_{i=1}^{4} x_i - 3\sum_{i=1}^{4} y_i + \sum_{i=1}^{4} 3 \qquad \text{rule 2}$$

$$= 2(12) - 3(11) + 4(3) \qquad \text{rule 1}$$
$$= 24 - 33 + 12 = 3 \qquad \text{and substitution}$$

PRACTICE 2 ☐ Consider these two data sets:

$$x_1 = 1 \qquad y_1 = -2$$
$$x_2 = 4 \qquad y_2 = 4$$
$$x_3 = -3 \qquad y_3 = 5$$

Find Σx, Σy, Σx^2, Σy^2, $\Sigma(2x + y)$, $\Sigma(3x - 2y)$, $\Sigma(3x + 2y - 1)$, and $\Sigma(x + 3y + 4)$.

Answers to Practice Problems

1. 7, 67, 21, 19, 10, 22, 16
2. 2, 7, 26, 45, 11, −8, 17, 35

APPENDIX B

TABLES OF PROBABILITY DISTRIBUTIONS

TABLE I CUMULATIVE BINOMIAL DISTRIBUTION

$$F_X(t) = P[X \le t] = \sum_{x \le t} \binom{n}{x} p^x (1-p)^{n-x}$$

						p					
n	r	0.10	0.20	0.25	0.30	0.40	0.50	0.60	0.70	0.80	0.90
5	0	0.5905	0.3277	0.2373	0.1681	0.0778	0.0312	0.0102	0.0024	0.0003	0.0000
	1	0.9185	0.7373	0.6328	0.5282	0.3370	0.1875	0.0870	0.0308	0.0067	0.0005
	2	0.9914	0.9421	0.8965	0.8369	0.6826	0.5000	0.3174	0.1631	0.0579	0.0086
	3	0.9995	0.9933	0.9844	0.9692	0.9130	0.8125	0.6630	0.4718	0.2627	0.0815
	4	1.0000	0.9997	0.9990	0.9976	0.9898	0.9688	0.9222	0.8319	0.6723	0.4095
	5	1.0000	1.0000	1.0000	1.0000	1.0000	1.0000	1.0000	1.0000	1.0000	1.0000
10	0	0.3487	0.1074	0.0563	0.0282	0.0060	0.0010	0.0001	0.0000	0.0000	0.0000
	1	0.7361	0.3758	0.2440	0.1493	0.0464	0.0107	0.0017	0.0001	0.0000	0.0000
	2	0.9298	0.6778	0.5256	0.3828	0.1673	0.0547	0.0123	0.0016	0.0001	0.0000
	3	0.9872	0.8791	0.7759	0.6496	0.3823	0.1719	0.0548	0.0106	0.0009	0.0000
	4	0.9984	0.9672	0.9219	0.8497	0.6331	0.3770	0.1662	0.0474	0.0064	0.0002
	5	0.9999	0.9936	0.9803	0.9527	0.8338	0.6230	0.3669	0.1503	0.0328	0.0016
	6	1.0000	0.9991	0.9965	0.9894	0.9452	0.8281	0.6177	0.3504	0.1209	0.0128
	7	1.0000	0.9999	0.9996	0.9984	0.9877	0.9453	0.8327	0.6172	0.3222	0.0702
	8	1.0000	1.0000	1.0000	0.9999	0.9983	0.9893	0.9536	0.8507	0.6242	0.2639
	9	1.0000	1.0000	1.0000	1.0000	0.9999	0.9990	0.9940	0.9718	0.8926	0.6513
	10	1.0000	1.0000	1.0000	1.0000	1.0000	1.0000	1.0000	1.0000	1.0000	1.0000
15	0	0.2059	0.0352	0.0134	0.0047	0.0005	0.0000	0.0000	0.0000	0.0000	0.0000
	1	0.5490	0.1671	0.0802	0.0353	0.0052	0.0005	0.0000	0.0000	0.0000	0.0000
	2	0.8159	0.3980	0.2361	0.1268	0.0271	0.0037	0.0003	0.0000	0.0000	0.0000
	3	0.9444	0.6482	0.4613	0.2969	0.0905	0.0176	0.0019	0.0001	0.0000	0.0000
	4	0.9873	0.8358	0.6865	0.5155	0.2173	0.0592	0.0094	0.0007	0.0000	0.0000
	5	0.9978	0.9389	0.8516	0.7216	0.4032	0.1509	0.0338	0.0037	0.0001	0.0000
	6	0.9997	0.9819	0.9434	0.8689	0.6098	0.3036	0.0951	0.0152	0.0008	0.0000
	7	1.0000	0.9958	0.9827	0.9500	0.7869	0.5000	0.2131	0.0500	0.0042	0.0000
	8	1.0000	0.9992	0.9958	0.9848	0.9050	0.6964	0.3902	0.1311	0.0181	0.0003
	9	1.0000	0.9999	0.9992	0.9963	0.9662	0.8491	0.5968	0.2784	0.0611	0.0023
	10	1.0000	1.0000	0.9999	0.9993	0.9907	0.9408	0.7827	0.4845	0.1642	0.0127
	11	1.0000	1.0000	1.0000	0.9999	0.9981	0.9824	0.9095	0.7031	0.3518	0.0556
	12	1.0000	1.0000	1.0000	1.0000	0.9997	0.9963	0.9729	0.8732	0.6020	0.1841
	13	1.0000	1.0000	1.0000	1.0000	1.0000	0.9995	0.9948	0.9647	0.8329	0.4510
	14	1.0000	1.0000	1.0000	1.0000	1.0000	1.0000	0.9995	0.9953	0.9648	0.7941
	15	1.0000	1.0000	1.0000	1.0000	1.0000	1.0000	1.0000	1.0000	1.0000	1.0000
20	0	0.1216	0.0115	0.0032	0.0008	0.0000	0.0000	0.0000	0.0000	0.0000	0.0000
	1	0.3917	0.0692	0.0243	0.0076	0.0005	0.0000	0.0000	0.0000	0.0000	0.0000
	2	0.6769	0.2061	0.0913	0.0355	0.0036	0.0002	0.0000	0.0000	0.0000	0.0000
	3	0.8670	0.4114	0.2252	0.1071	0.0160	0.0013	0.0001	0.0000	0.0000	0.0000
	4	0.9568	0.6296	0.4148	0.2375	0.0510	0.0059	0.0003	0.0000	0.0000	0.0000
	5	0.9887	0.8042	0.6172	0.4164	0.1256	0.0207	0.0016	0.0000	0.0000	0.0000
	6	0.9976	0.9133	0.7858	0.6080	0.2500	0.0577	0.0065	0.0003	0.0000	0.0000
	7	0.9996	0.9679	0.8982	0.7723	0.4159	0.1316	0.0210	0.0013	0.0000	0.0000
	8	0.9999	0.9900	0.9591	0.8867	0.5956	0.2517	0.0565	0.0051	0.0001	0.0000
	9	1.0000	0.9974	0.9861	0.9520	0.7553	0.4119	0.1275	0.0171	0.0006	0.0000
	10	1.0000	0.9994	0.9961	0.9829	0.8725	0.5881	0.2447	0.0480	0.0026	0.0000
	11	1.0000	0.9999	0.9991	0.9949	0.9435	0.7483	0.4044	0.1133	0.0100	0.0001
	12	1.0000	1.0000	0.9998	0.9987	0.9790	0.8684	0.5841	0.2277	0.0321	0.0004
	13	1.0000	1.0000	1.0000	0.9997	0.9935	0.9423	0.7500	0.3920	0.0867	0.0024
	14	1.0000	1.0000	1.0000	1.0000	0.9984	0.9793	0.8744	0.5836	0.1958	0.0113
	15	1.0000	1.0000	1.0000	1.0000	0.9997	0.9941	0.9490	0.7625	0.3704	0.0432
	16	1.0000	1.0000	1.0000	1.0000	1.0000	0.9987	0.9840	0.8929	0.5886	0.1330
	17	1.0000	1.0000	1.0000	1.0000	1.0000	0.9998	0.9964	0.9645	0.7939	0.3231
	18	1.0000	1.0000	1.0000	1.0000	1.0000	1.0000	0.9995	0.9924	0.9308	0.6083
	19	1.0000	1.0000	1.0000	1.0000	1.0000	1.0000	1.0000	0.9992	0.9885	0.8784
	20	1.0000	1.0000	1.0000	1.0000	1.0000	1.0000	1.0000	1.0000	1.0000	1.0000

Reprinted with permission of Macmillan Publishing Company, Inc., from Ronald Walpole and Raymond Myers, *Probability and Statistics for Engineers and Scientists*, 2d ed., 1978, p. 509.

TABLE II POISSON DISTRIBUTION FUNCTION

$$F_X(t) = P[X \leq t] = \sum_{x \leq t} e^{-\lambda s}(\lambda s)^x/x!$$

[t]	.50	1.0	2.0	3.0	4.0	5.0	6.0	7.0	8.0	9.0
0	.607	.368	.135	.050	.018	.007	.002	.001	.000	.000
1	.910	.736	.406	.199	.092	.040	.017	.007	.003	.001
2	.986	.920	.677	.423	.238	.125	.062	.030	.014	.006
3	.998	.981	.857	.647	.433	.265	.151	.082	.042	.021
4	1.000	.996	.947	.815	.629	.440	.285	.173	.100	.055
5	1.000	.999	.983	.961	.785	.616	.446	.301	.191	.116
6	1.000	1.000	.995	.966	.889	.762	.606	.450	.313	.207
7	1.000	1.000	.999	.988	.949	.867	.744	.599	.453	.324
8	1.000	1.000	1.000	.996	.979	.932	.847	.729	.593	.456
9	1.000	1.000	1.000	.999	.992	.968	.916	.830	.717	.587
10	1.000	1.000	1.000	1.000	.997	.986	.957	.901	.816	.706
11	1.000	1.000	1.000	1.000	.999	.995	.980	.947	.888	.803
12	1.000	1.000	1.000	1.000	1.000	.998	.991	.973	.936	.876
13	1.000	1.000	1.000	1.000	1.000	.999	.996	.987	.966	.926
14	1.000	1.000	1.000	1.000	1.000	1.000	.999	.994	.983	.959
15	1.000	1.000	1.000	1.000	1.000	1.000	.999	.998	.992	.978
16	1.000	1.000	1.000	1.000	1.000	1.000	1.000	.999	.996	.989
17	1.000	1.000	1.000	1.000	1.000	1.000	1.000	1.000	.998	.995
18	1.000	1.000	1.000	1.000	1.000	1.000	1.000	1.000	.999	.998
19	1.000	1.000	1.000	1.000	1.000	1.000	1.000	1.000	1.000	.999
20	1.000	1.000	1.000	1.000	1.000	1.000	1.000	1.000	1.000	1.000

λs

TABLE II POISSON DISTRIBUTION FUNCTION (*Continued*)

[t]	10.0	11.0	12.0	λs 13.0	14.0	15.0
2	.003	.001	.001	.000	.000	.000
3	.010	.005	.002	.001	.000	.000
4	.029	.015	.008	.004	.002	.001
5	.067	.038	.020	.011	.006	.003
6	.130	.079	.046	.026	.014	.008
7	.220	.143	.090	.054	.032	.018
8	.333	.232	.155	.100	.062	.037
9	.458	.341	.242	.166	.109	.070
10	.583	.460	.347	.252	.176	.118
11	.697	.579	.462	.353	.260	.185
12	.792	.689	.576	.463	.358	.268
13	.864	.781	.682	.573	.464	.363
14	.917	.854	.772	.675	.570	.466
15	.951	.907	.844	.764	.669	.568
16	.973	.944	.899	.835	.756	.664
17	.986	.968	.937	.890	.827	.749
18	.993	.982	.963	.930	.883	.819
19	.997	.991	.979	.957	.923	.875
20	.998	.995	.988	.975	.952	.917
21	.999	.998	.994	.986	.971	.947
22	1.000	.999	.997	.992	.983	.967
23	1.000	1.000	.999	.996	.991	.981
24	1.000	1.000	.999	.998	.995	.989
25	1.000	1.000	1.000	.999	.997	.994
26	1.000	1.000	1.000	1.000	.999	.997
27	1.000	1.000	1.000	1.000	.999	.998
28	1.000	1.000	1.000	1.000	1.000	.999
29	1.000	1.000	1.000	1.000	1.000	1.000

TABLE III CUMULATIVE DISTRIBUTION: STANDARD NORMAL

$$F_Z(z) = P[Z \leq z]$$

z	0.00	0.01	0.02	0.03	0.04	0.05	0.06	0.07	0.08	0.09
−3.4	0.0003	0.0003	0.0003	0.0003	0.0003	0.0003	0.0003	0.0003	0.0003	0.0002
−3.3	0.0005	0.0005	0.0005	0.0004	0.0004	0.0004	0.0004	0.0004	0.0004	0.0003
−3.2	0.0007	0.0007	0.0006	0.0006	0.0006	0.0006	0.0006	0.0005	0.0005	0.0005
−3.1	0.0010	0.0009	0.0009	0.0009	0.0008	0.0008	0.0008	0.0008	0.0007	0.0007
−3.0	0.0013	0.0013	0.0013	0.0012	0.0012	0.0011	0.0011	0.0011	0.0010	0.0010
−2.9	0.0019	0.0018	0.0017	0.0017	0.0016	0.0016	0.0015	0.0015	0.0014	0.0014
−2.8	0.0026	0.0025	0.0024	0.0023	0.0023	0.0022	0.0021	0.0021	0.0020	0.0019
−2.7	0.0035	0.0034	0.0033	0.0032	0.0031	0.0030	0.0029	0.0028	0.0027	0.0026
−2.6	0.0047	0.0045	0.0044	0.0043	0.0041	0.0040	0.0039	0.0038	0.0037	0.0036
−2.5	0.0062	0.0060	0.0059	0.0057	0.0055	0.0054	0.0052	0.0051	0.0049	0.0048
−2.4	0.0082	0.0080	0.0078	0.0075	0.0073	0.0071	0.0069	0.0068	0.0066	0.0064
−2.3	0.0107	0.0104	0.0102	0.0099	0.0096	0.0094	0.0091	0.0089	0.0087	0.0084
−2.2	0.0139	0.0136	0.0132	0.0129	0.0125	0.0122	0.0119	0.0116	0.0113	0.0110
−2.1	0.0179	0.0174	0.0170	0.0166	0.0162	0.0158	0.0154	0.0150	0.0146	0.0143
−2.0	0.0228	0.0222	0.0217	0.0212	0.0207	0.0202	0.0197	0.0192	0.0188	0.0183
−1.9	0.0287	0.0281	0.0274	0.0268	0.0262	0.0256	0.0250	0.0244	0.0239	0.0233
−1.8	0.0359	0.0352	0.0344	0.0336	0.0329	0.0322	0.0314	0.0307	0.0301	0.0294
−1.7	0.0446	0.0436	0.0427	0.0418	0.0409	0.0401	0.0392	0.0384	0.0375	0.0367
−1.6	0.0548	0.0537	0.0526	0.0516	0.0505	0.0495	0.0485	0.0475	0.0465	0.0455
−1.5	0.0668	0.0655	0.0643	0.0630	0.0618	0.0606	0.0594	0.0582	0.0571	0.0559
−1.4	0.0808	0.0793	0.0778	0.0764	0.0749	0.0735	0.0722	0.0708	0.0694	0.0681
−1.3	0.0968	0.0951	0.0934	0.0918	0.0901	0.0885	0.0869	0.0853	0.0838	0.0823
−1.2	0.1151	0.1131	0.1112	0.1093	0.1075	0.1056	0.1038	0.1020	0.1003	0.0985
−1.1	0.1357	0.1335	0.1314	0.1292	0.1271	0.1251	0.1230	0.1210	0.1190	0.1170
−1.0	0.1587	0.1562	0.1539	0.1515	0.1492	0.1469	0.1446	0.1423	0.1401	0.1379
−0.9	0.1841	0.1814	0.1788	0.1762	0.1736	0.1711	0.1685	0.1660	0.1635	0.1611
−0.8	0.2119	0.2090	0.2061	0.2033	0.2005	0.1977	0.1949	0.1922	0.1894	0.1867
−0.7	0.2420	0.2389	0.2358	0.2327	0.2296	0.2266	0.2236	0.2206	0.2177	0.2148
−0.6	0.2743	0.2709	0.2676	0.2643	0.2611	0.2578	0.2546	0.2514	0.2483	0.2451
−0.5	0.3085	0.3050	0.3015	0.2981	0.2946	0.2912	0.2877	0.2843	0.2810	0.2776
−0.4	0.3446	0.3409	0.3372	0.3336	0.3300	0.3264	0.3228	0.3192	0.3156	0.3121
−0.3	0.3821	0.3783	0.3745	0.3707	0.3669	0.3632	0.3594	0.3557	0.3520	0.3483
−0.2	0.4207	0.4168	0.4129	0.4090	0.4052	0.4013	0.3974	0.3936	0.3897	0.3859
−0.1	0.4602	0.4562	0.4522	0.4483	0.4443	0.4404	0.4364	0.4325	0.4286	0.4247
−0.0	0.5000	0.4960	0.4920	0.4880	0.4840	0.4801	0.4761	0.4721	0.4681	0.4641
0.0	0.5000	0.5040	0.5080	0.5120	0.5160	0.5199	0.5239	0.5279	0.5319	0.5359
0.1	0.5398	0.5438	0.5478	0.5517	0.5557	0.5596	0.5636	0.5675	0.5714	0.5753
0.2	0.5793	0.5832	0.5871	0.5910	0.5948	0.5987	0.6026	0.6064	0.6103	0.6141
0.3	0.6179	0.6217	0.6255	0.6293	0.6331	0.6368	0.6406	0.6443	0.6480	0.6517
0.4	0.6554	0.6591	0.6628	0.6664	0.6700	0.6736	0.6772	0.6808	0.6844	0.6879
0.5	0.6915	0.6950	0.6985	0.7019	0.7054	0.7088	0.7123	0.7157	0.7190	0.7224
0.6	0.7257	0.7291	0.7324	0.7357	0.7389	0.7422	0.7454	0.7486	0.7517	0.7549
0.7	0.7580	0.7611	0.7642	0.7673	0.7704	0.7734	0.7764	0.7794	0.7823	0.7852
0.8	0.7881	0.7910	0.7939	0.7967	0.7995	0.8023	0.8051	0.8078	0.8106	0.8133
0.9	0.8159	0.8186	0.8212	0.8238	0.8264	0.8289	0.8315	0.8340	0.8365	0.8389
1.0	0.8413	0.8438	0.8461	0.8485	0.8508	0.8531	0.8554	0.8577	0.8599	0.8621
1.1	0.8643	0.8665	0.8686	0.8708	0.8729	0.8749	0.8770	0.8790	0.8810	0.8830
1.2	0.8849	0.8869	0.8888	0.8907	0.8925	0.8944	0.8962	0.8980	0.8997	0.9015
1.3	0.9032	0.9049	0.9066	0.9082	0.9099	0.9115	0.9131	0.9147	0.9162	0.9177
1.4	0.9192	0.9207	0.9222	0.9236	0.9251	0.9265	0.9278	0.9292	0.9306	0.9319
1.5	0.9332	0.9345	0.9357	0.9370	0.9382	0.9394	0.9406	0.9418	0.9429	0.9441
1.6	0.9452	0.9463	0.9474	0.9484	0.9495	0.9505	0.9515	0.9525	0.9535	0.9545
1.7	0.9554	0.9564	0.9573	0.9582	0.9591	0.9599	0.9608	0.9616	0.9625	0.9633
1.8	0.9641	0.9649	0.9656	0.9664	0.9671	0.9678	0.9686	0.9693	0.9699	0.9706
1.9	0.9713	0.9719	0.9726	0.9732	0.9738	0.9744	0.9750	0.9756	0.9761	0.9767
2.0	0.9772	0.9778	0.9783	0.9788	0.9793	0.9798	0.9803	0.9808	0.9812	0.9817
2.1	0.9821	0.9826	0.9830	0.9834	0.9838	0.9842	0.9846	0.9850	0.9854	0.9857
2.2	0.9861	0.9864	0.9868	0.9871	0.9875	0.9878	0.9881	0.9884	0.9887	0.9890
2.3	0.9893	0.9896	0.9898	0.9901	0.9904	0.9906	0.9909	0.9911	0.9913	0.9916
2.4	0.9918	0.9920	0.9922	0.9925	0.9927	0.9929	0.9931	0.9932	0.9934	0.9936
2.5	0.9938	0.9940	0.9941	0.9943	0.9945	0.9946	0.9948	0.9949	0.9951	0.9952
2.6	0.9953	0.9955	0.9956	0.9957	0.9959	0.9960	0.9961	0.9962	0.9963	0.9964
2.7	0.9965	0.9966	0.9967	0.9968	0.9969	0.9970	0.9971	0.9972	0.9973	0.9974
2.8	0.9974	0.9975	0.9976	0.9977	0.9977	0.9978	0.9979	0.9979	0.9980	0.9981
2.9	0.9981	0.9982	0.9982	0.9983	0.9984	0.9984	0.9985	0.9985	0.9986	0.9986
3.0	0.9987	0.9987	0.9987	0.9988	0.9988	0.9989	0.9989	0.9989	0.9990	0.9990
3.1	0.9990	0.9991	0.9991	0.9991	0.9992	0.9992	0.9992	0.9992	0.9993	0.9993
3.2	0.9993	0.9993	0.9994	0.9994	0.9994	0.9994	0.9994	0.9995	0.9995	0.9995
3.3	0.9995	0.9995	0.9995	0.9996	0.9996	0.9996	0.9996	0.9996	0.9996	0.9997
3.4	0.9997	0.9997	0.9997	0.9997	0.9997	0.9997	0.9997	0.9997	0.9997	0.9998

Reprinted with permission of Macmillan Publishing Company, Inc., from Ronald Walpole and Raymond Myers, *Probability and Statistics for Engineers and Scientists*, 2d ed., 1978, p. 513.

TABLE IV   RANDOM DIGITS

Line/Col.	(1)	(2)	(3)	(4)	(5)	(6)	(7)	(8)	(9)	(10)	(11)	(12)	(13)	(14)
1	10480	15011	01536	02011	81647	91646	69179	14194	62590	36207	20969	99570	91291	90700
2	22368	46573	25595	85393	30995	89198	27982	53402	93965	34095	52666	19174	39615	99505
3	24130	48360	22527	97265	76393	64809	15179	24830	49340	32081	30680	19655	63348	58629
4	42167	93093	06243	61680	07856	16376	39440	53537	71341	57004	00849	74917	97758	16379
5	37570	39975	81837	16656	06121	91782	60468	81305	49684	60672	14110	06927	01263	54613
6	77921	06907	11008	42751	27756	53498	18602	70659	90655	15053	21916	81825	44394	42880
7	99562	72905	56420	69994	98872	31016	71194	18738	44013	48840	63213	21069	10634	12952
8	96301	91977	05463	07972	18876	20922	94595	56869	69014	60045	18425	84903	42508	32307
9	89579	14342	63661	10281	17453	18103	57740	84378	25331	12566	58678	44947	05585	56941
10	85475	36857	43342	53988	53060	59533	38867	62300	08158	17983	16439	11458	18593	64952
11	28918	69578	88231	33276	70997	79936	56865	05859	90106	31595	01547	85590	91610	78188
12	63553	40961	48235	03427	49626	69445	18663	72695	52180	20847	12234	90511	33703	90322
13	09429	93969	52636	92737	88974	33488	36320	17617	30015	08272	84115	27156	30613	74952
14	10365	61129	87529	85689	48237	52267	67689	93394	01511	26358	85104	20285	29975	89868
15	07119	97336	71048	08178	77233	13916	47564	81056	97735	85977	29372	74461	28551	90707
16	51085	12765	51821	51259	77452	16308	60756	92144	49442	53900	70960	63990	75601	40719
17	02368	21382	52404	60268	89368	19885	55322	44819	01188	65255	64835	44919	05944	55157
18	01011	54092	33362	94904	31273	04146	18594	29852	71585	85030	51132	01915	92747	64951
19	52162	53916	46369	58586	23216	14513	83149	98736	23495	64350	94738	17752	35156	35749
20	07056	97628	33787	09998	42698	06691	76988	13602	51851	46104	88916	19509	25625	58104
21	48663	91245	85828	14346	09172	30168	90229	04734	59193	22178	30421	61666	99904	32812
22	54164	58492	22421	74103	47070	25306	76468	26384	58151	06646	21524	15227	96909	44592
23	32639	32363	05597	24200	13363	38005	94342	28728	35806	06912	17012	64161	18296	22851
24	29334	27001	87637	87308	58731	00256	45834	15398	46557	41135	10367	07684	36188	18510
25	02488	33062	28834	07351	19731	92420	60952	61280	50001	67658	32586	86679	50720	94953
26	81525	72295	04839	96423	24878	82651	66566	14778	76797	14780	13300	87074	79666	95725
27	29676	20591	68086	26432	46901	20849	89768	81536	86645	12659	92259	57102	80428	25280
28	00742	57392	39064	66432	84673	40027	32832	61362	98947	96067	64760	64584	96096	98253
29	05366	04213	25669	26422	44407	44048	37937	63904	45766	66134	75470	66520	34693	90449
30	91921	26418	64117	94305	26766	25940	39972	22209	71500	64568	91402	42416	07844	69618
31	00582	04711	87917	77341	42206	35126	74087	99547	81817	42607	43808	76655	62028	76630
32	00725	69884	62797	56170	86324	88072	76222	36086	84637	93161	76038	65855	77919	88006
33	69011	65797	95876	55293	18988	27354	26575	08625	40801	59920	29841	80150	12777	48501
34	25976	57948	29888	88604	67917	48708	18912	82271	65424	69774	33611	54262	85963	03547
35	09763	83473	73577	12908	30883	18317	28290	35797	05998	41688	34952	37888	38917	88050
36	91567	42595	27958	30134	04024	86385	29880	99730	55536	84855	29080	09250	79656	73211
37	17955	56349	90999	49127	20044	59931	06115	20542	18059	02008	73708	83517	36103	42791
38	46503	18584	18845	49618	02304	51038	20655	58727	28168	15475	56942	53389	20562	87338
39	92157	89634	94824	78171	84610	82834	09922	25417	44137	48413	25555	21246	35509	20468
40	14577	62765	35605	81263	39667	47358	56873	56307	61607	49518	89656	20103	77490	18062
41	98427	07523	33362	64270	01638	92477	66969	98420	04880	45585	46565	04102	46880	45709
42	34914	63976	88720	82765	34476	17032	87589	40836	32427	70002	70663	88863	77775	69348
43	70060	28277	39475	46473	23219	53416	94970	25832	69975	94884	19661	72828	00102	66794
44	53976	54914	06990	67245	68350	82948	11398	42878	80287	88267	47363	46634	06541	97809
45	76072	29515	40980	07391	58745	25774	22987	80059	39911	96189	41151	14222	60697	59583
46	90725	52210	83974	29992	65831	38857	50490	83765	55657	14361	31720	57375	56228	41546
47	64364	67412	33339	31926	14883	24413	59744	92351	97473	89286	35931	04110	23726	51900
48	08962	00358	31662	25388	61642	34072	81249	35648	56891	69352	48373	45578	78547	81788
49	95012	68379	93526	70765	10593	04542	76463	54328	02349	17247	28865	14777	62730	92277
50	15664	10493	20492	38391	91132	21999	59516	81652	27195	48223	46751	22923	32261	85653

Reprinted with permission from W. H. Beyer (ed.), *CRC Handbook of Tables for Probability and Statistics*, 2d ed., 1968, p. 480. Copyright CRC Press, Inc., Boca Raton, Florida.

TABLE V CUMULATIVE T DISTRIBUTION

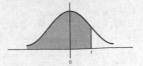

$$F(t) = P[T \leq t]$$

$\frac{F}{\gamma}$	.60	.75	.90	.95	.975	.99	.995	.9995
1	.325	1.000	3.078	6.314	12.706	31.821	63.657	636.619
2	.289	.816	1.886	2.920	4.303	6.965	9.925	31.598
3	.277	.765	1.638	2.353	3.182	4.541	5.841	12.924
4	.271	.741	1.533	2.132	2.776	3.747	4.604	8.610
5	.267	.727	1.476	2.015	2.571	3.365	4.032	6.869
6	.265	.718	1.440	1.943	2.447	3.143	3.707	5.959
7	.263	.711	1.415	1.895	2.365	2.998	3.499	5.408
8	.262	.706	1.397	1.860	2.306	2.896	3.355	5.041
9	.261	.703	1.383	1.833	2.262	2.821	3.250	4.781
10	.260	.700	1.372	1.812	2.228	2.764	3.169	4.587
11	.260	.697	1.363	1.796	2.201	2.718	3.106	4.437
12	.259	.695	1.356	1.782	2.179	2.681	3.055	4.318
13	.259	.694	1.350	1.771	2.160	2.650	3.012	4.221
14	.258	.692	1.345	1.761	2.145	2.624	2.977	4.140
15	.258	.691	1.341	1.753	2.131	2.602	2.947	4.073
16	.258	.690	1.337	1.746	2.120	2.583	2.921	4.015
17	.257	.689	1.333	1.740	2.110	2.567	2.898	3.965
18	.257	.688	1.330	1.734	2.101	2.552	2.878	3.922
19	.257	.688	1.328	1.729	2.093	2.539	2.861	3.883
20	.257	.687	1.325	1.725	2.086	2.528	2.845	3.850
21	.257	.686	1.323	1.721	2.080	2.518	2.831	3.819
22	.256	.686	1.321	1.717	2.074	2.508	2.819	3.792
23	.256	.685	1.319	1.714	2.069	2.500	2.807	3.767
24	.256	.685	1.318	1.711	2.064	2.492	2.797	3.745
25	.256	.684	1.316	1.708	2.060	2.485	2.787	3.725
26	.256	.684	1.315	1.706	2.056	2.479	2.779	3.707
27	.256	.684	1.314	1.703	2.052	2.473	2.771	3.690
28	.256	.683	1.313	1.701	2.048	2.467	2.763	3.674
29	.256	.683	1.311	1.699	2.045	2.462	2.756	3.659
30	.256	.683	1.310	1.697	2.042	2.457	2.750	3.646
40	.255	.681	1.303	1.684	2.021	2.423	2.704	3.551
60	.254	.679	1.296	1.671	2.000	2.390	2.660	3.460
120	.254	.677	1.289	1.658	1.980	2.358	2.617	3.373
∞	.253	.674	1.282	1.645	1.960	2.326	2.576	3.291

Reprinted with permission from W. H. Beyer (ed.), *CRC Handbook of Tables for Probability and Statistics*, 2d ed., 1968, p 283. Copyright CRC Press, Inc., Boca Raton, Florida.

TABLE VI CUMULATIVE CHI-SQUARE DISTRIBUTION

$$F(x^2) = P[X^2 \leq x^2]$$

γ	.005	.010	.025	.050	.100	.250	.500	.750	.900	.950	.975	.990	.995
1	.0000393	.000157	.000982	.00393	.0158	.102	.455	1.32	2.71	3.84	5.02	6.63	7.88
2	.0100	.0201	.0506	.103	.211	.575	1.39	2.77	4.61	5.99	7.38	9.21	10.6
3	.0717	.115	.216	.352	.584	1.21	2.37	4.11	6.25	7.81	9.35	11.3	12.8
4	.207	.297	.484	.711	1.06	1.92	3.36	5.39	7.78	9.49	11.1	13.3	14.9
5	.412	.554	.831	1.15	1.61	2.67	4.35	6.63	9.24	11.1	12.8	15.1	16.7
6	.676	.872	1.24	1.64	2.20	3.45	5.35	7.84	10.6	12.6	14.4	16.8	18.5
7	.989	1.24	1.69	2.17	2.83	4.25	6.35	9.04	12.0	14.1	16.0	18.5	20.3
8	1.34	1.65	2.18	2.73	3.49	5.07	7.34	10.2	13.4	15.5	17.5	20.1	22.0
9	1.73	2.09	2.70	3.33	4.17	5.90	8.34	11.4	14.7	16.9	19.0	21.7	23.6
10	2.16	2.56	3.25	3.94	4.87	6.74	9.34	12.5	16.0	18.3	20.5	23.2	25.2
11	2.60	3.05	3.82	4.57	5.58	7.58	10.3	13.7	17.3	19.7	21.9	24.7	26.8
12	3.07	3.57	4.40	5.23	6.30	8.44	11.3	14.8	18.5	21.0	23.3	26.2	28.3
13	3.57	4.11	5.01	5.89	7.04	9.30	12.3	16.0	19.8	22.4	24.7	27.7	29.8
14	4.07	4.66	5.63	6.57	7.79	10.2	13.3	17.1	21.1	23.7	26.1	29.1	31.3
15	4.60	5.23	6.26	7.26	8.55	11.0	14.3	18.2	22.3	25.0	27.5	30.6	32.8
16	5.14	5.81	6.91	7.96	9.31	11.9	15.3	19.4	23.5	26.3	28.8	32.0	34.3
17	5.70	6.41	7.56	8.67	10.1	12.8	16.3	20.5	24.8	27.6	30.2	33.4	35.7
18	6.26	7.01	8.23	9.39	10.9	13.7	17.3	21.6	26.0	28.9	31.5	34.8	37.2
19	6.84	7.63	8.91	10.1	11.7	14.6	18.3	22.7	27.2	30.1	32.9	36.2	38.6
20	7.43	8.26	9.59	10.9	12.4	15.5	19.3	23.8	28.4	31.4	34.2	37.6	40.0
21	8.03	8.90	10.3	11.6	13.2	16.3	20.3	24.9	29.6	32.7	35.5	38.9	41.4
22	8.64	9.54	11.0	12.3	14.0	17.2	21.3	26.0	30.8	33.9	36.8	40.3	42.8
23	9.26	10.2	11.7	13.1	14.8	18.1	22.3	27.1	32.0	35.2	38.1	41.6	44.2
24	9.89	10.9	12.4	13.8	15.7	19.0	23.3	28.2	33.2	36.4	39.4	43.0	45.6
25	10.5	11.5	13.1	14.6	16.5	19.9	24.3	29.3	34.4	37.7	40.6	44.3	46.9
26	11.2	12.2	13.8	15.4	17.3	20.8	25.3	30.4	35.6	38.9	41.9	45.6	48.3
27	11.8	12.9	14.6	16.2	18.1	21.7	26.3	31.5	36.7	40.1	43.2	47.0	49.6
28	12.5	13.6	15.3	16.9	18.9	22.7	27.3	32.6	37.9	41.3	44.5	48.3	51.0
29	13.1	14.3	16.0	17.7	19.8	23.6	28.3	33.7	39.1	42.6	45.7	49.6	52.3
30	13.8	15.0	16.8	18.5	20.6	24.5	29.3	34.8	40.3	43.8	47.0	50.9	53.7

Reprinted with permission from W. H. Beyer (ed.), *CRC Handbook of Tables for Probability and Statistics*, 2d ed., 1968, p. 294. Copyright CRC Press, Inc., Boca Raton, Florida.

TABLE VII CUMULATIVE F DISTRIBUTION

$$P[F_{\gamma_1,\gamma_2} \leq f] = .90$$

$\gamma_2 \backslash \gamma_1$	1	2	3	4	5	6	7	8	9	10	12	15	20	24	30	40	60	120	∞
1	39.86	49.50	53.59	55.83	57.24	58.20	58.91	59.44	59.86	60.19	60.71	61.22	61.74	62.00	62.26	62.53	62.79	63.06	63.33
2	8.53	9.00	9.16	9.24	9.29	9.33	9.35	9.37	9.38	9.39	9.41	9.42	9.44	9.45	9.46	9.47	9.47	9.48	9.49
3	5.54	5.46	5.39	5.34	5.31	5.28	5.27	5.25	5.24	5.23	5.22	5.20	5.18	5.18	5.17	5.16	5.15	5.14	5.13
4	4.54	4.32	4.19	4.11	4.05	4.01	3.98	3.95	3.94	3.92	3.90	3.87	3.84	3.83	3.82	3.80	3.79	3.78	3.76
5	4.06	3.78	3.62	3.52	3.45	3.40	3.37	3.34	3.32	3.30	3.27	3.24	3.21	3.19	3.17	3.16	3.14	3.12	3.10
6	3.78	3.46	3.29	3.18	3.11	3.05	3.01	2.98	2.96	2.94	2.90	2.87	2.84	2.82	2.80	2.78	2.76	2.74	2.72
7	3.59	3.26	3.07	2.96	2.88	2.83	2.78	2.75	2.72	2.70	2.67	2.63	2.59	2.58	2.56	2.54	2.51	2.49	2.47
8	3.46	3.11	2.92	2.81	2.73	2.67	2.62	2.59	2.56	2.54	2.50	2.46	2.42	2.40	2.38	2.36	2.34	2.32	2.29
9	3.36	3.01	2.81	2.69	2.61	2.55	2.51	2.47	2.44	2.42	2.38	2.34	2.30	2.28	2.25	2.23	2.21	2.18	2.16
10	3.29	2.92	2.73	2.61	2.52	2.46	2.41	2.38	2.35	2.32	2.28	2.24	2.20	2.18	2.16	2.13	2.11	2.08	2.06
11	3.23	2.86	2.66	2.54	2.45	2.39	2.34	2.30	2.27	2.25	2.21	2.17	2.12	2.10	2.08	2.05	2.03	2.00	1.97
12	3.18	2.81	2.61	2.48	2.39	2.33	2.28	2.24	2.21	2.19	2.15	2.10	2.06	2.04	2.01	1.99	1.96	1.93	1.90
13	3.14	2.76	2.56	2.43	2.35	2.28	2.23	2.20	2.16	2.14	2.10	2.05	2.01	1.98	1.96	1.93	1.90	1.88	1.85
14	3.10	2.73	2.52	2.39	2.31	2.24	2.19	2.15	2.12	2.10	2.05	2.01	1.96	1.94	1.91	1.89	1.86	1.83	1.80
15	3.07	2.70	2.49	2.36	2.27	2.21	2.16	2.12	2.09	2.06	2.02	1.97	1.92	1.90	1.87	1.85	1.82	1.79	1.76
16	3.05	2.67	2.46	2.33	2.24	2.18	2.13	2.09	2.06	2.03	1.99	1.94	1.89	1.87	1.84	1.81	1.78	1.75	1.72
17	3.03	2.64	2.44	2.31	2.22	2.15	2.10	2.06	2.03	2.00	1.96	1.91	1.86	1.84	1.81	1.78	1.75	1.72	1.69
18	3.01	2.62	2.42	2.29	2.20	2.13	2.08	2.04	2.00	1.98	1.93	1.89	1.84	1.81	1.78	1.75	1.72	1.69	1.66
19	2.99	2.61	2.40	2.27	2.18	2.11	2.06	2.02	1.98	1.96	1.91	1.86	1.81	1.79	1.76	1.73	1.70	1.67	1.63
20	2.97	2.59	2.38	2.25	2.16	2.09	2.04	2.00	1.96	1.94	1.89	1.84	1.79	1.77	1.74	1.71	1.68	1.64	1.61
21	2.96	2.57	2.36	2.23	2.14	2.08	2.02	1.98	1.95	1.92	1.87	1.83	1.78	1.75	1.72	1.69	1.66	1.62	1.59
22	2.95	2.56	2.35	2.22	2.13	2.06	2.01	1.97	1.93	1.90	1.86	1.81	1.76	1.73	1.70	1.67	1.64	1.60	1.57
23	2.94	2.55	2.34	2.21	2.11	2.05	1.99	1.95	1.92	1.89	1.84	1.80	1.74	1.72	1.69	1.66	1.62	1.59	1.55
24	2.93	2.54	2.33	2.19	2.10	2.04	1.98	1.94	1.91	1.88	1.83	1.78	1.73	1.70	1.67	1.64	1.61	1.57	1.53
25	2.92	2.53	2.32	2.18	2.09	2.02	1.97	1.93	1.89	1.87	1.82	1.77	1.72	1.69	1.66	1.63	1.59	1.56	1.52
26	2.91	2.52	2.31	2.17	2.08	2.01	1.96	1.92	1.88	1.86	1.81	1.76	1.71	1.68	1.65	1.61	1.58	1.54	1.50
27	2.90	2.51	2.30	2.17	2.07	2.00	1.95	1.91	1.87	1.85	1.80	1.75	1.70	1.67	1.64	1.60	1.57	1.53	1.49
28	2.89	2.50	2.29	2.16	2.06	2.00	1.94	1.90	1.87	1.84	1.79	1.74	1.69	1.66	1.63	1.59	1.56	1.52	1.48
29	2.89	2.50	2.28	2.15	2.06	1.99	1.93	1.89	1.86	1.83	1.78	1.73	1.68	1.65	1.62	1.58	1.55	1.51	1.47
30	2.88	2.49	2.28	2.14	2.05	1.98	1.93	1.88	1.85	1.82	1.77	1.72	1.67	1.64	1.61	1.57	1.54	1.50	1.46
40	2.84	2.44	2.23	2.09	2.00	1.93	1.87	1.83	1.79	1.76	1.71	1.66	1.61	1.57	1.54	1.51	1.47	1.42	1.38
60	2.79	2.39	2.18	2.04	1.95	1.87	1.82	1.77	1.74	1.71	1.66	1.60	1.54	1.51	1.48	1.44	1.40	1.35	1.29
120	2.75	2.35	2.13	1.99	1.90	1.82	1.77	1.72	1.68	1.65	1.60	1.55	1.48	1.45	1.41	1.37	1.32	1.26	1.19
∞	2.71	2.30	2.08	1.94	1.85	1.77	1.72	1.67	1.63	1.60	1.55	1.49	1.42	1.38	1.34	1.30	1.24	1.17	1.00

TABLE VII CUMULATIVE F DISTRIBUTION *(Continued)*

$$P[F_{\gamma_1, \gamma_2} \leq f] = .95$$

$\gamma_2 \backslash \gamma_1$	1	2	3	4	5	6	7	8	9	10	12	15	20	24	30	40	60	120	∞
1	161.4	199.5	215.7	224.6	230.2	234.0	236.8	238.9	240.5	241.9	243.9	245.9	248.0	249.1	250.1	251.1	252.2	253.3	254.3
2	18.51	19.00	19.16	19.25	19.30	19.33	19.35	19.37	19.38	19.40	19.41	19.43	19.45	19.45	19.46	19.47	19.48	19.49	19.50
3	10.13	9.55	9.28	9.12	9.01	8.94	8.89	8.85	8.81	8.79	8.74	8.70	8.66	8.64	8.62	8.59	8.57	8.55	8.53
4	7.71	6.94	6.59	6.39	6.26	6.16	6.09	6.04	6.00	5.96	5.91	5.86	5.80	5.77	5.75	5.72	5.69	5.66	5.63
5	6.61	5.79	5.41	5.19	5.05	4.95	4.88	4.82	4.77	4.74	4.68	4.62	4.56	4.53	4.50	4.46	4.43	4.40	4.36
6	5.99	5.14	4.76	4.53	4.39	4.28	4.21	4.15	4.10	4.06	4.00	3.94	3.87	3.84	3.81	3.77	3.74	3.70	3.67
7	5.59	4.74	4.35	4.12	3.97	3.87	3.79	3.73	3.68	3.64	3.57	3.51	3.44	3.41	3.38	3.34	3.30	3.27	3.23
8	5.32	4.46	4.07	3.84	3.69	3.58	3.50	3.44	3.39	3.35	3.28	3.22	3.15	3.12	3.08	3.04	3.01	2.97	2.93
9	5.12	4.26	3.86	3.63	3.48	3.37	3.29	3.23	3.18	3.14	3.07	3.01	2.94	2.90	2.86	2.83	2.79	2.75	2.71
10	4.96	4.10	3.71	3.48	3.33	3.22	3.14	3.07	3.02	2.98	2.91	2.85	2.77	2.74	2.70	2.66	2.62	2.58	2.54
11	4.84	3.98	3.59	3.36	3.20	3.09	3.01	2.95	2.90	2.85	2.79	2.72	2.65	2.61	2.57	2.53	2.49	2.45	2.40
12	4.75	3.89	3.49	3.26	3.11	3.00	2.91	2.85	2.80	2.75	2.69	2.62	2.54	2.51	2.47	2.43	2.38	2.34	2.30
13	4.67	3.81	3.41	3.18	3.03	2.92	2.83	2.77	2.71	2.67	2.60	2.53	2.46	2.42	2.38	2.34	2.30	2.25	2.21
14	4.60	3.74	3.34	3.11	2.96	2.85	2.76	2.70	2.65	2.60	2.53	2.46	2.39	2.35	2.31	2.27	2.22	2.18	2.13
15	4.54	3.68	3.29	3.06	2.90	2.79	2.71	2.64	2.59	2.54	2.48	2.40	2.33	2.29	2.25	2.20	2.16	2.11	2.07
16	4.49	3.63	3.24	3.01	2.85	2.74	2.66	2.59	2.54	2.49	2.42	2.35	2.28	2.24	2.19	2.15	2.11	2.06	2.01
17	4.45	3.59	3.20	2.96	2.81	2.70	2.61	2.55	2.49	2.45	2.38	2.31	2.23	2.19	2.15	2.10	2.06	2.01	1.96
18	4.41	3.55	3.16	2.93	2.77	2.66	2.58	2.51	2.46	2.41	2.34	2.27	2.19	2.15	2.11	2.06	2.02	1.97	1.92
19	4.38	3.52	3.13	2.90	2.74	2.63	2.54	2.48	2.42	2.38	2.31	2.23	2.16	2.11	2.07	2.03	1.98	1.93	1.88
20	4.35	3.49	3.10	2.87	2.71	2.60	2.51	2.45	2.39	2.35	2.28	2.20	2.12	2.08	2.04	1.99	1.95	1.90	1.84
21	4.32	3.47	3.07	2.84	2.68	2.57	2.49	2.42	2.37	2.32	2.25	2.18	2.10	2.05	2.01	1.96	1.92	1.87	1.81
22	4.30	3.44	3.05	2.82	2.66	2.55	2.46	2.40	2.34	2.30	2.23	2.15	2.07	2.03	1.98	1.94	1.89	1.84	1.78
23	4.28	3.42	3.03	2.80	2.64	2.53	2.44	2.37	2.32	2.27	2.20	2.13	2.05	2.01	1.96	1.91	1.86	1.81	1.76
24	4.26	3.40	3.01	2.78	2.62	2.51	2.42	2.36	2.30	2.25	2.18	2.11	2.03	1.98	1.94	1.89	1.84	1.79	1.73
25	4.24	3.39	2.99	2.76	2.60	2.49	2.40	2.34	2.28	2.24	2.16	2.09	2.01	1.96	1.92	1.87	1.82	1.77	1.71
26	4.23	3.37	2.98	2.74	2.59	2.47	2.39	2.32	2.27	2.22	2.15	2.07	1.99	1.95	1.90	1.85	1.80	1.75	1.69
27	4.21	3.35	2.96	2.73	2.57	2.46	2.37	2.31	2.25	2.20	2.13	2.06	1.97	1.93	1.88	1.84	1.79	1.73	1.67
28	4.20	3.34	2.95	2.71	2.56	2.45	2.36	2.29	2.24	2.19	2.12	2.04	1.96	1.91	1.87	1.82	1.77	1.71	1.65
29	4.18	3.33	2.93	2.70	2.55	2.43	2.35	2.28	2.22	2.18	2.10	2.03	1.94	1.90	1.85	1.81	1.75	1.70	1.64
30	4.17	3.32	2.92	2.69	2.53	2.42	2.33	2.27	2.21	2.16	2.09	2.01	1.93	1.89	1.84	1.79	1.74	1.68	1.62
40	4.08	3.23	2.84	2.61	2.45	2.34	2.25	2.18	2.12	2.08	2.00	1.92	1.84	1.79	1.74	1.69	1.64	1.58	1.51
60	4.00	3.15	2.76	2.53	2.37	2.25	2.17	2.10	2.04	1.99	1.92	1.84	1.75	1.70	1.65	1.59	1.53	1.47	1.39
120	3.92	3.07	2.68	2.45	2.29	2.17	2.09	2.02	1.96	1.91	1.83	1.75	1.66	1.61	1.55	1.50	1.43	1.35	1.25
∞	3.84	3.00	2.60	2.37	2.21	2.10	2.01	1.94	1.88	1.83	1.75	1.67	1.57	1.52	1.46	1.39	1.32	1.22	1.00

TABLE VII CUMULATIVE F DISTRIBUTION (Continued)

$$P[F_{\gamma_1,\gamma_2} \leq f] = .975$$

γ_2 \ γ_1	1	2	3	4	5	6	7	8	9	10	12	15	20	24	30	40	60	120	∞
1	647.8	799.5	864.2	899.6	921.8	937.1	948.2	956.7	963.3	968.6	976.7	984.9	993.1	997.2	1001	1006	1010	1014	1018
2	38.51	39.00	39.17	39.25	39.30	39.33	39.36	39.37	39.39	39.40	39.41	39.43	39.45	39.46	39.46	39.47	39.48	39.49	39.50
3	17.44	16.04	15.44	15.10	14.88	14.73	14.62	14.54	14.47	14.42	14.34	14.25	14.17	14.12	14.08	14.04	13.99	13.95	13.90
4	12.22	10.65	9.98	9.60	9.36	9.20	9.07	8.98	8.90	8.84	8.75	8.66	8.56	8.51	8.46	8.41	8.36	8.31	8.26
5	10.01	8.43	7.76	7.39	7.15	6.98	6.85	6.76	6.68	6.62	6.52	6.43	6.33	6.28	6.23	6.18	6.12	6.07	6.02
6	8.81	7.26	6.60	6.23	5.99	5.82	5.70	5.60	5.52	5.46	5.37	5.27	5.17	5.12	5.07	5.01	4.96	4.90	4.85
7	8.07	6.54	5.89	5.52	5.29	5.12	4.99	4.90	4.82	4.76	4.67	4.57	4.47	4.42	4.36	4.31	4.25	4.20	4.14
8	7.57	6.06	5.42	5.05	4.82	4.65	4.53	4.43	4.36	4.30	4.20	4.10	4.00	3.95	3.89	3.84	3.78	3.73	3.67
9	7.21	5.71	5.08	4.72	4.48	4.32	4.20	4.10	4.03	3.96	3.87	3.77	3.67	3.61	3.56	3.51	3.45	3.39	3.33
10	6.94	5.46	4.83	4.47	4.24	4.07	3.95	3.85	3.78	3.72	3.62	3.52	3.42	3.37	3.31	3.26	3.20	3.14	3.08
11	6.72	5.26	4.63	4.28	4.04	3.88	3.76	3.66	3.59	3.53	3.43	3.33	3.23	3.17	3.12	3.06	3.00	2.94	2.88
12	6.55	5.10	4.47	4.12	3.89	3.73	3.61	3.51	3.44	3.37	3.28	3.18	3.07	3.02	2.96	2.91	2.85	2.79	2.72
13	6.41	4.97	4.35	4.00	3.77	3.60	3.48	3.39	3.31	3.25	3.15	3.05	2.95	2.89	2.84	2.78	2.72	2.66	2.60
14	6.30	4.86	4.24	3.89	3.66	3.50	3.38	3.29	3.21	3.15	3.05	2.95	2.84	2.79	2.73	2.67	2.61	2.55	2.49
15	6.20	4.77	4.15	3.80	3.58	3.41	3.29	3.20	3.12	3.06	2.96	2.86	2.76	2.70	2.64	2.59	2.52	2.46	2.40
16	6.12	4.69	4.08	3.73	3.50	3.34	3.22	3.12	3.05	2.99	2.89	2.79	2.68	2.63	2.57	2.51	2.45	2.38	2.32
17	6.04	4.62	4.01	3.66	3.44	3.28	3.16	3.06	2.98	2.92	2.82	2.72	2.62	2.56	2.50	2.44	2.38	2.32	2.25
18	5.98	4.56	3.95	3.61	3.38	3.22	3.10	3.01	2.93	2.87	2.77	2.67	2.56	2.50	2.44	2.38	2.32	2.26	2.19
19	5.92	4.51	3.90	3.56	3.33	3.17	3.05	2.96	2.88	2.82	2.72	2.62	2.51	2.45	2.39	2.33	2.27	2.20	2.13
20	5.87	4.46	3.86	3.51	3.29	3.13	3.01	2.91	2.84	2.77	2.68	2.57	2.46	2.41	2.35	2.29	2.22	2.16	2.09
21	5.83	4.42	3.82	3.48	3.25	3.09	2.97	2.87	2.80	2.73	2.64	2.53	2.42	2.37	2.31	2.25	2.18	2.11	2.04
22	5.79	4.38	3.78	3.44	3.22	3.05	2.93	2.84	2.76	2.70	2.60	2.50	2.39	2.33	2.27	2.21	2.14	2.08	2.00
23	5.75	4.35	3.75	3.41	3.18	3.02	2.90	2.81	2.73	2.67	2.57	2.47	2.36	2.30	2.24	2.18	2.11	2.04	1.97
24	5.72	4.32	3.72	3.38	3.15	2.99	2.87	2.78	2.70	2.64	2.54	2.44	2.33	2.27	2.21	2.15	2.08	2.01	1.94
25	5.69	4.29	3.69	3.35	3.13	2.97	2.85	2.75	2.68	2.61	2.51	2.41	2.30	2.24	2.18	2.12	2.05	1.98	1.91
26	5.66	4.27	3.67	3.33	3.10	2.94	2.82	2.73	2.65	2.59	2.49	2.39	2.28	2.22	2.16	2.09	2.03	1.95	1.88
27	5.63	4.24	3.65	3.31	3.08	2.92	2.80	2.71	2.63	2.57	2.47	2.36	2.25	2.19	2.13	2.07	2.00	1.93	1.85
28	5.61	4.22	3.63	3.29	3.06	2.90	2.78	2.69	2.61	2.55	2.45	2.34	2.23	2.17	2.11	2.05	1.98	1.91	1.83
29	5.59	4.20	3.61	3.27	3.04	2.88	2.76	2.67	2.59	2.53	2.43	2.32	2.21	2.15	2.09	2.03	1.96	1.89	1.81
30	5.57	4.18	3.59	3.25	3.03	2.87	2.75	2.65	2.57	2.51	2.41	2.31	2.20	2.14	2.07	2.01	1.94	1.87	1.79
40	5.42	4.05	3.46	3.13	2.90	2.74	2.62	2.53	2.45	2.39	2.29	2.18	2.07	2.01	1.94	1.88	1.80	1.72	1.64
60	5.29	3.93	3.34	3.01	2.79	2.63	2.51	2.41	2.33	2.27	2.17	2.06	1.94	1.88	1.82	1.74	1.67	1.58	1.48
120	5.15	3.80	3.23	2.89	2.67	2.52	2.39	2.30	2.22	2.16	2.05	1.94	1.82	1.76	1.69	1.61	1.53	1.43	1.31
∞	5.02	3.69	3.12	2.79	2.57	2.41	2.29	2.19	2.11	2.05	1.94	1.83	1.71	1.64	1.57	1.48	1.39	1.27	1.00

TABLE VII CUMULATIVE F DISTRIBUTION (Continued)

$$P[F_{\gamma_1,\gamma_2} \leq f] = .99$$

γ_2 \ γ_1	1	2	3	4	5	6	7	8	9	10	12	15	20	24	30	40	60	120	∞
1	4052	4999.5	5403	5625	5764	5859	5928	5982	6022	6056	6106	6157	6209	6235	6261	6287	6313	6339	6366
2	98.50	99.00	99.17	99.25	99.30	99.33	99.36	99.37	99.39	99.40	99.42	99.43	99.45	99.46	99.47	99.47	99.48	99.49	99.50
3	34.12	30.82	29.46	28.71	28.24	27.91	27.67	27.49	27.35	27.23	27.05	26.87	26.69	26.60	26.50	26.41	26.32	26.22	26.13
4	21.20	18.00	16.69	15.98	15.52	15.21	14.98	14.80	14.66	14.55	14.37	14.20	14.02	13.93	13.84	13.75	13.65	13.56	13.46
5	16.26	13.27	12.06	11.39	10.97	10.67	10.46	10.29	10.16	10.05	9.89	9.72	9.55	9.47	9.38	9.29	9.20	9.11	9.02
6	13.75	10.92	9.78	9.15	8.75	8.47	8.26	8.10	7.98	7.87	7.72	7.56	7.40	7.31	7.23	7.14	7.06	6.97	6.88
7	12.25	9.55	8.45	7.85	7.46	7.19	6.99	6.84	6.72	6.62	6.47	6.31	6.16	6.07	5.99	5.91	5.82	5.74	5.65
8	11.26	8.65	7.59	7.01	6.63	6.37	6.18	6.03	5.91	5.81	5.67	5.52	5.36	5.28	5.20	5.12	5.03	4.95	4.86
9	10.56	8.02	6.99	6.42	6.06	5.80	5.61	5.47	5.35	5.26	5.11	4.96	4.81	4.73	4.65	4.57	4.48	4.40	4.31
10	10.04	7.56	6.55	5.99	5.64	5.39	5.20	5.06	4.94	4.85	4.71	4.56	4.41	4.33	4.25	4.17	4.08	4.00	3.91
11	9.65	7.21	6.22	5.67	5.32	5.07	4.89	4.74	4.63	4.54	4.40	4.25	4.10	4.02	3.94	3.86	3.78	3.69	3.60
12	9.33	6.93	5.95	5.41	5.06	4.82	4.64	4.50	4.39	4.30	4.16	4.01	3.86	3.78	3.70	3.62	3.54	3.45	3.36
13	9.07	6.70	5.74	5.21	4.86	4.62	4.44	4.30	4.19	4.10	3.96	3.82	3.66	3.59	3.51	3.43	3.34	3.25	3.17
14	8.86	6.51	5.56	5.04	4.69	4.46	4.28	4.14	4.03	3.94	3.80	3.66	3.51	3.43	3.35	3.27	3.18	3.09	3.00
15	8.68	6.36	5.42	4.89	4.56	4.32	4.14	4.00	3.89	3.80	3.67	3.52	3.37	3.29	3.21	3.13	3.05	2.96	2.87
16	8.53	6.23	5.29	4.77	4.44	4.20	4.03	3.89	3.78	3.69	3.55	3.41	3.26	3.18	3.10	3.02	2.93	2.84	2.75
17	8.40	6.11	5.18	4.67	4.34	4.10	3.93	3.79	3.68	3.59	3.46	3.31	3.16	3.08	3.00	2.92	2.83	2.75	2.65
18	8.29	6.01	5.09	4.58	4.25	4.01	3.84	3.71	3.60	3.51	3.37	3.23	3.08	3.00	2.92	2.84	2.75	2.66	2.57
19	8.18	5.93	5.01	4.50	4.17	3.94	3.77	3.63	3.52	3.43	3.30	3.15	3.00	2.92	2.84	2.76	2.67	2.58	2.49
20	8.10	5.85	4.94	4.43	4.10	3.87	3.70	3.56	3.46	3.37	3.23	3.09	2.94	2.86	2.78	2.69	2.61	2.52	2.42
21	8.02	5.78	4.87	4.37	4.04	3.81	3.64	3.51	3.40	3.31	3.17	3.03	2.88	2.80	2.72	2.64	2.55	2.46	2.36
22	7.95	5.72	4.82	4.31	3.99	3.76	3.59	3.45	3.35	3.26	3.12	2.98	2.83	2.75	2.67	2.58	2.50	2.40	2.31
23	7.88	5.66	4.76	4.26	3.94	3.71	3.54	3.41	3.30	3.21	3.07	2.93	2.78	2.70	2.62	2.54	2.45	2.35	2.26
24	7.82	5.61	4.72	4.22	3.90	3.67	3.50	3.36	3.26	3.17	3.03	2.89	2.74	2.66	2.58	2.49	2.40	2.31	2.21
25	7.77	5.57	4.68	4.18	3.85	3.63	3.46	3.32	3.22	3.13	2.99	2.85	2.70	2.62	2.54	2.45	2.36	2.27	2.17
26	7.72	5.53	4.64	4.14	3.82	3.59	3.42	3.29	3.18	3.09	2.96	2.81	2.66	2.58	2.50	2.42	2.33	2.23	2.13
27	7.68	5.49	4.60	4.11	3.78	3.56	3.39	3.26	3.15	3.06	2.93	2.78	2.63	2.55	2.47	2.38	2.29	2.20	2.10
28	7.64	5.45	4.57	4.07	3.75	3.53	3.36	3.23	3.12	3.03	2.90	2.75	2.60	2.52	2.44	2.35	2.26	2.17	2.06
29	7.60	5.42	4.54	4.04	3.73	3.50	3.33	3.20	3.09	3.00	2.87	2.73	2.57	2.49	2.41	2.33	2.23	2.14	2.03
30	7.56	5.39	4.51	4.02	3.70	3.47	3.30	3.17	3.07	2.98	2.84	2.70	2.55	2.47	2.39	2.30	2.21	2.11	2.01
40	7.31	5.18	4.31	3.83	3.51	3.29	3.12	2.99	2.89	2.80	2.66	2.52	2.37	2.29	2.20	2.11	2.02	1.92	1.80
60	7.08	4.98	4.13	3.65	3.34	3.12	2.95	2.82	2.72	2.63	2.50	2.35	2.20	2.12	2.03	1.94	1.84	1.73	1.60
120	6.85	4.79	3.95	3.48	3.17	2.96	2.79	2.66	2.56	2.47	2.34	2.19	2.03	1.95	1.86	1.76	1.66	1.53	1.38
∞	6.63	4.61	3.78	3.32	3.02	2.80	2.64	2.51	2.41	2.32	2.18	2.04	1.88	1.79	1.70	1.59	1.47	1.32	1.00

Reprinted with permission from W. H. Beyer (ed.), *CRC Handbook of Tables for Probability and Statistics*, 2d ed., 1968, pp. 305–308. Copyright CRC Press, Inc., Boca Raton, Florida.

TABLE VIII DUNCAN'S TABLES

least significant studentized ranges r_p $\alpha = 0.05$ P					least significant studentized ranges r_p $\alpha = 0.01$ P				
r	2	3	4	5	6	r	2	3	4	5	6
1	17.97	17.97	17.97	17.97	17.97	1	90.03	90.03	90.03	90.03	90.03
2	6.085	6.085	6.085	6.085	6.085	2	14.04	14.04	14.04	14.04	14.04
3	4.501	4.516	4.516	4.516	4.516	3	8.261	8.321	8.321	8.321	8.321
4	3.927	4.013	4.033	4.033	4.033	4	6.512	6.677	6.740	6.756	6.756
5	3.635	3.749	3.797	3.814	3.814	5	5.702	5.893	5.898	6.040	6.065
6	3.461	3.587	3.649	3.680	3.694	6	5.243	5.439	5.549	5.614	5.655
7	3.344	3.477	3.548	3.588	3.611	7	4.949	5.145	5.260	5.334	5.383
8	3.261	3.399	3.475	3.521	3.549	8	4.746	4.939	5.057	5.135	5.189
9	3.199	3.339	3.420	3.470	3.502	9	4.596	4.787	4.906	4.986	5.043
10	3.151	3.293	3.376	3.430	3.465	10	4.482	4.671	4.790	4.871	4.931
11	3.113	3.256	3.342	3.397	3.435	11	4.392	4.579	4.697	4.780	4.841
12	3.082	3.225	3.313	3.370	3.410	12	4.320	4.504	4.622	4.706	4.767
13	3.055	3.200	3.289	3.348	3.389	13	4.260	4.442	4.560	4.644	4.706
14	3.033	3.178	3.268	3.329	3.372	14	4.210	4.391	4.508	4.591	4.654
15	3.014	3.160	3.250	3.312	3.356	15	4.168	4.347	4.463	4.547	4.610
16	2.998	3.144	3.235	3.298	3.343	16	4.131	4.309	4.425	4.509	4.572
17	2.984	3.130	3.222	3.285	3.331	17	4.099	4.275	4.391	4.475	4.539
18	2.971	3.118	3.210	3.274	3.321	18	4.071	4.246	4.362	4.445	4.509
19	2.960	3.107	3.199	3.264	3.311	19	4.046	4.220	4.335	4.419	4.483
20	2.950	3.097	3.190	3.255	3.303	20	4.024	4.197	4.312	4.395	4.459
24	2.919	3.066	3.160	3.226	3.276	24	3.956	4.126	4.239	4.322	4.386
30	2.888	3.035	3.131	3.199	3.250	30	3.889	4.506	4.168	4.250	4.314
40	2.858	3.006	3.102	3.171	3.224	40	3.825	3.988	4.098	4.180	4.244
60	2.829	2.976	3.073	3.143	3.198	60	3.762	3.922	4.031	4.111	4.174
120	2.800	2.947	3.045	3.116	3.172	120	3.702	3.858	3.965	4.044	4.107
∞	2.772	2.918	3.017	3.089	3.146	∞	3.643	3.796	3.900	3.978	4.040

Abridgement of H. L. Harter's "Critical Values for Duncan's New Multiple Range Test", *Biometrics*, Vol. 16, No. 4 (1960). With permission from the Biometric Society.

TABLE IX WILCOXON SIGNED-RANK TEST

One-sided	Two-sided	$n = 5$	$n = 6$	$n = 7$	$n = 8$	$n = 9$	$n = 10$
$P = .05$	$P = .10$	1	2	4	6	8	11
$P = .025$	$P = .05$		1	2	4	6	8
$P = .01$	$P = .02$			0	2	3	5
$P = .005$	$P = .01$				0	2	3

One-sided	Two-sided	$n = 11$	$n = 12$	$n = 13$	$n = 14$	$n = 15$	$n = 16$
$P = .05$	$P = .10$	14	17	21	26	30	36
$P = .025$	$P = .05$	11	14	17	21	25	30
$P = .01$	$P = .02$	7	10	13	16	20	24
$P = .005$	$P = .01$	5	7	10	13	16	19

One-sided	Two-sided	$n = 17$	$n = 18$	$n = 19$	$n = 20$	$n = 21$	$n = 22$
$P = .05$	$P = .10$	41	47	54	60	68	75
$P = .025$	$P = .05$	35	40	46	52	59	66
$P = .01$	$P = .02$	28	33	38	43	49	56
$P = .005$	$P = .01$	23	28	32	37	43	49

One-sided	Two-sided	$n = 23$	$n = 24$	$n = 25$	$n = 26$	$n = 27$	$n = 28$
$P = .05$	$P = .10$	83	92	101	110	120	130
$P = .025$	$P = .05$	73	81	90	98	107	117
$P = .01$	$P = .02$	62	69	77	85	93	102
$P = .005$	$P = .01$	55	61	68	76	84	92

One-sided	Two-sided	$n = 29$	$n = 30$	$n = 31$	$n = 32$	$n = 33$	$n = 34$
$P = .05$	$P = .10$	141	152	163	175	188	201
$P = .025$	$P = .05$	127	137	148	159	171	183
$P = .01$	$P = .02$	111	120	130	141	151	162
$P = .005$	$P = .01$	100	109	118	128	138	149

One-sided	Two-sided	$n = 35$	$n = 36$	$n = 37$	$n = 38$	$n = 39$
$P = .05$	$P = .10$	214	228	242	256	271
$P = .025$	$P = .05$	195	208	222	235	250
$P = .01$	$P = .02$	174	186	198	211	224
$P = .005$	$P = .01$	160	171	183	195	208

One-sided	Two-sided	$n = 40$	$n = 41$	$n = 42$	$n = 43$	$n = 44$	$n = 45$
$P = .05$	$P = .10$	287	303	319	336	353	371
$P = .025$	$P = .05$	264	279	295	311	327	344
$P = .01$	$P = .02$	238	252	267	281	297	313
$P = .005$	$P = .01$	221	234	248	262	277	292

One-sided	Two-sided	$n = 46$	$n = 47$	$n = 48$	$n = 49$	$n = 50$
$P = .05$	$P = .10$	389	408	427	446	466
$P = .025$	$P = .05$	361	379	397	415	434
$P = .01$	$P = .02$	329	345	362	380	398
$P = .005$	$P = .01$	307	323	339	356	373

Reprinted with permission from W. H. Beyer (ed.), *CRC Handbook of Tables for Probability and Statistics,* 2d ed., 1968, p. 400. Copyright CRC Press, Inc., Boca Raton, Florida.

TABLE X WILCOXON RANK SUM TEST

$m = 3(1)25$ and $n = m(1)m + 25$
$P = .05$ one-sided; $P = .10$ two-sided

n	$m = 3$	$m = 4$	$m = 5$	$m = 6$	$m = 7$	$m = 8$	$m = 9$	$m = 10$	$m = 11$	$m = 12$	$m = 13$	$m = 14$
$n = m$	6,15	12,24	19,36	28,50	39,66	52,84	66,105	83,127	101,152	121,179	143,208	167,239
$n = m + 1$	7,17	13,27	20,40	30,54	41,71	54,90	69,111	86,134	105,159	125,187	148,216	172,248
$n = m + 2$	7,20	14,30	22,43	32,58	43,76	57,95	72,117	89,141	109,166	129,195	152,225	177,257
$n = m + 3$	8,22	15,33	24,46	33,63	46,80	60,100	75,123	93,147	112,174	134,202	157,233	182,266
$n = m + 4$	9,24	16,36	25,50	35,67	48,85	62,106	78,129	96,154	116,181	138,210	162,241	187,275
$n = m + 5$	9,27	17,39	26,54	37,71	50,90	65,111	81,135	100,160	120,188	142,218	166,250	192,284
$n = m + 6$	10,29	18,42	27,58	39,75	52,95	67,117	84,141	103,167	124,195	147,225	171,258	197,293
$n = m + 7$	11,31	19,45	29,61	41,79	54,100	70,122	87,147	107,173	128,202	151,233	176,266	203,301
$n = m + 8$	11,34	20,48	30,65	42,84	57,104	73,127	90,153	110,180	132,209	155,241	181,274	208,310
$n = m + 9$	12,36	21,51	32,68	44,88	59,109	75,133	93,159	114,186	136,216	159,249	185,283	213,319
$n = m + 10$	13,38	22,54	33,72	46,92	61,114	78,138	96,165	117,193	139,224	164,256	190,291	218,328
$n = m + 11$	13,41	23,57	34,76	48,96	63,119	80,144	100,170	120,200	143,231	168,264	195,299	223,337
$n = m + 12$	14,43	24,60	36,79	50,100	65,124	83,149	103,176	124,206	147,238	172,272	199,308	228,346
$n = m + 13$	15,45	25,63	37,83	52,104	68,128	86,154	106,182	127,213	151,245	177,279	204,316	234,354
$n = m + 14$	15,48	26,66	39,86	53,109	70,133	88,160	109,188	131,219	155,252	181,287	209,324	239,363
$n = m + 15$	16,50	27,69	40,90	55,113	72,138	91,165	112,194	134,226	159,259	185,295	214,332	244,372
$n = m + 16$	17,52	28,72	42,93	57,117	74,143	94,170	115,200	138,232	163,266	190,302	218,341	249,381
$n = m + 17$	17,55	29,75	43,97	59,121	77,147	96,176	118,206	141,239	167,273	194,310	223,349	254,390
$n = m + 18$	18,57	30,78	44,101	61,125	79,152	99,181	121,212	145,245	171,280	198,318	228,357	260,398
$n = m + 19$	19,59	31,81	46,104	62,130	81,157	102,186	124,218	148,252	175,287	203,325	233,365	265,407
$n = m + 20$	19,62	32,84	47,108	64,134	83,162	104,192	127,224	152,258	178,295	207,333	237,374	270,416
$n = m + 21$	20,64	33,87	49,111	66,138	86,166	107,197	130,230	155,265	182,302	211,341	242,382	275,425
$n = m + 22$	21,66	34,90	50,115	68,142	88,171	109,203	133,236	159,271	186,309	216,348	247,390	280,434
$n = m + 23$	21,69	35,93	52,118	70,146	90,176	112,208	136,242	162,278	190,316	220,356	252,398	285,443
$n = m + 24$	22,71	37,95	53,122	72,150	92,181	115,213	139,248	166,284	194,323	224,364	257,406	291,451
$n = m + 25$	23,73	38,98	54,126	73,155	94,186	117,219	142,254	169,291	198,330	229,371	261,415	296,460

$m = 3(1)25$ and $n = m(1)m + 25$
$P = .05$ one-sided; $P = .10$ two-sided

n	$m = 15$	$m = 16$	$m = 17$	$m = 18$	$m = 19$	$m = 20$	$m = 21$	$m = 22$	$m = 23$	$m = 24$	$m = 25$
$n = m$	192,273	220,308	249,346	280,386	314,427	349,471	386,517	424,566	465,616	508,668	552,723
$n = m + 1$	198,282	226,318	256,356	287,397	321,439	356,484	394,530	433,579	474,630	517,683	562,738
$n = m + 2$	203,292	232,328	262,367	294,408	328,451	364,496	402,543	442,592	483,644	527,697	572.753
$n = m + 3$	209,301	238,338	268,378	301,419	336,462	372,508	410,556	450,606	492,658	536,712	582,768
$n = m + 4$	215,310	244,348	275,388	308,430	343,474	380,520	418,569	459,619	501,672	546,726	592,783
$n = m + 5$	220,320	250,358	281,399	315,441	350,486	387,533	427,581	468,632	511,685	555,741	602,798
$n = m + 6$	226,329	256,368	288,409	322,452	358,497	395,545	435,594	476,646	520,699	565,755	612,813
$n = m + 7$	231,339	262,378	294,420	329,463	365,509	403,557	443,607	485,659	529,713	574,770	622,828
$n = m + 8$	237,348	268,388	301,430	336,474	372,521	411,569	451,620	494,672	538,727	584,784	632,843
$n = m + 9$	242,358	274,398	307,441	342,486	380,532	419,581	459,633	502,686	547,741	594,798	642,858
$n = m + 10$	248,367	280,408	314,451	349,497	387,544	426,594	468,645	511,699	556,755	603,813	652,873
$n = m + 11$	254,376	286,418	320,462	356,508	394,556	434,606	476,658	520,712	565,769	613,827	662,888
$n = m + 12$	259,386	292,428	327,472	363,519	402,567	442,618	484,671	528,726	574,783	622,842	672,903
$n = m + 13$	265,395	298,438	333,483	370,530	409,579	450,630	492,684	537,739	584,796	632,856	682,918
$n = m + 14$	270,405	304,448	340,493	377,541	416,591	458,642	501,696	546,752	593,810	642,870	692,933
$n = m + 15$	276,414	310,458	346,504	384,552	424,602	465,655	509,709	554,766	602,824	651,885	702,948
$n = m + 16$	282,423	316,468	353,514	391,563	431,614	473,667	517,722	563,779	611,838	661,899	712,963
$n = m + 17$	287,433	322,478	359,525	398,574	438,626	481,679	526,734	572,792	620,852	670,914	723,977
$n = m + 18$	293,442	328,488	366,535	405,585	446,637	489,691	534,747	581,805	629,866	680,928	733,992
$n = m + 19$	299,451	334,498	372,546	412,596	453,649	497,703	542,760	589,819	639,879	690,942	743,1007
$n = m + 20$	304,461	340,508	379,556	419,607	461,660	505,715	550,773	598,832	648,893	699,957	753,1022
$n = m + 21$	310,470	347,517	385,568	426,618	468,672	512,728	559,785	607,845	657,907	709,971	763,1037
$n = m + 22$	315,480	353,527	392,577	433,629	475,684	520,740	567,798	615,859	666,921	718,986	773,1052
$n = m + 23$	321,489	359,537	398,588	439,641	483,695	528,752	575,811	624,872	675,935	728,1000	783,1067
$n = m + 24$	327,498	365,547	405,598	446,652	490,707	536,764	583,824	633,885	684,949	738,1014	793,1082
$n = m + 25$	332,508	371,557	411,609	453,663	498,718	544,776	592,836	642,898	694,962	747,1029	803,1097

TABLE X   WILCOXON RANK SUM TEST (*Continued*)

$m = 3(1)25$ and $n = m(1)m + 25$
$P = .025$ one-sided; $P = .05$ two-sided

n	$m = 3$	$m = 4$	$m = 5$	$m = 6$	$m = 7$	$m = 8$	$m = 9$	$m = 10$	$m = 11$	$m = 12$	$m = 13$	$m = 14$
$n = m$	5,16	11,25	18,37	26,52	37,68	49,87	63,108	79,131	96,157	116,184	137,214	160,246
$n = m + 1$	6,18	12,28	19,41	28,56	39,73	51,93	66,114	82,138	100,164	120,192	141,223	165,255
$n = m + 2$	6,21	12,32	20,45	29,61	41,78	54,98	68,121	85,145	103,172	124,200	146,231	170,264
$n = m + 3$	7,23	13,35	21,49	31,65	43,83	56,104	71,127	88,152	107,179	128,208	150,240	174,274
$n = m + 4$	7,26	14,38	22,53	32,70	45,88	58,110	74,133	91,159	110,187	131,217	154,249	179,283
$n = m + 5$	8,28	15,41	24,56	34,74	46,94	61,115	77,139	94,166	114,194	135,225	159,257	184,292
$n = m + 6$	8,31	16,44	25,60	36,78	48,99	63,121	79,146	97,173	118,201	139,233	163,266	189,301
$n = m + 7$	9,33	17,47	26,64	37,83	50,104	65,127	82,152	101,179	121,209	143,241	168,274	194,310
$n = m + 8$	10,35	17,51	27,68	39,87	52,109	68,132	85,158	104,186	125,216	147,249	172,283	198,320
$n = m + 9$	10,38	18,54	29,71	41,91	54,114	70,138	88,164	107,193	128,224	151,257	176,292	203,329
$n = m + 10$	11,40	19,57	30,75	42,96	56,119	72,144	90,171	110,200	132,231	155,265	181,300	208,338
$n = m + 11$	11,43	20,60	31,79	44,100	58,124	75,149	93,177	113,207	135,239	159,273	185,309	213,347
$n = m + 12$	12,45	21,63	32,83	45,105	60,129	77,155	96,183	117,213	139,246	163,281	190,317	218,356
$n = m + 13$	12,48	22,66	33,87	47,109	62,134	80,160	99,189	120,220	143,253	167,289	194,326	222,366
$n = m + 14$	13,50	23,69	35,90	49,113	64,139	82,166	101,196	123,227	146,261	171,297	198,335	227,375
$n = m + 15$	13,53	24,72	36,94	50,118	66,144	84,172	104,202	126,234	150,268	175,305	203,343	232,384
$n = m + 16$	14,55	24,76	37,98	52,122	68,149	87,177	107,208	129,241	153,276	179,313	207,352	237,393
$n = m + 17$	14,58	25,79	38,102	53,127	70,154	89,183	110,214	132,248	157,283	183,321	212,360	242,402
$n = m + 18$	15,60	26,82	40,105	55,131	72,159	92,188	113,220	136,254	161,290	187,329	216,369	247,411
$n = m + 19$	15,63	27,85	41,109	57,135	74,164	94,194	115,227	139,261	164,298	191,337	221,377	252,420
$n = m + 20$	16,65	28,88	42,113	58,140	76,169	96,200	118,233	142,268	168,305	195,345	225,386	256,430
$n = m + 21$	16,68	29,91	43,117	60,144	78,174	99,205	121,239	145,275	171,313	199,353	229,395	261,439
$n = m + 22$	17,70	30,94	45,120	61,149	80,179	101,211	124,245	148,282	175,320	203,361	234,403	266,448
$n = m + 23$	17,73	31,97	46,124	63,153	82,184	103,217	127,251	152,288	179,327	207,369	238,412	271,457
$n = m + 24$	18,75	31,101	47,128	65,157	84,189	106,222	129,258	155,295	182,335	211,377	243,420	276,466
$n = m + 25$	18,78	32,104	48,132	66,162	86,194	108,228	132,264	158,302	186,342	216,384	247,429	281,475

$m = 3(1)25$ and $n = m(1)m + 25$
$P = .025$ one-sided; $P = .05$ two-sided

n	$m = 15$	$m = 16$	$m = 17$	$m = 18$	$m = 19$	$m = 20$	$m = 21$	$m = 22$	$m = 23$	$m = 24$	$m = 25$
$n = m$	185,280	212,316	240,355	271,395	303,438	337,483	373,530	411,579	451,630	493,683	536,739
$n = m + 1$	190,290	217,327	246,366	277,407	310,450	345,495	381,543	419,593	460,644	502,698	546,754
$n = m + 2$	195,300	223,337	252,377	284,418	317,462	352,508	389,556	428,606	468,659	511,713	555,770
$n = m + 3$	201,309	229,347	258,388	290,430	324,474	359,521	397,569	436,620	477,673	520,728	565,785
$n = m + 4$	206,319	234,358	264,399	297,441	331,486	367,533	404,583	444,634	486,687	529,743	574,801
$n = m + 5$	211,329	240,368	271,409	303,453	338,498	374,546	412,596	452,648	494,702	538,758	584,816
$n = m + 6$	216,339	245,379	277,420	310,464	345,510	381,559	420,609	460,662	503,716	547,773	593,832
$n = m + 7$	221,349	251,389	283,431	316,476	351,523	389,571	428,622	469,675	512,730	556,788	603,847
$n = m + 8$	227,358	257,399	289,442	323,487	358,535	396,584	436,635	477,689	520,745	565,803	612,863
$n = m + 9$	232,368	262,410	295,453	329,499	365,547	403,597	443,649	485,703	529,759	575,817	622,878
$n = m + 10$	237,378	268,420	301,464	336,510	372,559	411,609	451,662	493,717	538,773	584,832	632,893
$n = m + 11$	242,388	274,430	307,475	342,522	379,571	418,622	459,675	502,730	546,788	593,847	641,909
$n = m + 12$	248,397	279,441	313,486	349,533	386,583	426,634	467,688	510,744	555,802	602,862	651,924
$n = m + 13$	253,407	285,451	319,497	355,545	393,595	433,647	475,701	518,758	564,816	611,877	660,940
$n = m + 14$	258,417	291,461	325,508	362,556	400,607	440,660	482,715	526,772	572,831	620,892	670,955
$n = m + 15$	263,427	296,472	331,519	368,568	407,619	448,672	490,728	535,785	581,845	629,907	679,971
$n = m + 16$	269,436	302,482	338,529	375,579	414,631	455,685	498,741	543,799	590,859	638,922	689,986
$n = m + 17$	274,446	308,492	344,540	381,591	421,643	463,697	506,754	551,813	599,873	648,936	699,1001
$n = m + 18$	279,456	314,502	350,551	388,602	428,655	470,710	514,767	560,826	607,888	657,951	708,1017
$n = m + 19$	284,466	319,513	356,562	395,613	435,667	477,723	522,780	568,840	616,902	666,966	718,1032
$n = m + 20$	290,475	325,523	362,573	401,625	442,679	485,735	530,793	576,854	625,916	675,981	727,1048
$n = m + 21$	295,485	331,533	368,584	408,636	449,691	492,748	537,807	584,868	633,931	684,996	737,1063
$n = m + 22$	300,495	336,544	374,595	414,648	456,703	500,760	545,820	593,881	642,945	693,1011	747,1078
$n = m + 23$	306,504	342,554	380,606	421,659	463,715	507,773	553,833	601,895	651,959	703,1025	756,1094
$n = m + 24$	311,514	348,564	387,616	427,671	470,727	515,785	561,846	609,909	660,973	712,1040	766,1109
$n = m + 25$	316,524	353,575	393,627	434,682	477,739	522,798	569,859	618,922	668,988	721,1055	775,1125

Reprinted with permission from W. H. Beyer (ed.), *CRC Handbook of Tables for Probability and Statistics*, 2d ed., 1968, pp. 410-41. Copyright CRC Press, Inc., Boca Raton, Florida.

REFERENCES

1. Beyer, William, ed.: *Handbook of Tables for Probability and Statistics*, 2d ed., CRC Press, Boca Raton, Florida, 1968.

2. Bliss, C. T.: *Statistics in Biology*, McGraw-Hill, New York, 1967.

3. Bradley, James V.: *Distribution Free Statistical Tests*, Prentice-Hall, Englewood Cliffs, N.J., 1968.

4. Conover, W. J.: *Practical Non-parametic Statistics*, Wiley, New York, 1971.

5. Conover, W. J.: "Some Reasons for Not Using the Yates Continuity Correction on a 2 × 2 Contingency Table" *Journal of the American Statistical Association*, vol. 69, no. 346, June 1974, page 374.

6. Hoel, Paul: *Introduction to Mathematical Statistics*, Wiley, New York, 1971.

7. Larson, Harold: *Introduction to Probability Theory and Statistical Inference*, Wiley, New York, 1969.

8. Miller, I., and J. Freund: *Probability and Statistics for Engineers*, Prentice-Hall, Englewood Cliffs, N.J., 1965.

9. Milton, J. S., and C. P. Tsokos: *Probability Theory with the Essential Analysis*, Addison-Wesley, Reading, Mass., 1976.

10. Milton, J. S., and J. J. Corbet: *Applied Statistics with Probability*, Van Nostrand, New York, 1979.

11. *SAS User's Guide*, 1979 ed., SAS Institute Inc., Raleigh, N.C.

12. Snedecor, G. W., and William Cochran: *Statistical Methods*, 6th ed., Iowa State University Press, Ames, 1967.

13. Sokal, R., and James Rohlf: *Biometry*, Freeman, San Francisco, 1969.

14. Tsokos, C. P.: *Probability Distributions: An Introduction to Probability Theory with Applications*, Duxbury Press, Belmont, Calif., 1972.

15. Tukey, John: *Exploratory Data Analysis*, Addison-Wesley, Reading, Mass., 1977.

16. Walpole, Ronald, and R. Myers: *Probability and Statistics for Engineers and Scientists*, 2d ed., Macmillan, New York, 1978.

ANSWERS TO ODD-NUMBERED PROBLEMS IN THE EXERCISES

EXERCISES □ 1.1

1. **a.** 8.8, 4.2, 11.5, .5, 32.3, 30.7, 12; 3.6, 11.5, 3.6, 8.8, 6.8, 12.5, 14.1, 16.7, 22.4

   b. The vertical axis is always scaled from 0 to 1.

EXERCISES □ 1.2

1. **a.** 12130; 737

   b. 11393

   c. 1627.57

   d. 1628

   e. 736.5

   f.

CATEGORY	BOUNDARIES		FREQUENCY	RELATIVE FREQUENCY
1	736.5 to	2364.5	6	.133
2	2364.5 to	3992.5	5	.111
3	3992.5 to	5620.5	10	.222
4	5620.5 to	7248.5	12	.267
5	7248.5 to	8876.5	7	.156

| 6 | 8876.5 to 10504.5 | 4 | .089 |
| 7 | 10504.5 to 12132.5 | 1 | .022 |

3. **a and b**

CATEGORY	BOUNDARIES	FREQUENCY	RELATIVE FREQUENCY	CUMULATIVE FREQUENCY	RELATIVE CUMULATIVE FREQUENCY
1	1499.5 to 2320.5	9	.375	9	.375
2	2320.5 to 3141.5	1	.042	10	.417
3	3141.5 to 3962.5	10	.417	20	.834
4	3962.5 to 4783.5	0	0	20	.834
5	4783.5 to 5604.5	4	.166	24	1.00

  d. approximately 61%

EXERCISES ☐ 1.3

1. I: 2.1, 2.11, 1.45, 4, 2
    II: 3.5, 4.94, 2.22, 6, 3.5
3. **a.** Robin: 100.48, 75, 255, 3911.44, 62.54;
      Mourning dove: 224.66, 175.7, 1186.1, 55000.50, 234.52; no
    b. 184.02, 172.85, 355.8, 14308.12, 119.62; the median is least
      affected; the value 265.0 might be considered as an outlier.
5. **a.** Great Danes, CV = 33.33; Chihuahua, CV = 50; the Chihuahuas
      exhibit a greater variability relative to their mean weight; a
      direct comparison is misleading since the fact that Great
      Danes naturally weigh much more than Chihuahuas tends to
      lead to a larger value for the standard deviation in the former
      case.
    b. Great Britain, CV = 12.56; United States, CV = 6.85; Great
      Britain.

EXERCISES ☐ 1.4

1. **a.**

MIDPOINT	CUMULATIVE FREQUENCY
7	1
12	3
17	8
22	11

b. $\bar{x} \doteq 16.55$; $s^2 \doteq 22.7$; $s \doteq 4.72$;
$\tilde{x} = x_6 \doteq 14.5 + \frac{3}{5}[19.5 - 14.5] = 17.5$

3.

Men

MIDPOINT	CUMULATIVE FREQUENCY
7	1
12	5
17	12
22	35
27	51
32	58
37	68

$\bar{x} \doteq 25.09$; $s^2 \doteq 52.26$;
$s \doteq 7.23$;
$\tilde{x} = \dfrac{x_{34} + x_{35}}{2}$
$x_{34} \doteq 19.5 + \frac{22}{23}[24.5 - 19.5] = 24.28$
$x_{35} \doteq 19.5 + \frac{23}{23}[24.5 - 19.5] = 24.50$
$\tilde{x} \doteq 24.39$

Women

MIDPOINT	CUMULATIVE FREQUENCY
7	0
12	2
17	12
22	19
27	22
32	27
37	29

$\bar{x} \doteq 22.86$; $s^2 \doteq 51.91$;
$s \doteq 7.20$
$\tilde{x} = x_{15} \doteq 19.5 + \frac{3}{7}[24.5 - 19.5]$
$\qquad = 21.64$

The two groups appear to be similar with slight differences, perhaps, in the mean and median values.

EXERCISES □ 2.1

1. Personal or relative frequency
3. $p \doteq \frac{5}{150}$, relative frequency
5. $\frac{1}{4}$, classical
7. $p \doteq \frac{8}{100}$, relative frequency
9. $\frac{1}{5}$, classical

EXERCISES □ 2.2

1. $S = \{MMMM, MMMF, MMFM, MFMM, FMMM, FFMM, FMFM,$
$FMMF, MFMF, MFFM, MMFF, FFFM, FFMF, FMFF, MFFF,$
$FFFF\}$

$A = \{MMMM, MMMF, MMFM, MFMM, MFMF, MFFM, MMFF, MFFF\}$

$B = \{FFMM, FMFM, FMMF, MFMF, MFFM, MMFF\}$

$C = \{MMMM, MMFM, MFMM, MFFM\}$

$D = \varnothing$ (impossible)

3. **c.** $A = \{$GLAH, GLHA, GALH, GAHL, GHAL, GHLA, ALHG, AHLG, LHAG, HLAG, HALG, LAHG$\}$

   d. $P[A] = {}^{12}/_{24}$

   e. $B = \{$LAGH, LAHG, LGAH, LGHA, LHAG, LHGA$\}$
   $P[B] = {}^{6}/_{24}$

EXERCISES □ 2.3

1. Permutation
3. Combination
5. Permutation

EXERCISES □ 2.4

1. **a.** 8
   b. 4
   c. $^4/_8$

   d.

3. 4

5. $(64)^3 = 262,144; \quad 64 \cdot 63 \cdot 62 = 249,984; \quad \dfrac{12160}{262144};$

   $\dfrac{61 \cdot 60 \cdot 59}{262144} = \dfrac{215940}{262144}$

7. **a.** $7! = 5040$

   b. $\dfrac{2 \cdot 5!}{7!} = \dfrac{240}{5040} = .0475$

   c. Yes, the probability of this happening by chance is small (.0475)

9. $\dfrac{15!}{5!5!5!}$

11. **a.** Aa
    b. $\frac{1}{4}; \frac{1}{2}$
    c. $\frac{1}{2}$

EXERCISES ☐ 2.5

1. a. 15
   b. 56
   c. 1
   d. 1

3. $1/_{15}C_7 = 1/6435$; $\binom{7}{5}\Big/\binom{15}{7} = 21/6435$

5. $\binom{4}{2}\Big/\binom{10}{3}$

EXERCISES ☐ 3.1

1. b, c, d
3. .65
5. .10

EXERCISES ☐ 3.2

1. .82; .20
3. .16; .22

EXERCISES ☐ 3.3

1. a. $^6/_{16}$
   b. $^3/_8$
   c. $^1/_2$
   d. $^1/_2$
3. a. .04
   b. .10
   c. .02
   d. $^2/_{60}$
5. $^5/_{35}$; $^{35}/_{40}$

EXERCISES ☐ 3.4

1. $^{78}/_{129}$; $^{51}/_{147}$
3. $\alpha \doteq {}^7/_{402}$; $\beta \doteq {}^{19}/_{98}$
5. $^{130}/_{142}$; high; it is the probability of making a correct classification.
7.   Reported

	+	−	
True +	92	8	100
True −	13	62	75
	105	70	175

$\alpha \doteq {}^{13}/_{75}$

EXERCISES ☐ 3.5

1.
  1. Not independent; not mutually exclusive
  2. Not independent; not mutually exclusive
  3. Independent; not mutually exclusive
  4. Not independent; mutually exclusive
  5. Not independent; not mutually exclusive
  6. Not independent; not mutually exclusive
  7. Independent; not mutually exclusive

3. No, $P[A_1 \cap A_2] = .04 \neq P[A_1]P[A_2] = (.35)(.10) = .035$; $\frac{4}{35}$

5. $(.99)^2 \doteq .98$

7. $(.18)(.82) = .148$

9. $P[\text{hepatitis}] = P[\text{hepatitis and paid}] + P[\text{hepatitis and not paid}]$
$\qquad = P[\text{hepatitis} | \text{paid}]P[\text{paid}] + P[\text{hepatitis} | \text{not paid}]$
$\qquad\quad P[\text{not paid}]$
$\qquad = (.0144)(.67) + (.0012)(.33) = .01$

11. $P[\text{diabetes and unaware}] = P[\text{unaware} | \text{diabetes}]P[\text{diabetes}]$
$\qquad\qquad\qquad\qquad\qquad = (.5)(.02) = .01$

13.

PROBABILITY OF MATCH	POSSIBLE OFFSPRING GENOTYPE	PROBABLE OFFSPRING GENOTYPE	PATH PROBABILITY
$\frac{1}{4} \cdot \frac{1}{4}$	AA	1	$\frac{1}{16}$
$\frac{1}{4} \cdot \frac{1}{2}$	AA	$\frac{1}{2}$	$\frac{1}{16}$
	Aa	$\frac{1}{2}$	$\frac{1}{16}$
$\frac{1}{4} \cdot \frac{1}{4}$	Aa	1	$\frac{1}{16}$
$\frac{1}{2} \cdot \frac{1}{4}$	AA	$\frac{1}{2}$	$\frac{1}{16}$
	Aa	$\frac{1}{2}$	$\frac{1}{16}$
$\frac{1}{2} \cdot \frac{1}{2}$	AA	$\frac{1}{4}$	$\frac{1}{16}$
	Aa	$\frac{1}{2}$	$\frac{2}{16}$
	aa	$\frac{1}{4}$	$\frac{1}{16}$
$\frac{1}{2} \cdot \frac{1}{4}$	Aa	$\frac{1}{2}$	$\frac{1}{16}$
	aa	$\frac{1}{2}$	$\frac{1}{16}$
$\frac{1}{4} \cdot \frac{1}{4}$	Aa	1	$\frac{1}{16}$
$\frac{1}{4} \cdot \frac{1}{2}$	aA	$\frac{1}{2}$	$\frac{1}{16}$
	aa	$\frac{1}{2}$	$\frac{1}{16}$
$\frac{1}{4} \cdot \frac{1}{4}$	aa	1	$\frac{1}{16}$

15. $P[\text{error and observable}] = P[\text{observable} | \text{error}]P[\text{error}]$
$\qquad\qquad\qquad\qquad\qquad = (.35)(.4) = .14.$

EXERCISES □ 3.6

1. a.

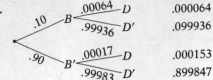

.00064 D	.000064
.99936 D'	.099936
.00017 D	.000153
.99983 D'	.899847

b. $x = ?$

.00022 D —   B   .000064
                   B'   .000153

.99978 D' — B   .099936
                   B'   .899847

c. $.00022x = .000064$

$$x = \frac{.000064}{.00022} \doteq .29$$

d. $P[B|D] = \dfrac{P[D|B]P[B]}{P[D|B]P[B] + P[D|B']P[B']}$

$$= \frac{(.00064)(.10)}{(.00064)(.10) + (.00017)(.90)} \doteq .29$$

3. .44
5. Specificity $\doteq {}^{60}/_{83}$; Sensitivity $\doteq {}^{44}/_{54}$;

$$\frac{{}^{44}/_{54} \cdot {}^{1}/_{10}}{{}^{44}/_{54} \cdot {}^{1}/_{10} + {}^{23}/_{83} \cdot {}^{9}/_{10}}$$

EXERCISES □ 4.1

1. Discrete
3. Continuous
5. Discrete
7. Continuous

EXERCISES □ 4.2

1. a. .09
    b. .41
    c. .11
    d. .19

3. a.

x	0	1	2	3	4	(from the
$f(x)$	$(.1)^4$	$4(.1)^3(.9)$	$6(.1)^2(.9)^2$	$4(.1)(.9)^3$	$(.9)^4$	tree)

    b. $(.1)^4 + 4(.1)^3(.9) = .0037$
    c. Yes; $P[X = 0] = (.1)^4 = .0001$
5. **a.** $P[5 \leq X \leq 10]$
    b. 0
7. **a.** $1 = \frac{1}{2} \cdot 4 \cdot h$, therefore, $h = \frac{1}{2}$
    b. $P[X \leq 1] = \frac{1}{2} \cdot 1 \cdot \frac{1}{4} = \frac{1}{8}$
    c. $P[X < 1] = \frac{1}{8}$
    d. $P[X > 3] = \frac{1}{8}$
    e. $P[X \leq 3] = 1 - P[X > 3] = \frac{7}{8}$
    f. $P[1 \leq X \leq 3] = \frac{6}{8}$
    g. $P[X = 2] = 0$

EXERCISES □ 4.3

1. **a.**

x	6	7	8	9	10
$F(x)$	.05	.15	.75	.90	1.00

    b. $P[X \leq 8] = F(8) = .75$
    c. $P[X > 7] = 1 - P[X \leq 7] = 1 - F(7) = 1 - .15 = .85$
    d. $P[7 \leq X \leq 9] = P[X \leq 9] - P[X \leq 6] = F(9) - F(6) = .90 - .05 = .85$

3. **a.**

x	0	1	2	3
$f(x)$	.15	.40	.90	1.0

    b. $P[X \leq 1] = F(1) = .40$
    c. $P[X \geq 2] = 1 - P[X \leq 1] = 1 - F(1) = 1 - .4 = .60$
5. **a.** I, II
    b. $P[2 \leq X \leq 6] = F(6) - F(2)$
    c. $P[X \geq 8] = 1 - F(8)$
    d. $P[X \leq 4] = P[X < 4] = F(4)$
7. **a.** I, II, III
    b. $P[X \geq 18] = 1 - F(18)$; III, IV, V
    c. $P[27 \leq X \leq 36] = F(36) - F(27)$; IV

EXERCISES □ 4.4

1. $E[X] = .2$; $\mu_X = .2$; $E[X^2] = 1.6$; Var $X = 1.56$;
    $\sigma_X^2 = 1.56$; $\sigma_X = 1.25$

3. **a.**

x	0	1	2	3
$f(x)$	$(.1)^3 = .001$	$3(.9)(.1)^2 = .027$	$3(.9)^2(.1) = .243$	$(.9)^3 = .729$

    b. $E[X] = 2.7$
    c. $\mu_X = 2.7$
    d. $E[X^2] = 3(.9)(.1)^2 + 4(3)(.9)^2(.1) + 9(.9)^3 = 7.56$
    e. Var $X = .27$; $\sigma_X = \sqrt{.27} \doteq .52$

5. **a.** $\sigma_X = 3$; $\sigma_Y = 4$

    b. $E[X^2] = 13$; $E[Y^2] = 52$

    c. 14; 73

    d. -8; 145

    e. 0; 1

    f. 0; 1

    g. $E\left[\dfrac{\text{variable} - \text{its mean}}{\text{its standard deviation}}\right] = 0$;

      $\text{Var}\left[\dfrac{\text{variable} - \text{its mean}}{\text{its standard deviation}}\right] = 1$

EXERCISES □ 5.1

1. **a.** Binomial; $n = 5$; $p = .006$

    b. Binomial; $n = 5$; $p = .001$

    c. Binomial; $n = 10$; $p = .9$

    d. Not binomial

    e. Binomial, $n = 8$; $p = .05$

    f. Not binomial; number of trials is not fixed

3. **a.** $f(x) = \binom{5}{x}(.006)^x(.994)^{5-x}$ $x = 0, 1, 2, 3, 4, 5$

       $f(x) = \binom{5}{x}(.001)^x(.999)^{5-x}$ $x = 0, 1, 2, 3, 4, 5$

       $f(x) = \binom{10}{x}(.9)^x(.1)^{10-x}$ $x = 0, 1, 2, \ldots, 10$

       $f(x) = \binom{8}{x}(.05)^x(.95)^{8-x}$ $x = 0, 1, 2, \ldots. 8$

    b. $E[X] = 5(.006) = .03$

       $E[X] = 5(.001) = .005$

       $E[X] = 10(.9) = 9$

       $E[X] = 8(.05) = .4$

    c, d. $\text{Var } X = 5(.006)(.994) \doteq .0298$ $\sigma_X = .1726$

          $\text{Var } X = 5(.001)(.999) \doteq .005$ $\sigma_X = .0707$

          $\text{Var } X = 10(.9)(.1) = .9$ $\sigma_X = .9487$

          $\text{Var } X = 8(.05)(.95) = .38$ $\sigma_X = .6164$

5. **a.**

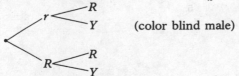

    (color blind male)

    b. $\frac{1}{4}$

    c. $\binom{3}{2}\left(\frac{1}{4}\right)^2\left(\frac{3}{4}\right)^1 \doteq .14$

    d. $\frac{5}{4}$; .8965; .1035

7. X = number alive; $n = 10$, $p = .8$; $P[X \geq 8] =$
$1 - P[X \leq 7] = .6778$

EXERCISES □ 5.2

1. a. 10
   b. $f(x) = \dfrac{e^{-10}10^x}{x!}$ $x = 0, 1, 2, 3, \ldots$
   c. .029
   d. $1 - P[X \leq 5] = 1 - .067 = .933$
   e. $P[4 \leq X \leq 12] = P[X \leq 12] - P[X \leq 3] = .782$
   f. $P[X = 9] = P[X \leq 9] - P[X \leq 8] = .125$
3. $\lambda = 2$; $s = 3$; $\lambda s = 6$
   $P[X \leq 4] = .285$; $P[X \geq 12] = 1 - P[X \leq 11] = .02$;
   yes — If $\lambda s = 6$, this is a rare event occurring with probability
   .0211
5. Unit = micrometer, $\lambda = \frac{1}{4}$, $s = 16$, $\lambda s = 4$;
   $P[X = 0] = .018$; $P[X \geq 9] = 1 - P[X \leq 8] = .021$
7. Unit = 5 hours, $\lambda = 1$, $s = \frac{1}{2}$, $\lambda s = .5$; $P[X = 0] = .607$;
   $P[X \geq 1] = 1 - P[X = 0] = .393$
9. $E[X] = 10$, $P[X \geq 1] = 1 - P[X = 0] \doteq 1$
11. $E[X] = 15$; .048

EXERCISES □ 5.3

1. a. $f(x) = \dfrac{1}{2\sqrt{2\pi}}e^{-1/2}[(x - 5)/2]^2$
   b. 5 ± 2 (3 and 7)
   c.

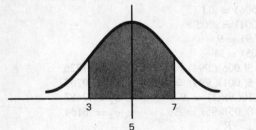

3. Standard normal
5. .6826
7. a. .0170
   b. .1401
   c. .7936
   d. .6826
   e. 121
   f. 192

9. a. .9599
    b. .4599
    c. .1915
    d. .0307
    e. 100.64

EXERCISES □ 5.4

1. a. .1112 (binomial .1071)
    b. .5512 (binomial .5725)
    c. .8888 (binomial .8929)
    d. .1215 (binomial .1304)
3. $E[X] = 30$; use the Poisson approximation to binomial and the normal approximation to the Poisson.

$$P[X \leq 25] \doteq P[Z \leq \frac{25.5 - 30}{\sqrt{30}} = P[Z \leq -.82] = .2061;$$

$$P[25 \leq X \leq 35] \doteq .6826$$

5. $P[X \geq 1] = 1 - P[X = 0] \doteq 1 - P\left[Z \leq \frac{.5 - 5}{\sqrt{5}}\right]$ (use the Poisson approximation to binomial first)

$$\doteq .9778$$

7. a. .7088
    b. .9744
    c. .7062
    d. .0397
9. $\lambda s = .5$; for each paramecium, $P[X = 0] = .607$ and $P[X \geq 1] = .393$; Let Y = number of paramecia emitting no killer particles, $P[Y = 20] = (.607)^{20}$; let K = number emitting at least 1 killer particle,

$$P[5 \leq K \leq 10] \doteq P\left[\frac{4.5 - 7.86}{\sqrt{4.77}} \leq Z \leq \frac{10.5 - 7.86}{\sqrt{4.77}}\right] = .8251$$

EXERCISES □ 6.1

1. Not statistical; birth data for each year can easily be obtained without having to sample.
3. Statistical; two populations—plants treated with indoleacetic acid and those not treated; potentially hypothetical
5. Statistical; petunia plants treated with infrared light; potentially hypothetical

EXERCISES □ 6.2

1. Estimation
3. Hypothesis testing
5. Hypothesis testing

7. $.2; .2 \pm 1.96 \sqrt{\dfrac{1}{4(500)}}$ or $.2 \pm .04$

9. 9; 106; 1598; 98; no, μ is unknown.

EXERCISES ☐ 6.3

1. **a.** $H_0: \mu \geq .08$ μ = average percentage metal in
   $H_1: \mu < .08$ household waste

   b. We will conclude that the percentage of metal in household waste on the average has decreased when in fact it has not.

   c. We will not detect the fact that the average percentage has decreased when in fact it has.

   d. There is a 5% chance that we will conclude that the percentage of metal among household waste has declined when in fact it has not.

3. **a.** $H_0: p \leq .38$
   $H_1: p > .38$

   b. We will conclude that the percentage of smokers has increased over the 38% figure when in fact it has not.

   c. We will not detect a situation in which the proportion of smokers has become larger than 38%.

   d. There is a 10% probability that we will conclude that the proportion of smokers is greater than 38% when in fact it is not.

5. **a.** $H_0: \mu \leq .3$
   $H_1: \mu > .3$

   b. We will conclude that the mean level has increased when in fact it has not; we will not detect the fact that the background level has increased.

   c. The probability of observing a value of the test statistic as large as, or larger than, that observed if H_0 is true is .01.

   d. No; .01 is usually considered to be small.

7. **a.** 10.5
   b. .1268
   c. .6020
   d. .3980
   e. No; II

9. **a.** $H_0: p \leq .15$
   $H_1: p > .15$

   b. 15

   c. $P = P[X \geq 20] \doteq P[Y \geq 19.5] = P[Z \geq 1.26] = .1038$; marginal

EXERCISES ☐ 7.1

1. 408.33

3. **a.** 13; $\dfrac{\sigma^2}{n} = \dfrac{9}{16}$, $\dfrac{\sigma}{\sqrt{n}} = \dfrac{3}{4}$

   b. 13.24; $13.24 \pm 2.575\frac{3}{4}$ or (11.31, 15.17); supports the value of
   13 since 13 does lie in the interval and is therefore a possible
   value for μ_x.

5. $4510 \pm 2.05\dfrac{300}{\sqrt{10}}$ or (4315.52, 4704.48); the interval tends to

   refute the proposed value of 4200 since this value does not lie in
   the interval; that is, we are 96% confident that μ is at least as large
   as 4315.52—this tends to cast doubt on the proposed figure
   of 4200.

EXERCISES □ 7.2

1. 12; 34; 2; 2; $\sqrt{2}$
3. **a.** 1.753
   b. 2.131
   c. −1.753
   d. −2.131
   e. .01
   f. .10
   g. .90
   h. 2.131
   i. 2.947
5. $\hat{\mu} = 175.76$; $\hat{\sigma}^2 = 432.36$; $\hat{\sigma} = 20.79$; $175.76 \pm 1.711\dfrac{20.79}{5}$

   or (168.65, 182.87); yes, we are 90% confident that the mean
   number of gallons used is between 168.65 and 182.87 gallons, and
   160 does not lie in this interval.

7. $9.5 \pm 1.96\dfrac{.5}{\sqrt{1000}}$ or (9.47, 9.53)

EXERCISES □ 7.3

1. **a.** H_0: $\mu \leq 10$
      H_1: $\mu > 10$
   b. $\bar{x} = 11$, $s = 1.94$, $t = 1.55$, the critical point is 1.397, reject H_0;
      conclude that the radiation level is above the safe limit;
      Type I.
3. $\bar{x} = 6.15$, $s = .26$, $t = 2.31$; $P = P[T_{15} \geq 2.31]$
   lies between .01 and .025; conclude that $\mu > 6$; Type I.
5. **a.** H_0: $\mu \leq .035$
      H_1: $\mu > .035$
   b. $t = 2.64$, $P < .005$; yes

EXERCISES □ 7.4

1. a. .01
   b. .25
   c. .05
   d. 19.0
   e. 2.09
   f. .90

3. a. $\hat{\mu} = 3840.22$
   b. $\hat{\sigma}^2 = 1261.69$
   c. $3840.22 \pm 1.86 \sqrt{\dfrac{1261.69}{3}}$ or   (3818.20, 3862.24)
   d. $\left(\dfrac{8(1261.69)}{15.5}, \dfrac{8(1261.69)}{2.73}\right)$ or   (651.19, 3697.26); $(\sqrt{651.19}, \sqrt{3697.26})$ or   (25.52, 60.81)

5. a. $\hat{\mu} = 12.11$, $\hat{\sigma}^2 = 2.19$, $\hat{\sigma} = 1.48$
   b. $t = -2.08$; $.025 < P < .05$, yes
   c. $\chi^2 = \dfrac{11(2.19)}{(1.5)^2} = 10.71$, $.5 < P < .75$, no

7. a. $t = -.59$, the critical point for an $\alpha = .05$ level test is -1.711, unable to conclude that the mean oxygen content is below 6.5 ppm.
   b. 36.4; $\chi^2 = \dfrac{24(1.7)^2}{(1.2)^2} = 48.17$, yes.

EXERCISES □ 8.1

1. $\hat{p} = {}^{32}/_{36} = .889$

3. a. $\hat{p} = {}^{11}/_{15} = .733$
   b. $.733 \pm 1.645 \sqrt{\dfrac{(.733)(.267)}{15}}$ or   (.545, .920)

5. $.2 \pm 2.05 \sqrt{\dfrac{1}{4(1000)}}$ or   (.167, .232)

7. $\hat{p} = \dfrac{42}{50} = .84$; $.84 \pm 1.88 \sqrt{\dfrac{.84(.16)}{50}}$ or   (.742; .937)

9. $n \doteq 1879$

11. $n \doteq \dfrac{(1.645)^2}{4(.02)^2} = 1692$

EXERCISES □ 8.2

1. a. $H_0: p \leq \frac{1}{2}$ $p = $ percent opposed to the dam
      $H_1: p > \frac{1}{2}$
   b. 1.645

    c. Yes, the observed value of the test statistic is 1.79.

    d. Type I; we might erroneously conclude that a majority of residents oppose the dam when in fact 50% or less are in opposition.

3. The observed value of the test statistic is -6.48; the P value is approximately 0; we conclude that the drug is effective in reducing the death rate.

5. We must have

$$\frac{\dfrac{x}{50} - .7}{\sqrt{\dfrac{.7(.3)}{50}}} > 1.96$$

solving for x we must have $x \geq 42$.

EXERCISES □ 8.3

1. $\widehat{p}_1 - \widehat{p}_2 = {}^{29}\!/_{742} - {}^{13}\!/_{733} = .0391 - .0177 = .0214 \doteq .02$; the death rate appears to be higher in the placebo group.

3. $\widehat{p}_1 - \widehat{p}_2 = .40 - .19 = .21$

5. $.32 \pm 1.645 \sqrt{\dfrac{(.89)(.11)}{19} + \dfrac{(.58)(.42)}{19}}$

    or (.0995, .5405); the interval found using method II would be longer; (.0531, .5869); yes, we are 90% confident that the difference between the two proportions is positive.

EXERCISES □ 8.4

1. Type II: we would doubt the effectiveness of vitamin C in the treatment of cancer; it is not correct to claim that we have shown that vitamin C does not help; we have been unable *at this time* to show its effectiveness; one does not show anything by failing to reject H_0 due to the inability to determine β.

3. $H_0: p_1 \leq p_2$ $p_1 =$ probability of detecting the cancer by
    $H_1: p_1 > p_2$ mammography alone in older women
    The observed value of the test statistic is 2.13; reject H_0 at the $\alpha = .05$ level (critical point, 1.645).

5. The observed value of the test statistic is 1.7558; this result is significant at the $\alpha = .1$ level (critical point, 1.28), the $\alpha = .05$ level (critical point, 1.645) but not at the $\alpha = .01$ level (critical point, 2.33).

EXERCISES □ 9.1

1. .15 (subtraction in the order men minus women)
3. 5; $^{16}\!/_{20} + {}^{18}\!/_{25} = 1.52$; 1.23; Z

EXERCISES □ 9.2

1. a. .95
   b. .975
   c. .99
   d. 2.62
   e. 9.38
   f. 2.23
   g. approximately 2.23 (a little larger than necessary)
   h. $^{1}\!/_{1.78} \doteq .56$
   i. $^{1}\!/_{1.74} \doteq .57$
   j. $^{1}\!/_{2.46} \doteq .41$
   k. $^{1}\!/_{2.69} \doteq .37$ (actually a litttle larger than necessary)

3. The right critical point is 3.66; the observed value of the test statistic is 3.92; reject H_0 and conclude that $\sigma_1^2 \neq \sigma_2^2$.

5. $s_M^2 = .092$, $s_W^2 = .291$; .316; the critical point is $^{1}\!/_{3.29} = .304$; since .316 $\not<$ .304 we are unable to conclude that $\sigma_M^2 < \sigma_W^2$.

7. $s_1^2/s_2^2 = .62$; yes; the tabled left critical point is 1.

EXERCISES □ 9.3

1. a. $\dfrac{9(42) + 13(37)}{10 + 14 - 2} = 39.05$
   b. 29
   c. $\dfrac{9(20) + 49(40)}{10 + 50 - 2} = 36.896$; $n_2 > n_1$

3. $s_p^2 = \dfrac{9(.092) + 7(.291)}{16} = .179$;

   $.15 \pm 2.12 \sqrt{.179(^{1}\!/_{10} + {}^{1}\!/_{8})} = .15 \pm .43$ or $(-.28, .58)$; no, because 0 lies in the confidence interval.

5. $s_1^2/s_2^2 = 1.02$; unable to detect a difference in the population variances, $f_{.1} = 2.59$; $s_p^2 = 101.005$.

   $1 \pm 1.746 \sqrt{101.005(^{1}\!/_{9} + {}^{1}\!/_{9})} = 1 \pm 8.272$ or $(-7.272, 9.272)$; since 0 lies in this interval, we cannot conclude that there is a difference in mean survival times.

7. $s_2^2/s_1^2 = 1.15$; unable to detect a difference in the population variances, $f_{.1} = 2.59$; $s_p^2 = 30661$; yes; the observed value of the test statistic is $\dfrac{1702 - 1509}{\sqrt{30661(^{1}\!/_{9} + {}^{1}\!/_{9})}} = 2.34$; $.01 < P < .025$.

9. $s_1^2/s_2^2 = 1.25$; unable to detect a difference in population variances, $f_{.1} = 2.27$; yes; $s_p^2 = \dfrac{9(1.9)^2 + 11(1.7)^2}{20} = 3.21$; the

observed value of the test statistic is $\dfrac{27.3 - 23.5}{\sqrt{3.21(\frac{1}{10} + \frac{1}{12})}} = 4.95$;

$P < .0005$.

EXERCISES □ 9.4

1. $s_p^2 = .0000157$; $\dfrac{.0167 - .0144}{\sqrt{.0000157(\frac{1}{57} + \frac{1}{12})}} = 1.83$; 67; yes, the new P
value would be between .05 and .025.

3. $s_1^2/s_2^2 = {}^{42.25}\!/_{12.96} = 3.26$, conclude that $\sigma_1^2 \neq \sigma_2^2$; yes; the
approximate number of degrees of freedom is 34; the observed
value of the test statistic is 15.53; P value $< .0005$.

5. Variances are unequal; do not pool; yes; the approximate number
of degrees of freedom is 3978; the observed value of the test
statistic is -810.9; P value $< .0005$.

7. **a.** $s_1^2/s_2^2 = .42$; variances appear to be unequal $f_{.975} =$

$\dfrac{1}{2.27} = .44$; $\gamma \doteq 32$; $(2.73 - 1.27) \pm 2.042 \sqrt{\dfrac{(.65)^2}{25} + \dfrac{1}{25}}$ or

(.97, 1.95); yes; 0 does not lie in the confidence interval.

b. Variances are unequal; $\gamma \doteq 11$;

$(26.05 - 30.19) \pm 1.796 \sqrt{\dfrac{(6.34)^2}{9} + \dfrac{(3.2)^2}{12}}$ or $(-8.28, .002)$; no,

0 lies in this interval.

c. $\gamma \doteq 19$; $(9.48 - 9.46) \pm 2.093 \sqrt{\dfrac{(.53)^2}{16} + \dfrac{(.25)^2}{25}}$ or $(-.28, .32)$;

no, 0 lies in the interval.

EXERCISES □ 9.5

1. $\bar{d} = -12.55$; $s_d = 24.47$; $-12.55 \pm 1.812\dfrac{(24.47)}{\sqrt{11}}$ or $(-25.92, .82)$;

no, because 0 lies in this interval.

3. yes; the observed value of the test statistic is $\dfrac{2.78(\sqrt{36})}{6.05} = 2.76$,

$P \doteq .005$.

EXERCISES □ 10.1

1. **a.** The levels were not selected randomly.
   b. $H_0: \mu_1 = \mu_2 = \mu_3 = \mu_4 = \mu_5$
   c. $T_{1.} = 591.4 \qquad \bar{X}_{1.} = 59.14 \qquad T_{..} = 1835.4$
   $T_{2.} = 460.4 \qquad \bar{X}_{2.} = 46.04 \qquad \bar{X}_{..} = 36.71$
   $T_{3.} = 364.5 \qquad \bar{X}_{3.} = 36.45 \qquad \Sigma\Sigma X_{ij}^2 = 79896.22$

$T_{4.} = 254.7 \qquad \bar{X}_{4.} = 25.47$

$T_{5.} = 164.4 \qquad \bar{X}_{5.} = 16.44$

d. $SS_{Total} = 12522.36$

$SS_{Tr} = 11274.32$

$SS_E = 1248.04$

e. $MS_{Tr} = SS_{Tr}/4 = 2818.58$

$MS_E = SS_E/45 = 27.73$

f. $F_{4,45} = 2818.58/27.73 = 101.64$

g. Yes; critical point is approximately 3.38; we are assuming normality, equal variances, and independent sampling.

3.

ANOVA

SOURCE	DF	SS	MS	F
Treatments	4	3.93	.98	8.17
Error	37	4.5	.12	
Total	41	8.43		

$\Sigma\Sigma X_{ij}^2 = 67.86 \qquad T_{4.} = 7.04$

$T_{1.} = 11.62 \qquad T_{5.} = 8.8$

$T_{2.} = 9.36 \qquad T_{..} = 49.96$

$T_{3.} = 13.14$

H_0 can be rejected; the P value is less than .01.

5.

ANOVA

SOURCE	DF	SS	MS	F
Treatments	2	7.73	3.87	96.75
Error	29	1.03	.04	
Total	31	8.76		

$T_{1.} = 12.08 \qquad T_{..} = 36.48$

$T_{2.} = 16.75 \qquad \Sigma\Sigma X_{ij}^2 = 50.35$

$T_{3.} = 7.67$

Reject H_0; the P value is less than .01.

EXERCISES ☐ 10.2

1.

p	2	3	4	5	$\alpha = .01$
r_p	3.825	3.988	4.098	4.180	$\gamma \doteq 40$
$(SSR)_p$	6.369	6.441	6.824	6.961	

$$\sqrt{\frac{MS_E}{n}} = \sqrt{\frac{27.73}{10}} = 1.6652$$

$\bar{x}_{5\cdot}$	$\bar{x}_{4\cdot}$	$\bar{x}_{3\cdot}$	$\bar{x}_{2\cdot}$	$\bar{x}_{1\cdot}$
16.44	25.47	36.45	46.04	59.14

3.

p	2	3	4	5	$\alpha = .01$
r_p	3.825	3.988	4.098	4.180	$\gamma \doteq 40$
$(SSR)_p'$	1.325	1.3815	1.4196	1.4480	

$\sqrt{MS_E} = .3464$

$\bar{x}_{5\cdot}$	$\bar{x}_{4\cdot}$	$\bar{x}_{2\cdot}$	$\bar{x}_{3\cdot}$	$\bar{x}_{1\cdot}$
.88	.88	1.17	1.46	1.66

5.

p	2	3	$\alpha = .05$
r_p	2.888	3.035	$\gamma \doteq 30$
$(SSR)_p'$	2.917	3.065	

$\sqrt{MS_E} = 1.01$

$\bar{x}_{3\cdot}$	$\bar{x}_{1\cdot}$	$\bar{x}_{2\cdot}$
.637	1.098	1.861

EXERCISES ☐ 10.3

1.

ANOVA				
SOURCE	DF	SS	MS	F
Treatments	3	586.6	195.53	2.9
Error	76	5124.2	67.42	
Total	79	5710.8		

Yes; the P value lies between .05 and .025.

EXERCISES ☐ 10.4

1. a. No interaction.
   b. Interaction—treatments B and C differ over blocks.
   c. Interaction—treatments A and B differ over blocks.
3. a. $T_{1\cdot} = 1872.3$ $\bar{X}_{1\cdot} = 936.15$
      $T_{2\cdot} = 1618.9$ $\bar{X}_{2\cdot} = 809.45$
      $T_{3\cdot} = 1781.3$ $\bar{X}_{3\cdot} = 890.65$
      $T_{4\cdot} = 1878.9$ $\bar{X}_{4\cdot} = 939.45$
      $T_{\cdot 1} = 3967.9$ $T_{\cdot\cdot} = 7151.4$
      $T_{\cdot 2} = 3183.5$ $\bar{X}_{\cdot\cdot} = 893.925$
      $\bar{X}_{\cdot 1} = 991.975$
      $\bar{X}_{\cdot 2} = 795.875$ $\sum_{i=1}^{4} \sum_{j=1}^{2} X_{ij}^2 = 6501860.16$

b.

ANOVA

SOURCE	DF	SS	MS	F
Treatments	3	22004.46	7334.82	2.17
Blocks	1	76910.42	76910.42	22.78
Error	3	10130.04	3376.68	
Total	7	109044.92		

Reject H_0': $\mu_{\cdot 1} = \mu_{\cdot 2}$ P values $< .01$

c. Unable to reject H_0: $\mu_{1\cdot} = \mu_{2\cdot} = \mu_{3\cdot} = \mu_{4\cdot}$.

5.

$\bar{x}_{3\cdot}$	$\bar{x}_{4\cdot}$	$\bar{x}_{2\cdot}$	$\bar{x}_{1\cdot}$	$b = 10$	$\sqrt{MS_E/b} = .429$
19.9	51.1	59.5	89.0	$MS_E = 1.84$	

p	2	3	4
r_p	3.956	4.126	4.239
$(SSR)_p$	1.6969	1.7699	1.8183

EXERCISES ☐ 10.5

1. b. $SS_{Total} = 12710.42$

c. $SS_{Tr} = 12489$; $SS_E = 221.42$

d. $SS_A = 10842$; $SS_B = 1225$; $SS_{AB} = 422$

e.

ANOVA

SOURCE	DF	SS	MS	F	
Treatments	5	12489	2497.8	338.42	$^*p < .01$
A	2	10842	5421	734.48	
B	1	1225	1225	165.97	
AB	2	422	211	28.59	$^*p < .01$
Error	30	221.42	7.3807		
Total	35	12710.42			

Reject the null hypothesis of no interaction; reject the null hypothesis of no difference among treatment combinations.

f.

$\bar{x}_{12\cdot}$	$\bar{x}_{11\cdot}$	$\bar{x}_{22\cdot}$	$\bar{x}_{21\cdot}$	$\bar{x}_{32\cdot}$	$\bar{x}_{31\cdot}$
71	73	86	102	106	123

$\sqrt{MS_E/n} = \sqrt{7.3807/6} = 1.1091$

p	2	3	4	5	6	
r_p	3.889	4.506	4.168	4.250	4.314	($\alpha = .01$
$(SSR)_p$	4.3133	4.9976	4.6227	4.7137	4.7842	DF = 30)

3. **b.** $SS_{Total} = 953.21$
   c. $SS_{Tr} = 471.45$; $SS_E = 481.76$
   d. $SS_A = 151.25$; $SS_B = .2$; $SS_{AB} = 320$
   e. Yes; there is a crossover indicating an inconsistency in the behavior of the two capsules.

   f.

   ANOVA

SOURCE	DF	SS	MS	F	
Treatments	3	471.45	157.15	5.22	$+.01 < p < .025$
A	1	151.25	151.25	5.02	
B	1	.2	.2	.007	
AB	1	320	320	10.62	$^*p < .01$
Error	16	481.76	30.11		
Total	19	953.21			

   We reject the null hypothesis of no interaction and turn attention to the 4 treatment combinations.

$\bar{x}_{21.}$	$\bar{x}_{12.}$	$\bar{x}_{22.}$	$\bar{x}_{11.}$
36.3	41.6	44.1	49.8

   $$\sqrt{MS_E/5} = \sqrt{30.11/5} = 2.454$$

p	2	3	4	$(\alpha = .05, DF = 16)$
r_p	2.998	3.144	3.235	
$(SSR)_p$	7.357	7.7153	7.9386	

EXERCISES □ 11.1

1. Yes
3. Questionable

EXERCISES □ 11.2

1. 36.2; 105.66; 85.6; 244.8; 2.59; 6.11
   $\hat{\alpha} = 1.08$ $\hat{\beta} = 1.95$;
   $\mu_{Y|x} = 1.08 + 1.95x$; 8.30
3. $\hat{\alpha} = 23.65$ $\hat{\beta} = 27.66$
   $\hat{\mu}_{Y|x} = 23.65 + 27.66x$; 175.78;
   no, out of range of the data.
5. **a.** 56.6, 117.68, 151.1, 311.96
   b. 1.36, 1.996, 1.36 + 1.996x
   c. 5.85

EXERCISES ☐ 11.3

1. **b.** close to 1
   c. 15; 47.5; 30.1; 183.65; 92.75
   d. .99
3. **b.** 0
   c. 21; 67.12; 38.2; 228.98; 114.46
   d. −.015
5. **a.** 2405; 900775; 2503; 919489; 902475
   b. .98

EXERCISES ☐ 11.4

1. **a.** Close to 1
   b. 1776; 322062; 3018; 941056; 549705; .967
   c. .9351; 93.51% of the variability in Y can be attributed to a linear relationship with X.
   d.

   ANOVA

SOURCE	DF	SS	MS	F
Regression	1	28238.89	28238.89	113.83
Error	8	1984.71	248.09	
Total	9	30223.6		

   Reject H_0; assume linearity
   $\widehat{\mu}_{Y|x} = -64.61 + 2.06x$
   $\widehat{y} = 347.39$ pounds

3.

   ANOVA

SOURCE	DF	SS	MS	F
Regression	1	21.98	21.98	.95
Error	8	184.62	23.08	
Total	9	206.6		

   Unable to reject H_0; linear model is not appropriate.
5. **a.** .9561; 95.61% of the variation in Y is due to a linear association with X; yes.

   b.

   ANOVA

SOURCE	DF	SS	MS	F
Regression	1	279468.26	279468.26	165.37
Error	8	13519.84	1689.98	
Total	9	292988.1		

Reject H_0

$\widehat{\mu}_{Y|x} = 26.12 + .93x$

$\widehat{y} = 119.12$

EXERCISES ☐ 11.5

1. a. Yes

b.

ANOVA

SOURCE	DF	SS	MS	F
Regression	1	4263.46	4263.46	11.23
Error	9	3417.09	379.68	
Total	10	7680.55		

Reject H_0; assume linearity

c. $\widehat{\alpha} = 163.13 \qquad \widehat{\beta} = -2.14$

d. $163.13 \pm 2.262\sqrt{379.68}\,\dfrac{\sqrt{28230}}{\sqrt{11(929.64)}}$

or 163.13 ± 73.23;

$-2.14 \pm 2.262\,\dfrac{\sqrt{379.68}}{\sqrt{929.64}} \quad$ or $\quad -2.14 \pm 1.45$

e. 88.23 days;

$88.23 \pm 2.262\sqrt{379.68}\sqrt{\dfrac{1}{11} + \dfrac{(35 - 49.82)^2}{929.64}}$

or

88.23 ± 25.21

f. 88.23 days;

$88.23 \pm 2.262\sqrt{379.68}\sqrt{1 + \dfrac{1}{11} + \dfrac{(35 - 49.82)^2}{929.64}}$

or

88.23 ± 50.78

EXERCISES ☐ 12.1

1. 30, 33.75, 11.25

3. 2.30, 17.5, 2.5; yes, there appear to be too many who never have considered suing and too few who have considered this action.

EXERCISES ☐ 12.2

1. a. H_0: $p_1 = .41$, $p_2 = .09$, $p_3 = .50$

H_1: at least one of these probabilities is not as stated.

b. 82, 18, 100

c. Yes; each expected cell frequency is greater than 5.

d. The critical point for an X_2^2 random variable, $\alpha = .1$, is 4.61.

e. $\chi^2 = \dfrac{(72-82)^2}{82} + \dfrac{(20-18)^2}{18} + \dfrac{(108-100)^2}{100} = 2.08;$

unable to reject H_0: there is no evidence based on these data of a change in smoking habits.

3. H_0: $p_1 = .4$, $p_2 = .3$, $p_3 = .2$, $p_4 = .1$; $DF = 3$;

$\chi^2 = \dfrac{(42-60)^2}{60} + \dfrac{(61-45)^2}{45} + \dfrac{(33-30)^2}{30} + \dfrac{(14-15)^2}{15} = 11.45;$

reject H_0; the P value is less than .01.

5. a, b, c.

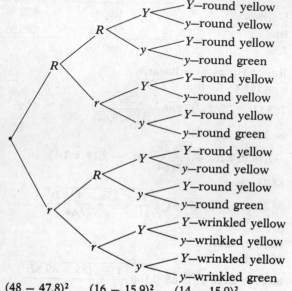

d. $\chi^2 = \dfrac{(48-47.8)^2}{47.8} + \dfrac{(16-15.9)^2}{15.9} + \dfrac{(14-15.9)^2}{15.9}$

$+ \dfrac{(7-5.3)^2}{5.3} = .77$; unable to reject H_0: $p_1 = \frac{9}{16}$, $p_2 = \frac{3}{16}$,

$p_3 = \frac{3}{16}$, $p_4 = \frac{1}{16}$ at the $\alpha = .05$ level (critical point is 7.81, $DF = 3$).

7.

	NONALCOHOLICS		
BOUNDARIES	MIDPOINT	0_i	$\widehat{E}_i$
$-\infty$ to .395	.255	2	.868 ⎫
.395 to .675	.535	1	3.58 ⎬ combine
.675 to .955	.815	10	9.04
.955 to 1.235	1.095	13	12.43
1.235 to 1.515	1.375	9	9.32
1.515 to ∞	1.655	5	4.76

$\hat{\mu}_X = 1.102$
$\hat{\sigma}_X^2 = .1226$
$\hat{p}_1 = .0217 \qquad \hat{p}_3 = .2260 \qquad \hat{p}_5 = .2330$
$\hat{p}_2 = .0895 \qquad \hat{p}_4 = .3108 \qquad \hat{p}_6 = .1190$
$\chi^2 = .6226$ unable to reject the null hypothesis of normality
$(DF = 2)$

ALCOHOLICS

BOUNDARIES	MIDPOINT	0_i	$\hat{E}_i$
$-\infty$ to .505	.405	2	1.71
.505 to .705	.605	3	4.26
.705 to .905	.805	12	8.26
.905 to 1.105	1.005	6	10.49
1.105 to 1.305	1.205	8	8.74
1.305 to ∞	1.405	9	6.54

$\hat{\mu}_Y = 1.015$
$\hat{\sigma}_Y^2 = .0881$
$\hat{p}_1 = .0427 \qquad \hat{p}_3 = .2065 \qquad \hat{p}_5 = .2186$
$\hat{p}_2 = .1065 \qquad \hat{p}_4 = .2622 \qquad \hat{p}_6 = .1635$
$\chi^2 = 5.025$ unable to reject the null hypothesis of normality; $DF = 3$; there is no reason to suspect that the T test is inappropriate.

EXERCISES ☐ 12.3

1. a. No
   b. $H_0: p_{11} = p_{1\cdot} \cdot p_{\cdot 1}$ (contracting flu is independent of the innoculation status)
   c. $\hat{E}_{11} = 175 \qquad \hat{E}_{21} = 275$
      $\hat{E}_{12} = 175 \qquad \hat{E}_{22} = 275$
   d. $\chi^2 = 11.69$; reject H_0; P value is less than .005; $DF = 1$.

3. a, c.

	HIGH	LOW	
Present	12 (6.67)	2 (7.33)	14
Absent	18 (23.33)	31 (25.67)	49
	30	33	63

b. $H_0: p_1 = p_2$ where p_1 = proportion of those with ulcers
with a high pepsinogen level
p_2 = proportion of those without ulcers
with a high pepsinogen level

d. $\chi^2 = 10.46$; reject H_0 at the $\alpha = .01$ level (critical point, 3.84, $DF = 1$).

5. $\chi^2 = 48.24$; conclude that the classification variables are not independent, $DF = 1$.

EXERCISES ☐ 12.4

1. Group A .36, .42; group B .08, .09; group AB .02, .04; there appear to be differences among patients and controls in all groups with the possible exception of group B.

3. **a.** H_0: fragrance is independent of color.
or
$H_0: p_{ij} = p_i \cdot p_{\cdot j}$ $i = 1,2$ $j = 1,2,3$

   b. $\hat{E}_{11} = 40.3$ $\hat{E}_{21} = 21.7$
$\hat{E}_{12} = 45.5$ $\hat{E}_{22} = 24.5$
$\hat{E}_{13} = 44.2$ $\hat{E}_{23} = 23.8$
$\chi^2 = 82.29$; reject H_0, $P < .005$; conclude that there is an association between flower color and fragrance.

5. **a.** H_0: the chloroplast distribution is the same regardless of the SO_2 level
or
$H_0: p_{1j} = p_{2j} = p_{3j}$ $j = 1,2,3$

   b. $\hat{E}_{11} = 5$ $\hat{E}_{21} = 5$ $\hat{E}_{31} = 5$
$\hat{E}_{12} = 8.33$ $\hat{E}_{22} = 8.33$ $\hat{E}_{32} = 8.33$
$\hat{E}_{13} = 6.67$ $\hat{E}_{23} = 6.67$ $\hat{E}_{33} = 6.67$
$\chi^2 = 14.73$; reject H_0 (critical point 9.49, $DF = 4$), conclude that the chloroplast level is affected by the SO_2 level.

   c. .65; .25; .10; it appears that SO_2 suppresses the chloroplast level in the leaf cells of trees.

EXERCISES ☐ 13.1

1. $P[N \leq 5] = .0207$; yes
3. $P[N \leq 1] \doteq 0$; yes
5. $\dfrac{n(n+1)}{2} = \dfrac{10(11)}{2} = 55$ $W_+ + |W_-| = 42.5 + 12.5 = 55$

7.

$\lvert X_i - 8 \rvert$	.09	.09	.15	.2	.29	.30	.31	.4	.48	.59	.59	.64	.67	.83
R_i	1.5	1.5	3	4	5	6	7	8	9	10.5	10.5	12	13	14
Signal rank	−	−	−	+	−	+	+	−	−	−	−	−	−	+

$W_+ = 31$ $|W_-| = 74$ $P[W_+ \leq 31] > .05$ unable to reject the proposed median of .8 km.

9. **a.** 137
   b. The smaller of W_+ and $|W_-|$
   c. $W_+ = 200$ $|W_-| = 265$, H_0 cannot be rejected, Type II.

11. **a.** .0778
    b. .2843

EXERCISES □ 13.2

1. **a.** N', the number of positive signs
   b. No, $P[N' \leq 3] = .1719$
3. Yes, $P[N \leq 1] = .0107$

5. **a.**

$|X_i - Y_i|$	.11	1.86	2.3	3.04	4.12	4.49	5.36	9.0	9.05	10.52
R_i	1	2	3	4	5	6	7	8	9	10
Signed rank	+	+	+	+	+	−	−	+	+	+

$|W_-| = 13$; the critical point for an $\alpha = .05$ level test is 11, unable to reject H_0.

   b. No, $P[N \leq 2] = .0547 > .05$.

EXERCISES □ 13.3

1.

OBSERVATION	.09	.12	.13	.17	.19	.19	.20	.20
Group	U	U	U	U	U	M	U	M
Rank	1	2	3	4	5.5	5.5	7.5	7.5

OBSERVATION	.21	.21	.21	.22	.23
Group	U	M	M	M	M
Rank	10	10	10	12	13

The test statistic is based on the sum of the ranks of those from group M (smaller sized sample); if the research hypothesis is true, then W_m should be large; the critical point from Table X is 54; the observed value of W_m is 58; reject H_0.

3.

OBSERVATION	604.1	646.8	688.1	739.4	760.5	793.4	797.0
Group	$<$	$<$	$<$	$\geq$	$<$	$<$	$\geq$
Rank	1	2	3	4	5	6	7

OBSERVATION	806.8	812.4	818.9	843.6	850.0	856.6	899.1
Group	$<$	$\geq$	$\geq$	$\geq$	$\geq$	$<$	$<$
Rank	8	9	10	11	12	13	14

OBSERVATION	906.5	909.3	940.7	961.8	968.1	979.1	1009.9
Group	$<$	$\geq$	$\geq$	$\geq$	$<$	$\geq$	$\geq$
Rank	15	16	17	18	19	20	21

OBSERVATION	1100.6	1330.3	1335.8
Group	$\geq$	$\geq$	$\geq$
Rank	22	23	24

The test statistic is based on the sum of the ranks of group ($<$); the critical point for a left-tailed test ($\alpha = .025$) is 91; the observed value of W_m is 86; reject H_0, the data tend to support the research hypothesis.

5. **a.** .4522
  b. .0722

EXERCISES □ 13.4

1. **a.** $R_1 = 72.5$ $R_2 = 170$ $R_3 = 163.5$
  b. $H = \dfrac{12}{28(29)} \left[\dfrac{(72.5)^2}{8} + \dfrac{(170)^2}{10} + \dfrac{(163.5)^2}{10} \right] - 3(29) = 4.9$; the

  critical point for an $\alpha = .1$ level test based on the X_2^2 distribution is 4.61; H_0 can be rejected at this level but not at $\alpha = .05$ (critical point 5.99).

3. $R_1 = 35$ $R_2 = 23$ $R_3 = 102$ $R_4 = 103$ $R_5 = 62$
  $H = 20.25$; the null hypothesis of no differences in exposure times among the groups can be rejected; based on the X_4^2 distribution the P value is $<.005$.

5. $R_1 = 39$ $R_2 = 163$ $R_3 = 98$
  $H = 19.23$; based on the X_2^2 distribution it can be concluded that the lead concentrations differ; the P value is $<.005$.

EXERCISES ☐ 13.5

1. $E[R_i] = \dfrac{b(k+1)}{2} = \dfrac{8(5)}{2} = 20;$

   $R_1 = 18 \qquad S = 51.5$
   $R_2 = 21.5 \qquad DF = 3$
   $R_3 = 25$
   $R_4 = 15.5 \qquad \chi^2 = \dfrac{12(51.5)}{8(4)(5)} = 3.86$

   The P value lies between .5 (critical point 2.37) and .25 (critical point 4.11).

3. $E[R_i] = \dfrac{b(k+1)}{2} = \dfrac{8(6)}{2} = 24$

   $R_1 = 25 \qquad S = 68$
   $R_2 = 17 \qquad DF = 4$
   $R_3 = 25$
   $R_4 = 25 \qquad \chi^2 = \dfrac{12(68)}{8(5)(6)} = 3.4$
   $R_5 = 28$

   The P value is between .25 and .5; there is no evidence that real differences are perceived.

EXERCISES ☐ 13.6

1. a. $\Sigma r_x = \Sigma r_y = 300 \qquad \Sigma r_x r_y = 3196$
       $\Sigma r_x^2 = \Sigma r_y^2 = 4900 \qquad r_s = -.48$

    b. $\Sigma d_i^2 = 3408 \qquad r_s = 1 - \dfrac{6(3408)}{24(24^2 - 1)} = -.48$

    c. They differ by .01.
    d. No; $r^2 \doteq (-.48)^2 = .23.$

3. $\Sigma r_x = \Sigma r_y = 78 \qquad \Sigma r_x r_y = 588.25$
    $\Sigma r_x^2 = \Sigma r_y^2 = 649.5 \qquad r_s = .57$

    Since $r^2 \doteq r_s^2 = .32$, there appears to be a slight positive association between blood alcohol content and the percentage decrease in the maximum smooth pursuit velocity.

INDEX